TWO WHEELS
AND A TENT

MARK GOWAN

Printed Worldwide
First Printing 2023
First Edition 2023

ISBN: 978-1-7363518-3-3

10 9 8 7 6 5 4 3 2 1

TWO WHEELS
AND A TENT

Table of Contents

Preface

I like to do what I would call "mild" adventure touring. I go off road to an extent and quite a bit when the chance offers itself. My adventure bike of choice is a 2008 Suzuki V-Strom that I call Mabel. She and I have done a lot of miles together and in doing so have shared a lot of thoughts with each other. Now this may seem strange to some. To those who might not know, motorcyclists, at least those not embarrassed to admit it, often talk "to themselves" in their helmets. I'm most definitely a culprit of this. But a lot of riders come to feel that their motorcycle becomes more than just a machine. Over time and with the miles that Mabel and I have ridden these "conversations" have evolved to being conversations with Mabel.

The conversations that Mabel and I have range from the practical to the philosophical, and are sometimes even a jumble of meaningless songs that I will sing to myself (Mabel will have to put up with these). I've been in predicaments out on tours where I've "asked" Mabel to get me out, mostly unseen difficulties with weather and roads, and sometimes I've not paid attention to Mabel's needs (like gasoline). But she has always got me out of any predicament without fail and without complaining too much. If all of this seems a bit, well, schizophrenic, then you've either not ridden motorcycles, or hung around motorcyclists for very much. The personification of our beloved machines is par for the course. Perhaps it's an American thing, with Americans having a long and deep love affair with motor vehicles? Either way, I've written this book with the idea that Mabel is my partner in adventure-crime, which she is.

As you read this book don't worry when Mabel answers me. I realize it's all just in my head, and I hope in yours after you've read this book.

So why tour on a motorcycle? Motorcycle touring is about roads and scenery, sure, but it is also about the people you meet. And so, in these pages are some of the conversations that I remember having in the many places that Mabel and I have visited. It is also important, at least to me, to realize that these tours are not a culmination of "the best" tours that we've taken nor are they a collection of *all* the tours that we've taken. They are a collection of stories that I've taken from my motorcycle journals. I've withheld some either because I don't think that most people want all of the tedious details of hours and hours in the saddle careening down the road on two wheels. With that said, these writings are a collection of different tours that I've taken, both long and short, and most of the dialogue between Mabel and I is what I would call typical. Sure, some of it has been imagined, but what would a motorcycle tour be without imagination?! In fact, motorcycle touring is steeped imagination: the imagining of open roads and freedom. Motorcycle touring allows you to give control over to your curiosity and follow your instincts. Just listen to and look at the commercials at any motorcycle dealer. Imagination comes in many different motorcycle-forms. From the Iron Butt Riders that push the limits of endurance to the weekend cruisers, to the café racers and the long-distance highway tourers, imagination is in them all. I've done a little of all of the above over the years and so I would argue that I am a good candidate for either the looney bin or just an artist with a two-wheeled canvas. Either way, Mabel and I have had our fun and our difficulties. Both she and I are getting up there in years but I like to think that both of us have a few thousand miles left in us. I know that when I get back from a long tour and park Mabel it's not too much time before I'm thinking of my next adventure, and I think I can hear Mabel contemplating the same thing.

So why books about travelling around on a motorcycle? I hope that these stories will motivate someone to get a bike and do some two-wheeled travelling themselves. And for those who don't find that their future includes a motorized two-wheeled contraption I hope that this book will remind them that adventure is just outside your door. I will end this little preface by saying that motorcycle touring doesn't take much and pays off in dividends. Maybe you'll find your own special friend to have long conversations with as I did. And if you're as lucky as me, you will.

Good reading!

Chapter 1

Colorado, New Mexico, Nevada, Utah, Idaho, Wyoming

1.1

Mabel stood silently in the garage loaded up and ready to go. I had changed her oil and checked everything that I knew how to check and now there was nothing left to do except ride.

"Are you ready to go?!" my wife asked, smiling and knowing that I was both excited and a little nervous.

"I think I am. I've checked everything. I think I've checked everything a lot."

She laughed.

"You've got everything?"

"Probably more than I need." I answered, taking a swig of my chilled Colorado IPA.

"Well, if you've forgotten anything it's not worse than you can stop and buy it."

"That's true, but I'd rather not have to do that."

"I know…but you can."

Mabel and I were leaving in the morning on our first long adventure together. I had planned for a month and was as giddy as a schoolboy going to his first dance.

"Just a sec…" I said, getting up and walking to the garage for the fourth or fifth time that evening.

A few minutes later I came back, sat down, and took another swig of my IPA.

"I'm gonna try to get off early in the morning if I can."

Helle smiled.

"I'll get up and say goodbye." She said.

"That'd be great, but you don't have to. It'll be early."

"Of course I will!" she replied, almost surprised.

I took another swig of my IPA and headed for the garage again. I could feel Helle shaking her head.

I was awake about 4am and lay in the dark doing nothing more than waiting to get up. And so, I did. I made coffee and checked on Mabel, still waiting in the garage. Helle sauntered out of our bedroom, bleary eyed. She yawned.

"It's early…" she said as she poured herself a cup of coffee. Our dog, Maggie, reluctantly got up and followed us, laying in the living room where we finally lighted in our usual chairs. Soon she was asleep again on the floor in the middle of the living room.

We sat drinking our coffee and I was fidgety with excitement. A few more cups of coffee and I simply couldn't wait any longer.

"Well. This is it. I think I'll try to beat traffic." I said, knowing that there probably would not be any traffic at 5:30 on a Sunday morning.

"Alright." Helle answered, putting her coffee cup down and coming over to give me a last hug before I took off. Maggie didn't bother getting up, but I kneeled down and hugged her anyway. We walked into the garage and I checked the tank bag for the necessities: wallet? Check. Journal? Check. Charging cord and phone? Check and check. I had a paper map in the clear top compartment of the little waterproof tank bag. Putting on my motorcycle jacket I kissed Helle one more time and then put on my helmet and gloves. I turned the key and pushed the starter button. Mabel instantly came to life. The journey had begun, just like that.

Months before I had bought Mabel without telling Helle. I knew she'd be mad (Helle, that is) when I did, and she was. I explained that I was getting older and had always wanted a motorcycle after giving up motocross when I was younger. She just glared at me the first day. We argued for a little bit, but she realized it was a lost cause. We'd been married for a long time and we'd both come to the conclusion that most arguments ended the same way: we forgave each other.

"I'll tell you what. You can be mad for two days. I'll sleep in the garage or out in the mountains. Wherever you want me to."

"You can't go in the mountains. That's fun for you! I'll think of something!" she had said with a mischievous gleam in her eyes.

My theory was that Helle just didn't want a second mistress in our lives. I had had one other mistress for years, and still had her. She was an old, cheap guitar that I had bought off the back of a truck in our first year of marriage. And now, I had Mabel.

That had been months ago and now I was pushing Mabel out of the garage, fully loaded and ready to go. Mabel was not old but was not new and I had spent months researching which bike I wanted, all in secret of course. She had not cost a lot and she wasn't the most exciting looking bike in the world but when I had ridden her, she just felt comfortable. She felt…right. She had plenty of power for me, handled great, and had a reputation for being a solid bike. Best of all, she was classified as an "adventure" bike, that loaded and very popular term in motorcycle circles. It could mean anything but for months I had tested what that word meant by taking her up into the Colorado mountains and veering off on fire roads and even dual track trails. I found her to be able enough for anything that I could throw at her. She wasn't a dirt bike but was willing to run on anything that I was brave enough to hand to her. I had put new "adventure" tires on her and they really helped more than anything. I added crash bars which I hoped never to test. Replacing her large window-like windscreen with a small, tinted Moose Racing screen and a little Puig touring screen on top of that gave her a sporty look. And for performance a 16-tooth counter sprocket for higher speed at lower RPM's. Mabel wasn't an off-road bike so I didn't really need the higher rpms at lower speeds and we weren't going to do any major off-roading, at least not yet. Of course, I installed a center stand and a fender extender for the front fender. She had come with luggage and a luggage rack.

All of the build-up, all of the planning and all of the practice-loading had led up to the moment of me pushing her off her center stand and gently setting her on her kickstand. Now I was backing her out of the garage on a dark, cool Sunday morning. I sat in the saddle and clicked her into first gear with a solid clunk then I lifted my visor.

"I love you!" I called to Helle through my helmet.

"I love you! Call!!" she demanded.

I smiled.

I rolled out of the driveway with Helle and now Maggie standing there watching me leave. The scene put a sense of reality to the whole trip instantly. I was excited that was true, but it had not fully sunk in that I was starting a month-long motorcycle adventure. That would take time. Pulling out of our neighborhood I rode north on an empty 85 and soon was leaning into curves on 285 which snaked into mountains out of Denver. I was eager to get out of the city and soon I was. The front range loomed invitingly in front of me, but in the dark. The flat, city landscape soon gave way to cliffs and switchbacks. 285 was a main road southwest out of Denver, but it wasn't exactly a highway. I took the switchbacks at the speed limit, something I wasn't in the habit of doing, in order to get a feel for Mabel fully loaded. I had ridden her fully loaded a few times, but I still wanted to take it easy, at least at first. Mabel's two lights lit up the road wonderfully and the little 650 pulled the endless hill to the little town of Bailey with no issues at all.

"I'm happy. I'm happy!" I yelled in my helmet with a smile on my face.

"I'm happy too!" Mabel answered.

I was a little surprised, thinking about a motorcycle answering me. But I soon settled with the idea.

"I guess we're both looking forward to this!"

It was colder than I expected and getting colder as we climbed in altitude. I watched as the sun started turning the darkness into a dark blue, and then blue-grey. In Grant, the cold had me shivering so I stopped at a gas station and used their bathroom as a changing room. I added long underwear to my motorcycle attire. Walking outside, I decided to add a sweater to the ensemble. Now looking like a walking balloon, I got a quick snack and got back on the bike and headed west. The sun was up and was gleaming off the dewy rocks and ponderosas. But it was cold. Waddling out to Mabel I had to quit smiling in order to get my helmet on.

"It's just part of the motorcycle adventure…" I told myself.

"The cold or you looking like the Michelin Man?" Mabel added.

Before I knew it, Mabel and I were weaving down 285 looking across the vast, beautiful valley of South Park Colorado. It spread out behind the Front Range and prefaced the Rocky's that spread in their glory over the far horizon, green and shiny from the iced dew that covered its miles and miles of fields and high mountain plains. I stopped and enjoyed the view from the peak of the Front Range in Bailey. The little highway, 285, was well traveled but still maintained its one-lane splendor. It changed direction the higher up I went and in Jefferson it veered south towards one of my favorite towns, Salida. Mabel and I had been riding for a couple of hours when I hit Buena Vista. It was a tiny spot that had been outshined by Salida but had its own charm. It also had a great little diner that I knew from my many camping excursions in the area, and so I stopped and had breakfast.

The waitress came over and handed me a menu. She had a coffee cup in her hand as she approached the table. I suppose that it was because I looked like a very round and very cold, water balloon. I nodded 'yes' and smiled appreciatingly while I took off layer after layer in order to sit down at the table comfortably.

"It's gotta be a little chilly on a bike this morning." She said, pouring my hot, black coffee.

"It is. That's why I look like a walking weather balloon."

She smiled, "I'll be back to take your order."

"I know what I want and I'll save you the trip."

"OK!" she said, taking out her notebook and pen in one rapid movement.

"I'll take a cheese omelet, cheddar, with jalapenos, home-fries and grits."

"Alright!"

She turned, taking up my menu and dropped a rolled-up bundle with my utensils on the table, again in one motion.

I sat enjoying a hot cup of fresh coffee and looked out the window at Mabel sitting in the sunshine. She was now a tour bike and I was proud of her. I was on my first motorcycle tour. And I was proud of that too. The excitement continued to fill my mind and kept a smile on my face for most of the day.

"You're not too bad lookin'." I said out loud but, in a whisper, looking out at Mabel.

"Who are you talking to, honey?" the waitress asked, standing at the table with the coffee pot and a smile.

"I'm talking to Mabel."

1.2

After my breakfast I was ready to make some time. This hurried feeling, I was soon to find out, would be a feeling to contend with for many trips to come. There's no real explanation for it other than an underlying push to get down the road for some reason or another. Perhaps it's because the natural state of a motorcycle is rolling and not sitting still? And without getting into all the platitudes about motorcycles I will say that they are, for the most part, true. There's something about a motorcycle and being a motorcyclist that lends itself to moving, progressing forward.

"Most motorcyclists, at least those that tour, would agree that we are most comfortable, happiest when we are astride a well-running, two-wheeled machine on a beautiful road." I thought out loud.

I rode towards Salida turning west on the "loneliest road" in America, Hwy 50. But it wasn't lonely this time. I hit construction around Maysville. With Mabel on her kickstand and the motor off, I sat and admired the amazing scenery of Colorado. The traffic finally moving again Gunnison was not far off. I stopped at a small park in town and made myself yet another cup of coffee, trying to slow down and shake the hurried feeling that was already building.

I had packed a full kitchen because it was my intention to camp most of the time. The little plastic French Press contraption I had packed was fair. I had used it for years hiking and camping in my little truck but for some reason the coffee was always a bit too weak. I kept it because it was small and light.

"I'll replace it after this trip." I thought to myself.

However, my camp stove worked like a charm. It was compact and super easy to use. I had a beat-up old pot that I used for everything from cooking to boiling, and I ate from it as well. It had a lid that allowed me to pack small, loose items in the pot when it was packed, and I also used the lid to hold ingredients while I cooked. I opened my side pannier and pulled out my kitchen gear which was packed in an old soft case that had come with my orbital sander. It worked great (the case that is). It carried my little stove, some sporks, a small spatula, some fire-starter materials such as a lighter, some bees wax and sawdust pellets that I'd made myself, and a fire-rod that came with its own striker. It also carried some toilet paper, a dishwashing brush and some handwipes. I had my Camelbak with its water bladder "spidered" to my seat. I carried the case, the ground coffee, my cup and my Camelbak to a small table and sat it all out. The process had become natural from truck-camping every summer for the past few years throughout Colorado. I got the water started and sat on top of the table watching the little town and listening to the whooshing sound of the stove. There were several other people sitting at tables around me but I was a fly on the wall and enjoyed it.

The water boiled in no time and I pressed the coffee through the little, plastic French Press and poured it carefully in my cup.

"This is…" I started, thinking to myself, "This is wonderful. This is life. I could live this way!"

I sat for about a half hour before I cleaned up my equipment, packed it all and put it back in its place in the pannier. Donning my motorcycle gear, I headed out of Gunnison already wondering where I would camp that night. There were plenty of places to pick from, most free, and I continued to remind myself that I wasn't in a hurry. And it was true. I wasn't in a hurry, at least not in a hurry to end the trip. I was, however, in a hurry to start my adventure.

"But it's already started! This is it. There's no need to hurry. Take your time. Enjoy." Mabel reminded me.

"You're right. Let's enjoy it." I said, and sat back down and made myself another cup of coffee and enjoyed the buzz of the little town.

Finally on the bike, I began philosophizing in my helmet as Mabel purred down the road, listening if not intently, then patiently.

"What is freedom and how do we know if we are actually free?"

"Change is the only consistent…"

Mabel hummed contentedly along Hwy 50 through the high desert plains while I thought out loud to myself. It was dry and it was hard to believe how much the scenery had changed from where I was careening down the road. All around me was desert and desert plants with flat-topped hills in the foreground. It was beautiful. It was wild. And it was warming up, finally.

Stopping on the south side of the Blue Mesa Reservoir just to take in the scenery before taking off towards Montrose I decided to pull my big map out of the top case. In Montrose a decision had to be made: which way to go.

"I need to beat the heat because if I go North first, I'll be coming back into the heat. But I really want to make it into Utah and spend some time there. If I take Hwy 145 and cut through Telluride…"

Mabel waited patiently for me to steer her in the direction she already knew I wanted to go. Closing the map and packing it back into the top case, I decided to wait until I came to Montrose and let Mabel choose. She chose Hwy 550, the Million Dollar Highway, but before then I needed to choose where I was going to camp for the night. I wanted some place quiet and not crowded which was, albeit, something not difficult to find in Colorado. Heading south towards the so-called money road, I decided to camp near Box Canyon Falls.

My camp setup was pretty simple. It consisted of a two-man tent, an underlay, and a sleeping bag rated to 35 degrees. I also brought a really old, mat that I laid out in front of the tent entrance to keep the dirt and mud out of the tent. It acted like a porch. I found a great place just south of Ouray. It was not a campsite, but was camp-able. I concentrated on taking my time. The process of setting up camp was simple. First, I took the panniers off the bike. One had all the camp gear in it and the other had the kitchen and other camp necessities. My top case had my clothes, a large map and some other odds and ends. I left it on Mabel. The tent went up easily and I threw my bed stuff and my tank bag into it. Then I read and wrote in my journal. Soon I was sitting on the ground readying my kitchen to cook the food I had bought a little earlier. It was a simple meal, rice and some veggies. I had bought bell pepper and some jalapenos as well as some par-boiled rice. After dinner I made my way to Ouray. I had done a little research and found a new brewery in town. Ouray was just down the road a few miles. There, I got into a conversation about beer with the brewer.

"I try to brew beer but it's not this good!"

"Well, if you like what you brew, it's good enough. That's how I got started."

"Well, you do a damn good job. This is great." I said, taking a second sip from my mug.

"I've got something you might like." He said, turning and walking towards the back of the building. He brought back two large cans of IPA.

"This is our new IPA. It's got a lot of Citra hops in it. You can have em' for the road."

"No, no! I'll buy them. I want to support the local artists!" I said smiling.

He reluctantly took money for one of the cans but insisted on giving me the other.

"I really appreciate it!"

"No problem. Enjoy your trip and be safe!"

I took the cans to go and rode the short distance back to camp. The day was now turning to night and the night cold was settling in. I had experienced my first day of my first motorcycle tour and I was already hooked.

"What's there not to like?!" Mabel added.

After setting my panniers behind my tent I rolled out my sleeping bag, blew up my pillow and underlay, and sat my tank bag and helmet next to the pillow. Back outside I sat enjoying one of the cans of the great beer I was given until the cold chased me in. It was early, but in the camping world bedtime was often when dark falls. Crawling into my sleeping bag I knew I was in for a cold night so kept my long underwear and socks on. I also kept my wool cap on. I lay there for a while listening to the bugs sing their nocturnal songs. I felt lucky for having the chance to do so. With the wilderness a thin sheet of waterproof material away I fell into slumber. It had been a long day. A very long and joy-filled day.

1.3

I woke up at day break. It was cold. It was very cold. The sleeping bag had done its job, but just barely. I would have been lying if I said it was not difficult to pull on the cold jeans that had laid beside me in the tent all night. Fortunately, I didn't much care how I looked and had kept my long sleeve shirt in the bag with me all night. It lay crumbled up in a ball at the foot of the sleeping bag and was wrinkled, but warm. I tried my best to put the shirt on while wriggling around in the sleeping bag, but finally gave up and unzipped my cocoon just enough to pull the garment over my cold body. And yes, it deserves repeating. It was cold. The jeans were, well, they were uncomfortable, at least at first. Slowly however I dressed myself and slid out of the tent onto my "porch" and put my boots on. Everything had a thin layer of frozen dew on it, including Mabel. I started my morning routine and noticed the ice as it sparkled off her tank in the morning sunlight.

"I wonder about the roads?" I said to myself, digging around in my kitchen bag to get coffee going.

"They'll be fine, but be careful." Mabel answered, "We are at high altitude."

At this point I was shivering and so found my jacket and put it on while the water boiled. I watched a cloud of white mist hover around my head as I breathed. I also looked around at the magnificent beauty that surrounded me. Mountains and rocky ledges, Pine trees everywhere and everything dipped in a sparkly, crystal cold. Nature was truly beautiful in a way that touched me deep down. It seemed I could never get enough of it. Of course, this is romanticizing truth a bit but I was on a motorcycle tour, a romantic thing in itself. Water boiled. Coffee made. A second cup. It was time to tear down camp.

I packed up the sleeping bag first while the underlay deflated. It was always the most difficult thing to pack. Getting it back into the compression sack was an endeavor in patience. Then the underlay was packed. The rainfly taken off and the tent un-staked, I kept the poles attached while turning the mesh-inner tent upside down to empty any dirt out and then took the poles down, folded everything and packed all of it away. The tent was wet from the dew, not frozen like everything else, but I'd be using it that night and so didn't worry much. Then more coffee. Then the panniers. First the camping gear was packed in one pannier and the pannier put on the bike. As I drank coffee the kitchen was slowly put away and my water container emptied, but only after filling my Camelbak (there was no spicket there). Coffee finished, kitchen put away, I gathered all the small stuff that I had left on the table and packed the second pannier. On Mabel it went. Then I rummaged through my tank bag to make sure the important stuff was in it, and slapped it on the tank. It had magnets and Mabel had a steel tank. My top pannier was already on the bike. It almost never came off for the rest of the trip. I double checked that my map was there and stuffed any forgotten nick-nacks in it as well. Before closing it up, I got my breakfast out: a protein cereal bar and some granola. This was to become a daily routine for the rest of the trips that I would take. It would become second hand quickly. Having camped quite a bit the only new step was the panniers. The process became a kind of meditative mental exercise for me, one that I looked forward to. Finishing the coffee and donning my gear I started Mabel, letting her motor warm up a bit.

"And we're...almost...off." she said, virtually rolling her headlights.

"I'm coming, I'm coming." I said, taking my helmet off to put in the earplugs I had forgotten to put in.

I was a bit nervous about ice on the roads and so took it slow, especially since we were gaining in altitude pretty quickly. To my left were the Uncompahgre Mountains (14,309 ft) and up ahead lay the so-called million-dollar highway. It was named that because it was said that a million dollars-worth of ore was driven on it by trucks back when mining was the leading industry in Colorado. Gladly, it was no longer the leading industry. At least I didn't think so. The highway was beautiful and the switchbacks were beginning to get a little tight but the light snow at the edges of the highway kept me from becoming too playful, especially on the parts of the road that were shaded by rock. They were places where ice could hide out. There was a pull-in with a gorgeous view that couldn't be passed up and so I took advantage of it to stop and make yet more coffee and to slow the trip down a bit. My hands had gotten instantly cold riding up the road and stayed cold for the next few hours until they were stiff. Mabel now glistened as the frozen dew became a glassy film of water on her which had been flying into my face and on my goggles while riding. The sun was now higher in the sky but it was still quite early and had not melted the morning freeze out yet. Even with the cold and the worry about ice I was in heaven. The nature, Mabel, the thought of the trip all gave me a sense of contentment. I sat on the rocky ledge, shivered, and drank my cup of coffee watching as the sun woke up the valleys down below and bluish, ethereal ledges lurked in the background where the sun had yet to shine. The colors were mesmerizing and I basked in the warm sun of the cold mountain-morning air at 11,008 ft. I sat with my eyes closed and my imagination soared.

"If life has purpose, this must be it!" I whispered, not wanting to disturb the holy place.

Onward, I made Silverton and passed through Moles Pass as the road slowly made its way down through the San Juan National Forest. South of me was Durango, a famous Colorado city. It was filled with the consumerism and urban sprawl created by the tourists that flocked there, especially during the winter. It seemed "anti" Colorado but the reality was that tourism was a major economic staple of the state, overtaking mining. I stopped at a busy gas station and filled Mabel's tank while I considered my options. I could follow Hwy 550 into New Mexico and to Aztec where the famous ruins were, or I could continue to head west. I had never been for visiting tourist attractions as a rule, preferring out-of-the-way places, the unknown corners of the world. My ultimate goal was the west and so I turned on Hwy 160 and followed it with the high desert on one side and the La Plata mountains on the other. Mabel was running like a little kitten. I didn't push her. I really never did. Even through earplugs her engine had a certain tone, a certain rhythm that it would sing. I had become accustomed to it and if it didn't sound a certain way it was a sign that something had changed, good or bad.

"What was that?!" I would sometimes say, thinking that I'd heard something odd.

"It was nothing. I know best." she would sometimes remind me.

Descending down the mountain road it had begun warming up. The scenery was changing quickly from mountains and ponderosas to desert and industrial areas. In Cortez we followed Hwy 160 into the Ute Mountain Indian reservation. I stopped and shed some of the clothing I'd put on early that morning in the mountains. By the time I reached the turn-off for Hwy 160 going west it was almost hot and the mountains had all but disappeared. But so had the industrial areas I had ridden through at the foot of the mountain range. The desert welcomed me now with its own beauty. Tinged brown and beige with dots of light green from the hardy plants that made their home there the landscape seemed to have an almost pink hue that changed as I rode. The road was well-kept but straight and soon I found myself at the Four Corners Monument where Colorado met with New Mexico, Arizona and Utah. I stopped for a bit, but the idea of the so-called "meeting of the states" was a bit meaningless to me. I decided not to visit the monument set up for the place and so rode on.

Taking time, stopping here and there to enjoy the scenery I rode with no particular plans until I got hungry. Lunch was simple, eating crackers and sitting on the ground next to Mabel. Nothing was planned.

"And we like it that way!"

A little further and I found myself deep in the Navajo Nation. Noticing the sparse but beautiful nature I couldn't imagine people farming or making a living off of this land. I had no idea how they survived or what they did. American history came welling up in my head. I felt bad for these people and the situation the migrating Europeans had put them in. Many of the houses were in pitiful disrepair and there were almost no services in the few small specks of "towns" that I did see. I finally saw a gas station with two pumps and a small grocery store. I stopped to scrounge up something for dinner that night and to fill Mabel up. While I was filling the tank two old Indian men who had been sitting on the curb on the side of the grungy building got up and approached me before I had my helmet off. They were dirty and scruffy with large hats on that covered their dark faces. Their baggy clothing hung off their bodies, rag-like.

"Anything?!" One asked quietly, as he held his hand out, "Cigarettes?"

"I'm sorry. I don't smoke. I don't have anything."

The other came up and they moved to the front of Mabel, in front of me.

"Money? You have money!" they demanded, speaking with a little more authority.

"No. I don't." I lied, "Just credit cards."

We stood there, me looking at them and they looking at the ground. After a few seconds they raised their heads and looked forlornly at me with dark, empty eyes. Then started to turn around, hesitating before walking back to the curb where they had been sitting. I stood staring at them as they settled in on the dirty curb and lowered their heads shielding themselves from the hot, morning sun.

The place was dusty and dry, but it was also dirty. There was trash alongside of the once white building. Some of it looked as if it had been there for a while. Beer cans, food wrappers and plastic bags lined the blank wall. I stood by the bike wondering about the two old men and about leaving Mabel there unattended. Looking around I didn't see anyone else. Thinking this way, with suspicion and concern, bothered me but I couldn't shake that little voice in my head.

"Don't stay here long." It seemed to say.

Needing groceries, I decided not to worry too much. After all what could two old men do? I did take the keys, something I rarely did. The panniers were all locked up and I took my wallet and my phone with me from the tank bag.

"Don't worry. I'll be fine." Mabel assured me as I walked into the store.

"That's fine for you. But without you I won't be."

In the store I was met with cheap, instant, boxed meals, junk food and a surly looking obese woman behind the counter who simply stared at me with dark, glaring eyes. Her long, beautiful black hair was tightly woven into a large bun on the back of her head. I looked around for a few minutes and finally gave up and went to the counter.

"Hi! Do you have any vegetables or something like that?" I asked her.

She stared at me and said nothing, and squeezed the big bun of her hair on her head.

"OK." I said slowly, staring at her blank face before walking away to search for something to eat for the night.

I walked around and wondered at the total lack of decent food there. It was the only grocery store I had seen for an hour or more. In fact, it was the only real store I had seen since leaving Durango. I picked up some canned beans and a box of macaroni and cheese as well as a small bottle vegetable oil for the mac-n-cheese. They had beer, but the cheap, watery kind. I passed remembering my now warm can of IPA from Ouray. Walking up to the counter with my few things, I set them down and pulled out my wallet.

"This is it." I said, looking at the cashier.

The lady rang me up and then stopped, robot-like, and stared, again saying nothing. I looked at the register and the number on the small screen and paid the total shown.

"Thank you." I said, smiling and leaving the amount on the counter.

Outside the two men seemed to be sleeping sitting up on the curb, their heads lowered to their bent knees but Mabel sat undisturbed. I packed up my few things and checked the Camelbak to see how much water I had.

"It's full! Great!!" I said to myself, wanting to camp that night. I just had to find a camping spot.

I walked over to the two men and handed them the change I had gotten from the cashier. They nodded their heads.

Hwy 160 was for the most part a straight line diagonally heading southwest. About every other mile there was a long dirt road that met it and so I decided to explore a little and took one. It soon turned to deep sand and I stood up and kept the gas on to keep the front wheel from plowing the sand as the road gave way under my tires.

"Keep gas in mind." Mabel reminded me.

"I just got some! Don't worry."

"Yes, but…" she continued.

The road circled back to the highway. A second dirt road appeared some miles down and I followed it for about a half hour. The landscape was flat and empty. It seemed that there was absolutely nothing around for miles and miles other than empty desert. The road was solid enough though, "baby heads" (rocks about the size of baby heads) and gravel mostly. In a day I had went from jetting through mountains and ledges covered with grass and pines to looking across flat, desert speckled with tough prickly plants. The horizon had gotten bigger, much wider. Out here the sky was expansive.

"This is what I love about the west." I said.

"I like the mountain roads!" Mabel answered.

The nature was truly beautiful. It didn't seem like the dirt road was going to circle back to the main road and so I decided to pull off into the desert, dodging cacti and found a spot that spoke to me about 200 yards in. I turned the motor off and found a rock to set under Mabel's kickstand. It was totally…utterly…silent. I soaked it in until I started feeling a bit strange. This kind of silence was a rare thing indeed in our modern world. It was a thing that sometimes made me nervous. But at the same time, I knew needed it. I desired it. I loved it. This was going to be my camp spot for the night.

The process of unpacking and settling in started. Parked beside a small Mexican Buckeye just a bit higher than Mabel and the tallest thing I could see on the horizon, I cooked my cheap meal and laid out in the desert on my sleeping pad looking up at the dish-like sky as the sun rounded the flat, western horizon. The light disappeared slowly and methodically. Then another world appeared: cool, dark and peaceful. The moon was bluish-white and brighter than I'd ever seen it. The stars in the night sky were a show in themselves and I got lost in thought thinking about how far they were from me and how many there were. I also remembered that there were things in the desert that would want to snuggle up to me now that it was cooling down.

"It's getting cold anyway." I thought, making an excuse.

I got up and gingerly made my way to the tent. But before going in I removed the rainfly and stuffed it inside with me. There was not a cloud to be seen. I knew this could change quickly, but decided to take a chance. The experience of laying in the desert and looking up at the huge, gaping blackness filled with sparkling specks of light was too much to pass up.

"Most of them are light years away, possibly non-existent!" I thought to myself.

These thoughts and others filled me with a kind of happiness. It was late but I had no idea what time it was. I didn't care because I didn't have to. I lay on my back and listened as coyotes began singing their songs. Their yelps and howls surrounded me from all sides but I couldn't see them. There must have been dozens. It sounded like it but I didn't know. I just knew that I loved laying there listening to them and fell into a deep sleep with the sounds of coyotes howling at the moon. It was magical.

1.4

The next morning, I woke early, just before daybreak. The night had been cooler than I thought but I had slept like a baby the whole way through. I lay in my sleeping bag looking up through the mesh of the tent at a bluish-grey sky. There were no sounds now. Nothing. It was the kind of silence that was deep and un-abiding. Unzipping the small doorway and getting out of the tent, I stood naked in the desert and felt a certain freedom and even courage. But even in the desert with nothing around for miles, I also felt a little self-conscious.

"It would be funny if there was someone, somewhere that just happen to be looking." I thought to myself.

"I have to look." Mabel reminded.

"Well. Who cares!"

"I do!"

Pulling some shorts on I started my morning routine. Boiling water for coffee and watching the world as it welcomed the day. I had a second cup before I started packing. Practicing not being in a hurry I did my best to take my time, but it started heating up pretty quick once the sun got a hold on the day. In no time Mabel's tires were swerving and dipping in the loose sand on the road. I took a few detours on some side-side roads but eventually made it back to Hwy 160 and to Tuba City. It was a hub full of the typical fast-food joints and luckily gas stations as well. I frowned in my helmet and tried to imagine how this area would have been before the invasion of corporate America. As I complained quietly I stopped to buy gasoline for the now complaining Mabel, realizing my hypocrisy.

"You're still far from empty!" I chided her.

"Yes, but you never know."

My phone was dying and I had not plugged it into the USB port wired on Mabel nor had I punched in directions. So, I decided to be adventuresome. I took a side road off the main drag to do a little exploring of the town and ended up in a poor neighborhood. I was now riding slowly past small, beige houses that all looked the same. They all had flat roofs and were square, looking much too worse for wear. I turned around at a dead-end road where there were three children playing in their yard and a woman who looked to be overly tired, pulling groceries and yet another small child out of the car as she tried to balance the grocery bag. I waved at the young boy who had stopped playing and now stood staring at me. He made a gun figure with his hand and "shot" me and then stared, unsmiling.

"Nice." I said in my helmet.

"Let's get out of here." Mabel said.

"I agree."

It was hot now and I was in no mood to explore poor neighborhoods in the middle of the desert so I made it to the main road and a nearby gas station to plug my phone into the USB cable that hung off the handlebars. Picking up my tank bag and bringing it in the store with me I bought a few candy bars. My Camelbak was empty from camping the night before. I approached the counter and a friendly looking young man.

"Do you have some place I could fill this up?" I asked, raising the Camelbak.

"Sure! I'll fill it up for you right here, if that's OK?"

"That'd be great!" I said, handing him the small backpack.

He returned with my Camelbak completely full.

Back with Mabel I stood in the parking lot eating one of my candy bars. I watched people who looked very exotic to me walk back and forth from the store. Long, beautiful black-haired women and men with high up and pronounced cheekbones, thin upper lips, and downward sloping mouth corners walked around the gas station. As I stood people watching and not paying attention, I suddenly heard a voice.

"Are you lost? Do you need some help?"

I turned around to see one of the beautiful, black-haired women standing and looking at Mabel. She had walked up behind me from her truck that now sat idling.

"Oh!" I exclaimed. "No, no. But thanks. I'm just taking a break."

"OK." She replied matter-of-factly.

"Where're you from?"

"I live in Denver."

"I've never been there. Where're you headed?" she asked, almost not taking a breath between questions.

I thought for a moment. First about why she told me she'd never been to Denver, and then answered.

"You know. I don't…really know. Right now, I'm going to the Grand Canyon."

She smiled and nodded.

"Have a good time."

"Thanks! Thanks. You too." I answered wondering why I had said "You too.".

She walked away slowly as I admired her long, bluish-black hair brushing her against back as she walked.

1.5

I had a long time to make a short distance but wanted to get on the road nevertheless. The nomadic motorcyclist to the end, it seemed that I was losing the battle to take my time. It was now late morning but I did my best to take it slow, sight-seeing as I made my way to Hwy 64, my turn-off to the Grand Canyon. 64 was a lonesome road that made its way through more hot, dry, flat desert. The sand was now reddish-white and there were some hills just ahead of me. I stopped at the Little Colorado River Gorge Navajo Tribal Park to take a look and after paying the small fee made my way to a beautiful gully in the ground. This was the start of the Grand Canyon area but was not a national park. Down below, the river continued cutting through the rock at a pace that I understood was incredibly slow and at the same time amazing to think about. The timespan was impossible for me to understand. Looking at the deep canyon it was hard to think that at one time this had probably been a small river running through the desert. As I neared the Grand Canyon the landscape started changing gradually. It began to get greener with small trees on the surrounding hillsides, and the road became better kept as well. By the time I had made it the park entrance, traffic had picked up and the area was more built up. I was riding outside of "tourist season" but there were still cars and lots of them. Watching car after car ride by going the other way I was glad I had not come in the middle of tourist season. I slowed and sped up with the traffic. As I followed 64 around to the entrance, I found Grand Canyon Village.

Grand Canyon Village was a monstrosity of a place that littered the south side of the Grand Canyon. The canyon was obviously magnificent but the "village" was just another sprawling consumer center. It was a small town packed with the "conveniences" geared towards modern life in a large RV. I stopped at the entrance.

"Hello sir!" the attendant said, amiably.

"Hi. Is there camping around here somewhere?" I asked.

"Yes. But the campgrounds in the Canyon are full. There's one just down the road. You passed it."

She pointed towards the way I had come.

"It's cheaper too, but it doesn't have too many full hookups." She continued.

"I don't need much. I don't need those for sure." I answered.

"Well, I don't know but I'd think they should have something. But we're full. I'm sorry!"

"It's no problem. Thanks. Can I turn around. I think I'll go check."

"Sure."

She waved me through and I made a U-turn.

The campground that I found was a nice one and not that small.

"All the full hook-ups are taken.", the attendant told me when I stopped.

"Yea. That's not a surprise, but I just need water."

"All of our sites have water."

"OK. Do you have any that are available?"

"Sure."

I filled out the requisite paperwork and got a site, a nice shady spot, and made camp in the busy campground. Afterwards I made my way back to the Grand Canyon "village" to have a look around the park.

Parking in one of the large, sprawling parking lots I started walking around, trying to find a quiet spot to sit and stare over the amazing views that I knew were in the place. I never quite found what I was looking for because of the buildings and cement. After an hour or two I just had to get out. It was too much, too many people. I made my way back to Mabel and decided to look for some more interesting roads to follow, which I found and was able to finally get some great views of the stunning canyon. There were turn-offs and small roads that led away from the main traffic routes. I found that they were much more to my taste. The "village" was of no interest to me, but the Grand Canyon was a place much too big and much to interesting to see in a day. I'd have to make another trip, just not to the so-called "village".

"Maybe I should go to the north rim?" I thought to myself.

"I don't know, but I think we've had enough of the traffic and the tourists." Mabel added.

"I agree!"

I spent the next few hours tooling around and finding quiet spots to sit, any spot away from the "village". There were several that I took advantage of and had a nice if not exciting time. Back at the entrance I asked the attendant about camping on the north side.

"Oh…the north rim camping is full up."

"Do you know about tomorrow?"

"It's full up the whole week." She replied.

"OK. Thanks." I responded, disappointedly.

"Well, that answers that!" I thought.

I stopped and got some beer and food, and after exploring a little more made my way back to the campground and the little site where my tent was up and waiting for me. It was fairly early, but I was tired and ready for a beverage. I settled in and watched as a small family started setting up their tent next to my spot. Three kids and a minivan. They were pulling out everything but the kitchen sink. It took them a good hour or more to set up. I popped open a can of local brew and snacked on some chips as I watched them set up, and wrote in my journal.

"I'm heading to Las Vegas tomorrow, at Helle's request, but I know I'll be back at the Grand Canyon. On the north side. If there is some nature left here, I'd like to experience it. I'll deal with the sinful city of Sodom albeit with some hesitation. A promise is a promise after all."

1.6

I woke suddenly, around 4am. It seemed dark in the tent but I could detect just a hint of light, a dark blue aura through the thick trees that surrounded me. I could also hear faint footsteps. I got my clothes on and unzipped the tent fly. I had the stove and the coffee set up for "instant" coffee and was eager to get the instant going as soon as possible. Outside it was somewhat cool and totally silent except for some faint rustling of leaves and limbs. I sat at the picnic table waiting for the cool morning to sweep the sleep away from my eyes when I heard the rustling again. It was directly behind me. Turning around I saw four or five deer quietly making their way through the campground, feeding. Some were no more than a few yards away from me. It was beautiful sight, and it was somewhat sad as well. I thought about the millennia that these animals must have come through this area before Grand Canyon Village and the numerous RV campgrounds like this one were built. They didn't seem to mind the change, munching on grass and other edibles and simply walking by all the RV's. They were oblivious to the intrusion of civilization on their world, at least for the moment. One looked up and saw me sipping coffee and seemed to think a for second. I was evidently not anything to worry about as it bent its head again and continued eating.

I watched the animals until they disappeared. Then the campground was silent and still, the only sound being me packing out. I kept the kitchen bag out as usual after I had packed everything else on Mabel and made a quick breakfast of instant oatmeal. While I would never eat the stuff at home, out camping it was actually pretty good and became my breakfast of choice. Camping was funny that way. The further out I went, the better anything tasted. It wasn't long before I started Mabel up and rolled out of the silent and still sleeping campground. The light was just beginning to show as I made my way back to Hwy 64 going east, and back to 89 north. I could have taken a dirt road by going south on 64 and turning towards Willaha but I wasn't sure of the condition of it, and it was going to be about fifty miles on dirt. I wasn't comfortable with that, yet, but I came to regret it later. Now, however, I would suggest taking an adventure over comfort any day but experience is often recognized in hindsight.

The drive north was, well, boring. Through the desert, highway 89 was full of dump trucks and construction traffic, industrial and metal were the themes. The road had lots of construction and it was hot. Finally, the scenery got much better but only when I turned on Alt 89. I reached Jacob Lake and the turn off for the North Rim and stopped at the intersection, considering another night at the Grand Canyon. I did remember what the park ranger had said about the camp ground being full but also thought about the multitudinous dirt roads that would probably lead to stealth-camping opportunities. Possibilities filled my head but the decision was made to wait and make a whole trip of it later. I took my time as I rode on the south side of the Grand Staircase mountains in Utah. I passed one after another small dirt road leading north through what I almost knew was an amazing area but again thought twice, a little nervous about the unknown, the dirt.

"I'm a coward!" I thought to myself, and rode on.

"Another time; when you're more comfortable with the thought." Mabel assured me.

I entered Zion National Park and rode through that beautiful but busy little place, poking along behind big RV's and often waiting while people pulled off or just stopped in the middle of the small road to take photographs. The park was just off the highway and so an easy mark for tourists looking for easy-to-get photos. Things starting getting really busy as the little road neared the highway itself. My wife had talked me into at least one night in Vegas and I was going to make good on my promise. It was against my wishes.

"But everyone needs to experience Las Vegas at least once." She had argued.

"I'm pretty sure I know what it is." I told her when I stopped and called. I found that I had cell service, something that had been lacking the past few days.

"And I'm pretty sure you're right. But you need to see it for yourself. You won't like it, but you need to experience it. Just go and quit questioning me." She chided.

"That's not really why I came on this trip. I came to see nature and experience landscapes." I continued.

"I know, I know…but…"

"Well. OK. But I won't stay longer than a day." I pouted.

"That's fine. Just enjoy yourself. Splurge a little. Have fun." She said with a smile in her voice.

"Be careful with what you ask for." I cautioned.

The highway to Las Vegas was no fun either. Just fast and busy. It was not what motorcycle adventures were about. At least not to me. But I was now on a mission to get Las Vegas behind me. And so, the highway it was. They did have their uses. I hit the city from the north and hurriedly found the infamous "strip". The new Vegas was a family-friendly affair with huge skyscrapers cutting the wide desert sky I had enjoyed the past several days. The big glass and steel monstrosities were separated by massive fountains in the middle of a naturally arid area. Everything about Las Vegas was wrong; oxymoronic. It was human debauchery at its best. But, for now, I was here. Just driving through the strip gave me a bad taste in my mouth. Mabel and I both felt out of place completely as minivans and Maserati's whizzed by. We were covered in dust and dirt and smelled of mountains and desert air.

"I just don't understand this!" I said to myself in my helmet.

"Well, I don't either." Mabel answered. "What are we doing here?!"

"We are fulfilling a promise."

"What did you get us into?!"

I had come to like the feeling of earth and the outside. But I decided to find a place to wash some clothes before getting into a hotel. I wasn't going to find anything on the strip and so rode out to the floundering outliers, the unseen and everyday Las Vegas where there was a washateria in a poor neighborhood. What I found was that most neighborhoods, in fact most of Las Vegas that was sans strip was a collection of poor houses, drab suburbs, and run down strip malls. Lost, I had accidentally run across the place. It was ironically a dirty looking washateria and I hurriedly found that no one spoke English and I had no Spanish skills. No one talked much in the place anyway. I sat and read a book waiting on my clothes. A few hours later, the clothes were clean, all except the ones I had on. I was back on Mabel and heading for the strip again. The city was almost as hot and dusty as the desert, until I reached the new-and-improved strip. Then it was immaculately clean and just hot.

There was not a lack of hotels and I looked for one close and with somewhere covered to park Mabel, preferably out of the way and out of sight. I spotted a parking garage just off the main drag and hurriedly found a spot a few floors up. Carrying my top case into the instantly cool and marbled hotel lobby I searched for a front desk which wasn't hard to find. I didn't know the name of the hotel as I chose it on the proximity and inclusion of the parking garage and not on the merits of the hotel itself. I was decked out in my dirty, black moto jacket, leather gloves and wore my helmet (because I couldn't carry it). I had the top case, and the tank bag in my hands. The concierge at the hotel looked at me for a second, but not for long. She was probably used to seeing all sorts here.

"Hello…" she said, and waited as I took my helmet off.

"Hello sir! And welcome." She repeated.

"Thanks! I'm hoping you have a room. Preferably one with a shower." I smiled.

"I think we can accommodate that request!" she grinned.

"Whatever you have, just not the most expensive."

"Have you been to Vegas before?"

"Nope. My first time. I'm only here because of my wife."

She stared not knowing what I meant by that. I remembered where I was and explained.

"My wife" I began, "said I needed to experience Vegas at least once, and so here I am."

She smiled, "Well, I would agree with your wife. I think you'll like it here. Do you like to gamble?"

"Not much. But I hear there's good food."

"That there is! And here's your key. You'll be on the 18th floor. Enjoy your stay!"

She handed me a key card and I took the elevator up to the eighteenth floor. She must have liked me because I got a corner room with windows as walls and a wide, expansive view of the city. The room had a little living room and a large bathroom. It was luxury suite by all accounts and had only cost me $65 dollars! I was amazed actually. Sitting on the bed I enjoyed the view and leaned back against the hardwood walls. I could see past a few skyscrapers and looked at the sprawling, beige desert just outside the city limits.

"I could do a road trip and find some nice roads." I thought to myself.

"Maybe to the Hoover Dam or just explore?!"

Then I heard my wife's voice in my head, "Spend time *in the city*. See the strip."

A promise was a promise and Mabel was safely parked in the parking garage, so I donned my shorts and a clean shirt and made my way down to the lobby. On the way out I saw the concierge again.

"Thanks for the great room!"

"No problem, sir. Have a great time!" she smiled and waved.

Outside, the sidewalks were full of people in tourist garb doing tourist things. There were buskers everywhere selling everything from counterfeit CD's to tickets to who knows what. It seemed like everyone was overweight, over-inundated with too much of everything, and oblivious to it all. I walked around in awe of all the cement until around 1 pm when the heat off the streets and sidewalks started getting to be a bit much. I ducked into one of the many, many casinos. Inside was the endless clang of ringing from the endless rows of gambling machines and money-grubbers. No one talked and the place had a smell that only casinos had: cheap chemicals and food. And it was freezing inside. I got lost in the rows of slot machines, flashing lights, and gambling tables and finally came out and into a hallway of restaurants. The large, covered hallway was stuffed with buffets and sit-down places as well as lots and lots of fast food. Outside again I walked, mostly following the herd of people which seemed to wander aimlessly taking pictures and "selfies". I ducked into another casino and found myself in yet another hall. This time an expansive hall with the sky painted on the ceiling. I heard the sound of birds chirping, being pumped in from somewhere through loudspeakers I presumed. I found a little bar with a few people lounging around, a place to get a snack. I stopped and sat down. A friendly young man decked out in fifties diner garb came up.

"Hello sir. What can I get you?"

"How about…some…French fries and…you know what…I'll take a beer too. Local if you've got it."

"We do! Do you like IPA's?" the attendant asked.

"Why, yes I do!" I answered with excitement in my voice.

About that time, I heard thunder and looked up. The blue ceiling with friendly white clouds had turned grey with ominous thunderclouds.

"That's pretty cool!" I said.

"Huh? Oh that. I don't even notice it anymore." He said before walking off with my order. The bar was small and the waiter was only a few feet away so I continued talking.

"Are you from Vegas?"

"Yea. My whole life."

"You haven't worked *here* your whole life?"

"NO!" he smiled. "But I've been in the service industry for a long time. I'm working on getting to be a dealer. They make great money!"

"So, you like gambling? Casinos?"

"I guess they're OK. It's work and its better than this."

"You don't seem like you like Las Vegas?" I asked.

"I don't know. I've never been anywhere. Maybe?"

"Maybe you should try leaving? Do something else?"

"I've thought of that, but don't know where I'd go. I don't know what I'd do. Are you here to gamble?"

"Me? No! I'm not much of a gambler. I'm here because my wife told me I needed to be here. I'm touring around on a motorcycle." I answered, smiling and waiting for the inevitable question.

"That sounds cool! But I've never heard that before!" he said, smiling.

"What?" I asked, sipping beer and chomping on the hot fries, knowing what was coming next.

"Your wife told you to be here?!" he asked.

"Yea. She said I needed to experience it. You know what. Hell with it. I'll take another beer. Do have any other local beers?"

"We have a Bock beer. It's from near here."

"I'll stick to the IPA, thanks."

He walked off and brought another frosty mug of hoppy ale.

"Well, don't experience too much of it or you'll get hooked." He said with a sly grin.

"I doubt it. The beer's good though. And so are the fries. Do have something that would go good with fries?"

He smiled.

As I sat there eating my fries and finishing a big chili dog that I "just had to have" the ceiling changed again to a wintery flurry, and then later back to the summer day. It was strange sitting in this place. I had no idea whether it was day or night, or what time it was for that matter. It was discombobulating. I finished, paid and made my way back to the street where I happened upon an upscale looking restaurant; in a casino of course. I made plans to have a nice dinner there that night, if I could find it again. That afternoon I flip-flopped from the hot streets of Las Vegas to the freezing temperatures of a few casinos getting lost in them every time I went in. I didn't gamble but I did enjoy many of the small restaurants and bars that were found in the casinos, sampling appetizers here and there and drinks at other places. I never got used to the casino-smell though.

"They must have it pumped in." I thought.

That night I put my "dress pants", jeans, on and my cleanest shirt and made my way back to the posh restaurant I had found earlier. It was late, around 9pm when I walked in the door. There were not many people in the place and I was sat quickly. I ordered a gin and cucumber martini and sat waiting for my dinner and enjoying a very good drink. Back in the corner I noticed a family with a small child. They weren't talking. In fact, they never said a single word the entire time I was there. The man had dark sunglasses on and was dressed to the hilt in what looked like an expensive Italian suit. He seemed to ignore the child and the lady, staring down at the table instead and fidgeting. The lady was also dressed highly fashionably. She was very thin and paid no attention to the little girl in the chair beside her. She sat staring blankly out over the restaurant, seeming not to notice anything or anybody, or the fact that she was obviously being ignored by her boyfriend or husband. I didn't know which. My dinner came and it was very good. The service was as good as the drink and so I ordered another martini and watched the silent table, studying them. Even the little girl said nothing but sat there as if waiting for something to happen. Their dinner came. They ate. And suddenly, as if they needed to be somewhere, they got up quickly. Him first and the thin lady slowly. She slumped over to pick up the child and they walked out. Silently.

1.7

Back at my room I settled in the huge, comfortable bed and stared out at the lights of Las Vegas through my window-walls. I wondered about that couple and I wondered about how a place like Las Vegas could exist. It was so, so out of place. It was empty and insubstantial and yet full of every extravagant thing and activity you could think of. It seemed that this little slice of the city was just a bubble surrounded by poverty and people just trying to get by. It was full of roaming, empty stares and circus acts, and casinos that never closed; people that never slept. It seemed like it was a bad dream full of good drinks and great food. Las Vegas was a place where things just seemed to appear out of nowhere, around corners and for no reason. It was a mirage, a temporary illusion, and yet it seemed so real. But it wasn't real. Reality was sitting on the floor in the form of my dirty, scratched up panniers that were surreal in a place like Las Vegas and yet there they were. There I was. But everything seemed to be out of place in this extravagance and luxury. I didn't know whether to thank or curse my wife for sending me to this place. But I reminded myself that adventures came in many forms including, perhaps, Las Vegas. This was an adventure that I had had enough of though, and I fell asleep and slept soundly. I knew I had a long day ahead of me. I knew I would leave the next day but I didn't know where to. I knew it was going to be out of Las Vegas though.

I slept late, wrapped in the luxurious comfort of a huge bed in an air-conditioned hotel room surrounded by the cityscape below me and the desert out in the distance. I instantly felt guilty about it.

"This is not what I came to do." I thought to myself, and shifted in the cool, comfortable sheets.

I forced myself to stand up, to get out of bed. It was late by my standards and I had a slight headache from the night's alcoholic debauchery and found a packet of aspirin neatly laid out with the other accoutrements that such places always had. There were towels perfectly folded. A spotless bathroom devoid of any offending odors or even dust for that matter. The perfectly padded rug under my feet and the cool temperature of the room all wrapped me in comfort while at the same time the reality of the desert lay just a quarter inch away through a glass wall.

"Don't look out there!" Las Vegas seemed to whisper, "keep your eyes on all *I have to offer*!"

Comfort is easy and tempting, but it is also our worst enemy. Mabel and the adventure that she symbolized was a quest. Las Vegas symbolized consumerism; a purpose empty of meaning other than materialism. But I enjoyed the cool shower, consumeristic or not. And I took my time packing. I had to admit that it was difficult to live up to my own ideals although I tried. Back down in the lobby I saw the concierge from the day before.

"Are you leaving us already?" she asked, feigning some sorrow.

"Yes. It's time for me to get back to reality." I answered.

"Aww. That doesn't sound fun. Where are you headed?" she followed up as she continued typing on her computer.

"I don't know. Probably north. It's getting hot here."

"Yes. It does do that. Did you have fun?" she asked.

"It was…different. I am glad I came though."

In the parking garage I hurriedly found Mable sitting in her spot among the sedans, the minivans and the expensive sport coupes. She was still dusty and dirty from a few weeks of riding, and seemed out of place and bored.

"We're leaving today. Don't worry." I said out loud to her.

And we did leave. But before we left the "new and improved" strip I accidently ran into the "old" part of Las Vegas. There was the infamous (or famous) Golden Nugget.

A thought instantly ran through my head, "Now *this* is Las Vegas!"

I couldn't help but stop. There was a small covered walking street with shops and restaurants and The Golden Nugget hotel sat close by. I walked in and walked through the hallways and into the casino instantly noticing the stench of cigarette smoke. I didn't gamble but I just had to see it. Some of my high school TV history was in this place. I envisioned Dean Martin and "The Rat Pack". It was a little after 8am and already the clanging of slot machines was deafening as I opened the old doors to the famous casino. Sprinkled throughout the aged but still well-kept place were aged and not so well-kept people, pulling levers, mesmerized by the lights and noise. I couldn't take anymore and made my way back when I noticed the hotel diner. It still maintained a sixties aura and smelled of cigarette smoke as well. I imagined the old actors and mafia types that might have sat in it after dirty deeds done the night before. It was perfect, even with the smoking patrons inside. I walked in an ordered a big breakfast and as much coffee as I could drink to wash it down. It was greasy and mediocre. It fit the place exactly! For a short period, I played with the idea of staying at the The Golden Nugget but decided against it in the end. Adventure called and I had had enough. And so back out to Mabel, again waiting patiently for me in the parking garage now along with a few other motorcycles.

"At least you have someone to talk to." I said.

"What are we still doing here?!" was the answer I got.

The mid-morning was hot. I headed north with the idea of exploring some nature. The twenty-miles or so on I-15 were horrendous. Construction trucks, cars and big rigs zoomed past and stirred up dust everywhere. It was hot but I had one more stop before shaking Las Vegas off of me. I needed a map of Nevada to put on my tank bag and found one just outside North Las Vegas. I also found that getting an old-fashion map was more difficult than I expected. I did find one in a truck stop and decided to head north on Hwy 93. It cut straight through the eastern section of Nevada. By the time I turned on 93 I was beat from battling the traffic and the heat. Hoping for better riding I hurriedly bid farewell to the strip of freeway that scarred the surrounding desert and started my trek north. The Great Basin Highway through Nevada was wide, straight and flat. In the distance lay mountain ranges that seemed out of place in the expanse of the hot, reddish desert but I was riding towards them with hopes of a cooler climate and less city. The road was not looking promising but I decided to press on anyway. Soon it turned into a two-lane road, but that was the only change. The landscape was still desert, and as beautiful as it was it was also scorching. I pressed on through the heat, packing my motorcycle jacket and riding in short sleeves for a while. Straight. About one hundred miles north of Vegas I came to a smaller highway, Hwy 318. The only sign of civilization was a small, metal building set far off the road at the intersection. I turned on 318 and headed north, checking my gasoline situation. It was good and so onward Mable and I sped. The road gradually became narrower but the landscape didn't seem to change. It was beautiful desert. Soon I saw entrances for ranches and wondered how those survived out in this beautiful but barren land. Then I passed a sign that warned no services until Lund, about 129 miles away. I looked down to check the gas again.

Hwy 318 was a beautiful straight stretch of road that gave me time to think, something that motorcycles were excellent at doing. In my helmet I talked out loud to myself and to Mabel about philosophical ideas and life in general. I commented on the nature and on Las Vegas while I kept a close ear on Mabel's motor, which hummed liked a bird. I didn't push her and kept a constant eye on the gas gauge. Mabel had a theoretical range of about 300 miles but I didn't want to test that range out here in the middle of nowhere Nevada. I saw a dirt road with what looked like a park service sign and stopped. The sign stated that there were campgrounds about twenty miles down the inviting dirt road and I was tempted. But alas, my camelback was about ½ full and I had minimal food, snacks basically, and no idea if the campground had any amenities or if it even had any spots. It was also extra mileage and Lund was still about sixty-five miles away. I was hoping that the services there were open or even existent, but I didn't know. Stores and gas stations could close their doors. I took a swig of water from my pack and pulled out one of two protein bars I always had in my tank bag, mainly for emergencies. Chewing on the bar I stared out in the distance towards the mountain ranges and possible adventures that lay down the dirt road. I thought of my wonderful night in the desert back on the Navajo reservation. But I chose the safety and relative security of the main road and decided to continue on 318 towards Lund.

318 was whitewashed from the sand and the heat that surrounded it, and the only "civilization" that I saw was the occasional metal building with worn out, rusted construction equipment strewn about. When I arrived in Lund there were no gas stations, just as I suspected, and while my gas situation wasn't quite critical yet, I instantly got nervous. From Lund I had about twenty miles to the next intersection and about thirty miles to Ely where there was supposed to be another gas station. I crossed my fingers.

"There's no problem." I reminded myself, but still for some reason worry set in.

I rode slowly through the tiny burg making sure to keep an eye out for any commercial building that might be a gas station but there were none. I had no choice but to keep going. Soon I realized that my worries were not necessary because about ten miles up the road in Preston I found a very small, sparse truck stop with two pumps.

"I hope they work!" I said to Mabel.

"We'll be good." She assured me, as I down geared to slow.

They worked! The intersection at Hwy 6 didn't have much to offer other than other empty metal buildings but now I had gas and was out for some adventure. I backtracked to the dirt road and spent the night at an empty, primitive campsite. I was the only camper in the small, desolate place. The next day, after stopping again at the small station, I decided to continue north hoping for some cooler weather. North on Hwy 6 trees started appearing, those short fir trees I had seen so many of in the mountains back in Colorado. They were promising signs to me because they meant some opportunity for stealth camping. The landscape changed from flat, reddish desert to hilly reddish desert with hundreds of trees dotting the hillsides. I was almost to Ely where I decided I would stop and make some more decisions. I quickly made the decision, though, to continue north. This was going to be a day of riding, desert heat and helmet discussions with Mabel.

In Wells Hwy 80 appeared and I continued north. The day was spent riding and taking detours up unknown dirt roads. I had decided to rid myself of that nervousness about riding in dirt and sand and the only way to do that, I proposed to myself and Mabel, was to ride in dirt and sand. Some roads were rutted and tough and I dropped Mabel a few times trying to circumvent the worst of the furrowed roads, and others were graded and smooth. Most dead-ended into a fence row or simply stopped, leaving the desert to itself. But the idea worked. I was getting more comfortable managing a fully loaded motorcycle on dirt and in sand. After a while I started thinking about camp sites. It was getting a little late and so about ten miles north of 80 I continued taking detours on dirt roads that looked interesting. They were now mostly access farm roads that led to and through ranch land. I rode across some cattle guards and considered camping behind the large water towers that fed several troughs for cattle but remembered the time I camped in a field in Denmark and woke up to a large, gritty cow tongue licking my face while I lay trapped in a sleeping bag surrounded by a herd of 2000 lb. animals. I turned Mabel around and found another dirt road that led up a steep, rutty incline where I dropped Mabel yet again in a deep rut. This time I had to unpack the luggage and maneuver her around and repack again in order to get back down to the main road.

"This is getting old!" she reprimanded me.

I turned around and headed towards the pavement. It was now getting late enough to start seriously looking for a campsite. The sun was down along the mountain peaks in the distance and I wanted to set up camp before dark. I rode on and found a wide dirt road that led up into the nearby hills which were covered with trees. I took a chance hoping for the best. Several miles up a graded but rocky road into the hills I found a spiderweb of trails and followed them until I found a nice, flat spot hidden by short, windblown trees and large boulders. I was high up on a hill. That night I had instant soup, some candy bars and a few cheap beers that I'd bought earlier after leaving the gas station in Preston. Sitting on the dusty ground next to Mabel my simple dinner was wonderful. That night I lay in my tent with the rainfly off staring up at a beautiful desert sky, clear and filled with stars. Full of cheap food and even cheaper beer and lying in the cool night air of northern Utah, I didn't miss that comfy bed at all.

1.8

I hadn't slept at any real altitude but I had slept high enough up to make the night just perfect for camping. I wasn't far from the Idaho border and was looking forward to seeing a little of that state and all it had to offer. As usual I began my morning camping ritual.

The morning and evening rituals were becoming times that I found I enjoyed almost as much as exploring the country on Mabel. Perhaps it was because the packing out and packing in were the only consistent things I had on such trips. Over the last few weeks these rituals had become second nature, and times that I looked forward to every day. Finding a camp spot and setting up camp, eating and having a beverage, sleeping out in the open, and waking up to instant oatmeal and strong coffee. They all added to my love of camping. That night up on the hill I had had a peaceful slumber with no interruptions, something that you're always happy about when stealthily camping. The next morning, I decided that I would do a little inspection on Mabel so I found the flattest spot I could and pulled out my little tool bag. There was nothing wrong, but I tightened and lubed the chain and checked her fluids. I inspected what wiring I could see and checked for signs of leaks. Everything was ship-shape.

I had bought the bike really cheaply about a year before. It had evidently been traded in with a boat for a big highway machine. Mabel had caught my eye right off the bat in the showroom and after a test ride there was no doubt. Since then, we had done a lot of miles through the mountains of Colorado. Now I was out touring a part of the west with her.

I made my way down the rocky, graded road I had climbed up the day before until I reached 93 heading north. I passed through Twin Falls Idaho and stopped at a gas station to top the fuel tank off and check the oil again; just to make sure. I always brought a quart to carry with me just in case. But, of course, there were no problems. The day was spent filled with perfect riding through southern Idaho. I didn't even know what road I had gotten on but it wasn't a main road. It wound through a colorful valley with green hills and wildflowers everywhere. It was just twisty enough to be interesting and not so twisty to force Mabel and I to "work". It was so beautiful that I decided to stop and take a nap and so started looking for a place to do just that. I found a little dirt road with just enough space to pull off and park. Walking up a grassy, colorful incline to a large group of trees I looked down at Mabel parked away from the non-existent traffic on the dirt pullout. I found an old, friendly-looking tree and rolled my jacket up for a pillow and lay looking up through the branches until my eyes started slowly closing. I faded away into a relaxing slumber. When I woke, I was refreshed but missing my home for the first time on the trip. I started thinking.

"If I started back now, I would have been gone for about three weeks."

"Who are you trying to impress?!" Mabel answered.

"No. It's not that…"

"Do what you want. That is the luxury of having time."

"You're right!"

"I usually am."

It was time to head back to Colorado and so we turned south and headed towards Wyoming. The backwoods of Idaho would have to wait.

"I'll be back!" I promised.

I crossed into Wyoming just south of Jackson and the Grand Tetons. A few hours north was Yellowstone. I had another decision to make and so stopped for a snack at a junction, and thought about it.

"North to some beautiful National Parks or wait for next time and take the time that they deserve. Or, onward through some un-explored and equally beautiful Colorado landscape.?"

I thought of the crowded park in Utah, with the masses of RV's and tourists. A cup of coffee later I decided to wait.

"They deserve more than a rushed run through."

"I'm not sure what the question was? You made your mind up a while ago." Mabel added.

I decided to forego the parks.

Continuing, I rode past a little road to get to Pinedale in order to buy some groceries and beer for the night. I stocked up on both and turned back to explore route 352. Wyoming is full of rolling hills and flat plains and 352 gently swung around them and dead ended at a BLM campground. It was a typical western campground with dirt roads and open space, nicely kept with a few group camp areas and several places with fire rings or a ring of rocks. Most had firewood stacked closed by, left by previous, thoughtful campers. There were never any amenities such as water or electricity which kept most of the weekend warriors and RVs at bay. I had found the same thing in many places in Colorado. But Wyoming had been the only place that I had found beer cans hanging off branches in trees put there by drunk or stupid (or both) people. For the most part out west most (I say most) campgrounds were nice, neat little out of the way spots. But today it seemed like I had the whole BLM land to myself. I explored a little once entering the national forest and found a rocky dirt road. It headed up and away from the obvious campgrounds I had found. I followed it a few miles, passing several welcoming spots and couldn't make my mind up.

"Maybe this one…Let's go up a bit and see if there's something better…"

"That's great! Oh, but it's not completely flat and it's a bit close to the road…"

"Oh this it. Oh wait…"

This is how it went and it went this way with many of the campers I had talked to over the years. I can't explain it. There I was in the middle of nowhere, where I hadn't seen a sign of civilization or even a person for hours and I was going through the same procedure as I would have in a crowded campground.

"C'mon!" Mabel scolded.

I finally lighted at a place that I had to ride through the woods to get to. The only thing that tipped me off was a small, rough trail that led into the forest. A few hundred feet of riding through trees and brush and I found a small trail that led to a cleared-out area with a rock fire ring. It had some firewood neatly stacked.

"I'm not the only one that likes to search for the perfect campground!" I told Mabel as I parked her on the most solid ground I could find.

"I'm glad I stopped and filled up my water tank! Maybe I'm getting smarter in my old age?"

There's no chance of that." Mabel retorted.

All around was the most amazing nature. A river ran nearby with mountains surrounding us on all sides. There were campgrounds everywhere, each one welcoming, inviting, and fairly private even if there had been anyone at the place. I started to realize that there was probably not enough time to see the amazing nature that the west had even if I did do this full time. That night I watched the sun go down through the thick forest leaving strips of orange-red light on the forest floor that seemed to move and quiver. My small fire was going before it was completely dark, and it got really dark out in these areas, especially in the forest. But the sky and the overall scenery was amazing. I looked through the trees as the night sky took the day over. It was a sight to behold with no light-pollution. I looked over at Mabel with the shadows from the fire making the sparkles in her black paint light up. I sipped my IPA. I had the night and my thoughts to myself.

"I could live like this, though." I thought, "This is all I need."

1.9

Rolling the thought of being a full-time motorcycle-nomad around in my head made me feel happy. Almost hopeful. Little did I know, but this trip would be the start of a new addiction. I finished the beer and crunched the can down, put it in my trash sack and picked the other can up. I had bought a bag of chips as a treat, and opened it up as well. This idea would take some pondering, and some snacks.

"Yep. This is it. This is what I want to do."

"Helle would never agree!" Mabel reminded me.

I rolled that thought around in my head and took a few more sips of beer.

"Of course not. It's just a thought." I said, taking yet another sip of the beer.

I spent a perfect night in the woods next to Mabel, sleeping like a baby with my sleeping bag half open and no tent. I had woken up to "sounds" during the night but they were wilderness sounds and not the sounds of people and so I hadn't worried much. It was cool and the sun hadn't come up yet when I woke up for the day the first time.

"My morning ritual is going to start late today." I thought. I felt it in my bones.

There was no hurry now and I was comfortable with my decision to head back. I laid back and fell asleep again. A few hours later I woke because it was getting hot in the sleeping bag and the bugs were starting up. The sun had come up and even though I was protected from the full glare by the trees, a few rays had found me and the sleeping bag. The heat index was rising. My morning ritual started, having gotten quite a bit more efficient throughout the trip. Mabel packed I cranked her up and let the motor warm up even though it wasn't really necessary.

"Thank you for a wonderful night." I said to the place and then made my way back to the main road and turned south.

"The wind has picked up." I thought to myself, "Well, it is Wyoming. But how bad can it be?!"

It was bad. It was worse than I had thought.

Travelling south down 191 the wind was at my back and I enjoyed the cool-ish breeze blowing through my riding jacket. The road was good and the desert was starting to spread over the horizon. I was going to make Denver by nightfall and surprise my waiting wife. When I reached Rock Springs the wind was strong and was pushing me every which way as I entered the north side of town. The freeway was in front of me and I stopped at a gas station to get a snack, gas up, and just get out of the wind for a bit. I knew I was heading home but maybe I could make it a little fun? I found a possibility, a road that headed south out of Rock Springs into the north-western most corner of Colorado. Part of it was unpaved and although I had done some dirt riding, and had motocross experience in my early days, I knew that unpaved roads in Colorado could be fire roads or they could be craggy, rutted nightmares, especially on a fully loaded bike. Even with my newly found courage I decided to forego the unknown road for now. I had it in my head to have a beer at home and so opted for the boring but fast freeway to make my way to a paved road that would still put me in the beautiful riding country of Colorado. Freeways were not my favorite way to travel for many reasons and I was going to be reminded of a few of those shortly. The pesky wind that I had at my back going south was now a nightmarish side-gale. Going 75 on the freeway had Mabel at a twenty-degree angle and I was getting buffeted as the wind twisted around mountains and gained speed over the ubiquitous flatlands of Wyoming. Every time I passed or was passed by a big rig I felt as if I was being grabbed by an invisible hand and thrown in the opposite direction of the lean almost instantaneously.

"This...is...interesting." I said aloud in my helmet to the rush of wind surrounding me in all directions, whipping Mabel back and forth.

Mabel flopped around and I felt like a ping-pong ball on a very short table. After about forty minutes of being slapped around by mother-nature, my shoulders hurt and my neck ached but I was adamant and kept the throttle twisted. In fact, I twisted the throttle right past my turn-off and ended up in the next town being whipped and snapped back and forth all the way. Now clouds were accumulating in the east. Dark clouds and out west they could turn wet in a hurry. I gave up my plans of hitting Denver that night. I was beat down and haggard from fighting eighteen-wheelers and the blustery wind. I turned off and found a not-so-exciting motel to waste my money on. In the past weeks, I had come to consider getting a motel as failure. But now I didn't care. It wasn't fun anymore. The freeway had sucked the joy out of riding.

"This will be the last freeway I take on any motorcycle tour!" I swore to myself. It wasn't true.

I walked in the lobby and it smelled…different. That kind of clean but not clean smell that some cheap motels have. The Indian man greeted me from behind the counter.

"Hello. May I help you?" he said with a friendly tone.

"Yes. Yes you can! I hope you have a room. On the first floor if possible. I'm on a bike.

"Yessir."

Outside it was getting dark fast. Clouds were rolling in and becoming black quickly. I knew that afternoon storms in the west had a way of sneaking up on you swiftly.

"I have several rooms. Two queens or a king?"

"It doesn't matter to me. Whichever one is cheaper." I said looking out the window at the dark clouds quickly marching towards us.

"They cost the same sir."

"OK. I'll take the king." I said hurriedly, looking out the window again.

"Yessir."

As he was typing on his keyboard I continued watching as the thunderstorm rolled in. I heard the wind pick up even more speed, rattling the cheap motel windows.

"Looks like some weather is moving in."

"Yes it does." I answered, unconsciously tapping my fingers on the counter.

Soon he handed me a key card and directed me towards the room at the far corner of the building, in the back. I rode the short distance to the room through the parking lot as large drops of rain started bombing me, slowly at first. As I took the top case off Mabel a down pour, like someone had tipped over a bucket, started.

"Shit!" I said, hurriedly taking my tank bag and trying to wrap my elbows around my helmet that I had taken off. I dropped helmet in the parking lot.

"Son of a…"

The downpour had me drenched in seconds as I fumbled around trying to hold the tank bag and pick up my helmet laying upside down in the parking lot like a pail. I looked at the key card for the number of the room.

"212?" I said wondering about a first-floor room.

I climbed the stairs with the tank bag, my gloves, and my helmet as a loud clap of thunder smashed the sky. Finding my room, I got in put my things down and went back down for the top case and to "settle" Mabel in. I put her on her center stand. Luckily, I had the foresight to leave my riding jacket in the room before going downstairs to get wetter. Finally settled in my dingy room on the second floor I ordered a pizza and made my way over to the gas station (yes, in the rain) for beer (I had my priorities). Anyway, I figured I was already drenched. Soon, after a hot shower, I was laid out over one of the queen beds, clean, in my dirty underwear, eating sub-par pizza, drinking cheap beer and listening as the air-conditioner fan ran full blast drying out my boots, socks and some clothing that I had hung over it. I looked out the window at Mabel sitting in the down pour, silent and stoic. She didn't like hotels nor did she care for freeways. Neither did I.

Sprawled out on the bed with a half-eaten pizza beside me I fell asleep. Waking up suddenly I started up and picked up my trash, put the fan on auto and crawled in bed for the night, sleeping soundly in the dingy little room. The blinds were pulled down and so had no idea what time it was when I woke up. It felt early, but the alarm clock didn't work. The motel interrupted my camp ritual and I felt strange walking around in the dingy room towards the little coffee maker to make my morning brew. It used those puck things that might be a good idea on paper, but made for a pitiful cup of coffee. I took advantage of the shower and then packed my things. I was going to head for the northwest corner of Colorado today. Opening the blinds, a bright laser of light hit me. Outside the sun was shining and the sky was blue; a perfect biking day. I took out my big map and draped it over the open top case and immediately started looking for a way to get off the highway. I found a possible road with a little dirt section and decided to take the chance. You had to be careful with dirt roads, especially in Colorado and especially after rain.

430 turned out to be a fine little road. It was basically all dirt but it was packed and wound its way through flat country with the beautiful mountains on the horizon. Mabel did wonderful on the packed dirt with no worries at all. Once I got used to the "loose" feeling of the tires as they wiggled their way on dirt and rock the ride was actually really fun. Standing up on the bike for most of the way, I enjoyed the wind in my face. 318 was even better. Paved and lonely, it was a motorcycle dream. Not too technical but lots of fun. I hit 40, another great, un-technical road and made my way to Craig riding fast and enjoying the road to myself. As I neared the mountains the landscape started slowly changing from desert to

more green high desert plains, the mountains still up ahead, always farther than you think they are. When I hit Craig it was strange to see the barren and lonely landscape change, almost instantly, into a town with buildings dotting the road on both sides. In Milner I took a detour to get off what I now considered a "big" road. It added some mileage but it also added a lot of scenery: pines, scraggy cliffs and mountains. Again, I had the road to myself at least until the dead end that I came to. I stopped and made a lunch out of it: water, some bread and left over candy bars. Afterwards, I took a nap in the silence sleeping on the little dirt road on my mat.

Back on 40 I rolled into Empire and hit Hwy 70 which would lead me into Denver. My trip was coming to an end now and although I didn't like it ending on a highway, I had the memories of all the great roads I was able to enjoy in the last three weeks. Hwy 70 has its fun side though, careening down the steep pitched front range, hanging on for dear life I kept a close eye on the cars that tried to keep up and sometimes passed me. I took the loop and then decided to take the back way circumventing the traffic around Denver. I wasn't watching my speed outside of Morrison and suddenly saw red flashing lights in my rearview mirror. I had no excuse.

"Hello sir. You were going a bit fast through here."

"Yes. I know. I'm coming home from a long tour and got excited I guess." I said, hoping he'd have a little pity on me.

"Yessir. I understand. But you were well over fifteen miles over the speed limit." he continued.

I didn't argue.

"Probably so. I'm, I'm sorry."

"Yessir. But because of that I'm going to have to issue you a citation. My I see your license and registration."

"Yep. The registration is under the seat." I answered, resigned to my stupidity.

I took off the top case and the seat and rummaged through the tools until I found the little red pouch and pulled out the paperwork.

"Thank you, sir."

He made his way back to the car and I put Mabel together again.

"Welcome home!" I said to myself.

The ticket wasn't much and I carefully road home well under the speed limit for the rest of the way. When I pulled up, I stopped in the driveway and walked to the front door. My wife looked around in surprise and our dog, Maggie, barked and then turned into a wiggle-butt when she realized it was me.

"Your home!" Helle said.

"Yep! Home again. The prodigal son!"

We hugged and I rode Mabel into the garage and parked her beside my little truck after I had unpacked all the bags and brought them into my little workshop to unload at a later time. It was good to be home but I already missed the roads and that night spent much of the time telling tales of adventure and serenity to Helle over a glass of wine.

"It's good to be home again. I missed you!"

"I missed you too! Did you have fun?!"

I smiled and thought, "If you only knew just how much fun I had!"

"Yes. Yes I did." I answered.

"Skal!"

"Skal!"

"Oh, by the way…"

I drank my wine, petted the dog and thought of all the places that I had seen. Having Mabel parked in the garage just outside the door made me smile a little. She had become more than just a motorcycle. She was more than just a machine. She was a ticket to an amazing world. Sometimes adventurous, sometimes tedious, sometimes hot, and sometimes freezing. But a world always full of wonder and surprises. Mabel was a ticket to understanding important and necessary aspects of living a life fully with meaning and purpose, and I realized that this trip was the start of a wonderful relationship that I would have as I searched for the answers to those illusive ideas.

Chapter 2

New Hampshire, Maine, Prince Edwards Island

We had moved to New Hampshire from my beloved state, Colorado. The move had been a mistake and we realized it too late, but the reasoning had been good. We wanted to get a small farm up and running. I loved the work but after a year I needed a little break, both from the farm and from the mistake I was learning to live with. I hadn't been able to ride much in the time since moving and decided that some time with Mabel was just the ticket.

"Hey Helle." I started one evening.

"Yes?"

"I was thinking. I need a cup of coffee and found a new coffee shop."

"Oh yea. Where is it?" she asked, not really paying attention.

"Prince Edwards Island."

"Prince…Edwards…is that off the coast somewhere?"

"You could say that. It's in Canada."

She hesitated.

"Canada?!"

The next weekend I packed Mabel up for a day ride and pulled out my trusty road atlas plotting a long weekend trip. It was going to be about 677 miles one way but I couldn't think of a better place to unwind than on the back of my motorcycle, Mabel. So, Mabel and I were going to make a trip to get some coffee and get out for a while. It wasn't going to be an overly long trip, just a long weekend, but any time on a motorcycle was a good time. I had made dozens of short, day trips since moving to New Hampshire and there were plenty of beautiful rides in the state. But it was time for a little longer one. It was late in the summer, and so I made the farm ready before leaving for my three-day hiatus and headed north on 16.

I had no other plans than a coffee shop I had found online, in Charlottetown New Brunswick. I kissed my wife and my dog Maggie good bye and was on the road again. It had been a while since my last tour throughout the west with Mable. She purred. And in a few hours we were winding our way through Maine on back roads towards Bangor and north. I had it in my mind to make the whole 677 miles one shot. From our home in the middle of the New Hampshire forests I made my way through winding roads north and east heading for the coastal road and hoped that I wouldn't have to stay on the freeway for long. The easiest and fastest way out of the east coast traffic mayhem was the 295 to Bangor. In Augusta I took Hwy 3 to Bangor, a small little road that headed north towards the coast. It was better than the freeway but still a busy little one-lane road. I then headed north on 9. Stopping in Bangor for a pre-cup cup of coffee I studied my map. I really just wanted to stop. I didn't really need to because I had the route written and stuck in my tank bag's clear cover. But I just liked reading maps, especially on motorcycle trips and Bangor was a small, quiet town just before the miles and miles of wilderness in the north. The weather was beautiful. Sunny skies and wonderful temps. North of Bangor the scenery changed quickly from busy northeastern traffic to sparse houses, and then to thick forest all around. There were remnants of traffic on the road but even that was thinning out. The road quieted the more northerly I rode until it seemed like there was only me and Mabel.

Heading northeast on Hwy 9 towards New Brunswick Canada Maine started showing its real beauty. Miles and miles of green, thick, lush forest, and I was riding the single lane road through it all. I took it in and wondered out loud how the United States must have once looked before all the shopping malls and highways took over. I got lost in my thoughts humming through the lush forest wonderland stopping only for gas and snacks until I was at the small, unassuming little town, Calais, close to the Canadian border. I turned on International Lane and headed for the border. There was a lone passport control officer eating a sandwich in his little booth. I stopped and took off my helmet and he finished chewing his food before speaking.

"How ya doin?" he said with a slight Canadian accent.

"Great! I'm on a motorcycle!"

"I can see that. What's your plans in Canada?"

"I plan on getting a cup of coffee."

He stared silently at me for moment.

"Where you coming from?"

"Middleton New Hampshire."

"I see...where's that?

"It's down close to Portsmouth."

He stared again, silently.

"That's quite a trip for a cup of coffee. It better be a good one, eh?!" he said, handing my passport back.

"I certainly hope so." I chuckled and he waved me through.

I followed an almost empty Hwy 1 in Canada. It was a little eerie as it was a big, two-lane highway with very little traffic. Deciding to get some gas I got off at the first exit that offered a station where I found my debit card didn't work. And neither did my cellphone.

"OK. This is interesting!" I thought.

With a little fenagling I was able to get the phone working and then called the bank and had the credit card working in a few minutes. Relieved I tanked up and got a Canadian coke. The Canadian landscape was beautiful, reminding me of riding through the Missouri Ozarks. As I rode north traffic started picking up and soon I hit St. John, the first major city I had to ride through. It wasn't bad but it wasn't too big either. Situated on the coast it was pretty with buildings that seemed to hang off the cliffs. It was a bit cooler but the sun was still shining bright. On the north side of St. John, I stopped for lunch at a little coffee shop in a small, quaint downtown area. I had spent quite a bit of time in Canada many years ago but didn't have many memories of it. But now, other than the metric measurements and the names of stores (unknown to me for the most part) Canada resembled America. The highway, now not so empty, led to Moncton, north of St. John and made its way up to 104. I hit the Trans-Canadian Highway and then the Confederation Bridge towards Prince Edwards Island. Traffic was now slow, bottle-necking on a narrow road and bridge. There were now a lot of cars, which I assumed were tourists like myself. I was tired. That cup of coffee sounded really good but I was some hours away yet.

"It's got to be getting close?!" I thought to myself as I droned on.

"We'll get there when we get there. What's the hurry?!" Mabel answered.

The bridge offered beautiful views of the Northumberland Strait but I was too exhausted to really enjoy them. Finally on

Prince Edwards Island, I turned towards Charlottetown. The last forty-five minutes were slow, tedious and seemed to take forever.

"This is the closest thing to "no fun" I can have on a motorcycle!" I complained.

Remember Wyoming?!" Mabel reminded me.

I was going at a slow enough pace to enjoy the island itself and it was beautiful. But when your butt hurts your eyes are dried out and you're just ready to stop, nothing is fun. The Kettle Black Coffee Shop was my goal and I wasn't going to stop until I got there.

Downtown Charlottetown was a busy little tourist trap with tons of shops and even more restaurants. With a little work I found the coffee shop and walked in. It was about two hours before they closed up. Tired and road weary, I walked up to the counter.

"You have coffee?" I asked, jokingly.

The server just stared at me.

"Yes. I think I can help you out."

"Alright! I just rode over six hundred miles cuz I heard you guys had good coffee here!"

"We do! What can I get for you?" she answered, oblivious to what I had said.

"I like black, strong coffee. So, how about an Americano with an extra shot. And I'll take that chocolate chip scone and that banana muffin too."

She rang up the price and I found a weathered wooden table and sat down. Soon she had my coffee and food sitting in front of me. I took a picture of it and then paused.

"Six hundred and seventy-seven miles!" I thought. And I took a long sip of the strong, hot coffee and sat back in my chair.

"I'm an idiot." I said out loud.

A couple of americanos more and I was headed out to find a seafood restaurant that the waitress had recommended.

"It's very good!" she assured me.

It was supposed to be close by but I got lost looking for it. When I found it, I also found that the fish and chips were top notch. I had a few ESB's as well, thinking about Mabel the whole time. I had decided that riding back that night was not in my future, although I had considered it over the crab cakes I had before my meal.

Outside Mabel asked, "Are you happy now?!"

"Happy and full, but we need to find a place to stay tonight."

It was dark and I had no idea where I was going to sleep, a situation that I didn't like. I had packed light though, foregoing the camping gear and so had to either sleep at a rest area on my mat or find a motel. Clouds were rolling in from the north and the weather was cooling down pretty quickly so I went for the latter. Anyway, I had no idea where a rest area might be. By the time I had found the little motel behind a dingy gas station there were large droplets hitting me. But I wasn't worried. The motel looked questionable from the outside but it was clean as a bug inside. I had a few more beers and some snacks and all night to write in my journal. I listened to the thunder and the rainfall outside, finished my beers and most of the snacks and dozed off content and full of food, ESB, and happiness. I had accomplished something, but I didn't know what.

The next morning, I slept in a little but was on the road by 9am looking for a quick bite to eat. I had a long way to ride on the same road back. But Mabel didn't mind and neither did I if I was honest. Before heading out I decided to explore the island a little and so took a random road out of the city towards the north coast. It wasn't long before I was riding little country roads, dodging oncoming cars on the narrow strip of asphalt that snaked its way through the lush, green, flat countryside. There were smaller roads that crisscrossed everywhere and there were cars heading to and from Charlottetown and Summerside, to work I presumed. On one road I found myself back at a store I had passed an hour earlier and decided to head back to the main road and start for home, New Hampshire. On my way south I thought about motorcycle touring and what it meant.

Motorcycles have been called many things from suicide machines to freedom on two wheels. There was no doubt: motorcycles offered something different. There was just something…something that they added to life. One had only to look at the history of motorcycles and their riders. For one thing, I would have never driven my little truck up here. I don't know why, but I think most people who loved riding motorcycles, who tour on them, would say the same thing. I hadn't come up to Canada just for a cup of coffee, of course. The place was arbitrary; the ride was not. There is a ghost in these machines that waits patiently for riders like us. It waits to haunt our dreams and give us crazy ideas in the middle of the night. Iron Butt Riders, of which I am one, know this. It puts ideas in our heads because it knows we will listen. And we do. Because we look for ghosts like those in motorcycles and like those in our heads. The ride through Canada went by quickly, me being lost in my thoughts and soon I was at the border crossing again. There was a new border guard at the station. She looked serious.

"Heading back, sir?"

"Yes."

"Did you bring anything with you, sir?"

"Just memories."

"Yes, I'm sure." She answered, not smiling.

"Did you *buy* anything?" she asked, continuing not to smile and waiting with as much patience as she could muster for someone like me.

"Uh…no." I answered, changing my light humored tone to a more serious one.

I thought about saying "a cup of coffee" but thought better for it.

"Would you mind if I looked in your cases?"

"I guess not." I answered, knowing I really didn't have a choice.

She picked up the phone while she stared at my passport. After a few minutes she handed my passport back.

"Alright. That's fine. Be careful, sir."

"No searching of cavities?" I thought to myself, again almost saying it out loud.

"OK…ma'am." I answered, feeling it necessary to add the last little gesture.

And off I went.

Beautiful weather, lush, green northern forests met me across the border again. The whole trip again, in reverse. The forests gave way to small towns which gave way to larger tourist areas. I detoured on the coastal highway, Hwy 1, for a while before tiring of the stop and go traffic. It didn't seem like much time passed before I was back in Middleton. I turned into the driveway of my little farm and was greeted by our dog, Maggie, and my wife. They were all smiles and welcomed me back.

"How was your trip?"

"It was good. It's beautiful up there, but Charlottetown is just another tourist town."

"That's not surprising, though." She said, pulling a frosty beer out of the fridge for me.

"No, but it is beautiful. Thanks!" I said, pouring the double-IPA in a frosty mug.

"You know you're kinda weird. That's a long way for a cup of coffee." She said, smiling.

"Yea. But it's not about the cup of coffee…"

"I know that." She interjected, "I know that. But you're still a little strange."

"That's probably why you married me!" I retorted, sitting back enjoying the beer.

Chapter 3

Texas, New Mexico, Colorado, Oklahoma, Missouri

New Hampshire didn't work out. We had had the idea of starting a farm and I had given up a great job teaching in Colorado to do so. That was a mistake. It didn't work out for numerous reasons, although I did really enjoy the work and there was a lot of it. So, after numerous nights of tears, wine and conversation we decided to throw in the towel. On the one hand the whole decision had been a botched mess. On the other hand, and a point that we had forgotten, not all adventures end up being what you expect. Helle's job had offices in Dallas Texas, my home town, and so we settled on moving back to a place I thought I had seen the last of. It was not a place that we longed for but was familiar and comfortable, and that's what we needed. We sold everything and packed a truck with a few belongings and some select pieces of furniture, and made the long and arduous journey to Dallas after finding a house there. Before long we were enjoying our new home in my old neighborhood. Helle enjoyed her work and I started a small business. Mabel sat in the garage, waiting. Things were going well, and then covid hit.

Soon after Covid I planned a motorcycle tour through south Texas and New Mexico. It was time. Dallas had changed quite a bit, mostly growing like a virus. Getting out of the city had always been a chore but now it had become even worse. So, I started early trying to beat the worst of the traffic, heading south through downtown. The idea was to stay clear of all highways once out of the city. About 7am I was through the nastiest of it. It felt good to have Mabel out on a long tour, loaded and rolling again. This time I had no plan but had given us up to a month. South of town I stopped at a small gas station to tank up before cutting off into unknown territory and smaller roads.

"Where you headed?" the attendant asked while I was milling around the store looking for snacks.

"I don't know." I answered without thinking.

"I guess that's a good enough place." She replied. I liked that answer and turned to talk.

"I'm on a long tour and the only thing I've got planned is Big Bend National Park."

"I've heard that's pretty down there but I've never been."

"Well, hop on the back!" I smiled.

She hesitated as if to ponder the possibility, "I got kids." She finally answered and rang me up, still looking like she was thinking about the offer.

I paid her and wished her well. Back on Mabel I headed towards the Three Sisters area, a collection of small roads that were great for motorcycling and famous in Texas for fun times and fun rides as well as good food. Finding State Rd. 16 and following it as the landscape turned from rough little towns and pines to more scrub brush and desert, I sat back and enjoyed the soft turns on the rough country asphalt. I had done an Iron Butt ride the year before and had ridden through the area from the east and on towards Van Horn in the west and back but I was trying to do 1500 miles in 36 hours so there was not much enjoying the scenery.

16 continued southwest turning into a smaller and smaller road, narrowing as the weeds and brush started taking over the shoulders, which I thought was nice. In Frederiksberg I rode through downtown past the tourists and the tourist traps. It was quaint and somewhat quiet but filled with tourists milling around

and taking pictures. From there I followed 16 to Kerrville, a folk music destination. The landscape turned from scrub brush to green forests and just past that, the hill country presented itself. It was still beautiful even though in the past decades there had been too much development. It was an inevitable consequence as more and more people moved from outside of Texas to Austin, Dallas and Houston. But there were still some wildflowers and they were in bloom. Pink and purple and blue, they decked the hillsides together with the bluebonnets. In Kerrville I stopped at a grocery store and endured the masses of people but outside of the now burgeoning town, valleys appeared again and the road returned to its peaceful rolls and subtle twists. I was riding in the last hours of daylight and feeling tiredness coming upon me so I watched for stealth camping possibilities. Most of the dirt roads led to a gate or a fence. The area had numerous hunting camps where rich city people came to shoot fenced-in wildlife. After about a half hour of turning down dirt roads only to be turned back by fences and gates, and "No Trespassing" signs, I headed towards the Lost Maple Natural Area hoping to score a camp spot so late in the day.

By the time I made it to the campground I was exhausted. The weather had started cool and gotten warm throughout the day and now the temperature was dropping again, rapidly. If this didn't work out, I would have to don my sweater and find a less than good stealth camp spot.

"How are you doing." I sighed, tired. "Got any spots? I don't need electricity."

"Hello!" the rotund ranger said almost gleefully.

"Yes! We have four spots left in fact. It's your lucky day! We're typically filled up by now. Especially with the weather likes it been. I bet it's been great riding, though. We have some good spots here too..."

She went on happily filling me in on several bits of information, some needed and some not so much.

"Just a quiet spot…" I interjected.

"No problem. Do you have a state park card?"

"No."

"Well! I think they're worth it. You get so much for so little and there are so many state parks here in Texas. Are you from Texas!"

I sat and listened while I rummaged through my tank bag to find my wallet.

"How much?" I interjected again.

"Oh…it'll be $15. You going to be staying more than one night? If so, I need to know so I don't overbook. I've done that before and people aren't real happy about it…"

"No. Just one." I interrupted again, pulling out some cash and my drivers' license.

"Well, alrighty then."

She hurriedly filled out some paperwork, took my cash and the wrote out a ticket.

"Here ya go. Just tape this to the windshield. Follow this road around and you'll come to. You're on a bike. Do you have a windshield?"

"Yes."

I listened to the directions and when she bid me good night, I started Mabel up and rode off in search of spot #4.

The spot was nice and the campground was beautiful. Located in a valley the sites were somewhat spread out. There were a few campers set up with Christmas lights strung around their sites and grills on the table still warm and smelling of charred meat and charcoal. For the first time on my trip I started the now rusty ritual of setting up camp. It was nice. I hadn't done it in a while and still had the old tent from Colorado. It went up pretty fast, the process returning to my memory quickly. My dinner was a ready-made Indian meal but I had no rice on hand. I didn't worry though. I had a few warm brown ales from Buffalo Brewing Company and a few bags of Zapps potato chips. As I was sitting and enjoying the first of my beers and waiting for the mediocre Indian food to warm up a dog started barking down at the other end of the camp. I wondered about that as I usually did.

"That's one reason I don't like campgrounds." I thought as the dog quieted down. I took another swig of beer.

It wasn't a problem for long though. Across the campground, just behind the campers on the other side of the small road that wound around the camp sites was a huge natural, granite wall. It was beautiful and the colors on the rock changed from bluish greys to bright oranges in the late, dying afternoon sun.

"The wonderful thing about camping is that it slows everything down." I now thought, taking some chips and forgetting about the dog barking, which had now quieted completely.

As the sun continued falling behind the cliff the weather continued cooling down. I ate and even the pre-made mediocre Indian food tasted edible. I read my book and wrote in my journal. It was good to be camping again with Mabel, even if it was in a campground, albeit a nice one. Putting my journal down as nightfall settled, I sat and thought about life, the shortness of it, and the purpose that we all seemed to be searching for. I was looking for something and was hoping to find it on two wheels while listening to Mabel's little motor that purred under me every day. Whatever it was I was looking for seemed to always lie just past the horizon, out of reach. But for now, I was content. I put away my things for the night and tucked myself into the old, reliable tent and the even older sleeping bag. They smelled dingy from unuse. They smelled good. The crickets chirped and people talked in soft murmurs. I went to sleep with the smell of a dying campfire in the background and excitement in my head for an unknown future.

"Welcome back." Mabel said quietly.

3.2

I was awake early and laid in my sleeping bag listening to the silent sounds of early morning at a campground. There were no voices but still there was life. I found that early mornings while camping are special somehow. The tent had a special smell; a good one. And the sleeping bag had that just-right feeling: warm and cozy. Early mornings tended to have an ambience and a feel that cannot be found at any other part of the day. The light outside on the cliff was blue-grey and I unzipped the bag letting the cool morning air in. I had slept soundly that night, woke only by the sounds of my sliding around in the sleeping bag during the night. When camping I always kept my essentials in the tent with me, including my clothes. I had one thing in mind, though: coffee. Unzipping the fly of the tent I put my camp shoes on and slid out onto the dewy grass. On the table just a few yards away was my gear, most if it locked up. But on the table itself sat my little stove with the pot full of water and my new metal French press, coffee in it. I had traded the old, plastic one in deciding that good coffee was worth the space. I lit the stove and enjoyed the little hiss it made as it warmed up the water. These were some of the camp sounds that made early morning at camp one of my favorite times of day. Before long I was pouring boiling water over the grounds and pressing the coffee through the hot water with the French press filter. I sat at the table enjoying my coffee and mentally starting my plans for the day.

"First, I need to figure out the best route to get to the Three Sisters." I thought. I looked at my watch. It was 6:45.

"I can get out of here by 8am."

"If you don't dilly-dally." Mabel added.

At 8:05 I had Mabel packed and was making my last look-around to make sure I hadn't inadvertently forgotten something. Clamping the phone to Mabel's handlebars, I switched it on and set the directions for the twisty roads that I knew awaited me. I rode out of the campground passing people just waking up and peaking outside of their campers at the day in front of them. In no time I was entering the "Three Sisters" area, which hadn't been that far away. Three roads that were famous in Texas for great motorcycle riding. And they didn't disappoint. The route was full of tight turns and beautiful scenery that opened up into small towns after miles of leaning around cliffs and great riding up and down hills and valleys. 335, 336 and 337 made a motorcyclist's dream loop and I rode the whole thing with a big, wide smile on my face. Leaning into corners and trying to follow that magical and sometimes illusive line I let Mabel work her magic and just tried to stay out of the way. One had a choice to make on roads like these, though. You could ride the road or enjoy the scenery, but not both. When my cheeks got sore from smiling so much, I followed 377 to Ranch Road 674 which cut across some beautiful, South Texas desert filled with wildflowers and cacti. The road even out-did itself when I hit Kickapoo State Park, and eventually free-grazing livestock started appearing. I slowed down as cattle grazed peacefully at the sides of the road. They paid no attention to me but I didn't want to spook them. The only plan in my head was Del Rio on Hwy 90. I was contemplating stopping at a Mexican restaurant but when I got to Del Rio the little downtown was dead, killed by the nearby Walmart. What once was a thriving little town filled with adobe buildings was now gutted and replaced by a busy thoroughfare pocked by the typical fast-food restaurants and of course, the Walmart. If there had been a Mexican restaurant there it wasn't there any longer which seemed wrong since Del Rio was a border town.

As I rode around the dead downtown area I noticed dark clouds gathering west on the horizon. I wasn't worried but they set the typical "motorcyclist battle" thoughts going in my head concerning weather.

"Gotta make some miles..." I thought. Mabel interjected.

"You don't have to do anything."

"Some miles would be good, though. Let's go to Big Bend..."

Mabel chimed in again. "Take it easy", she reminded me. "Take your time."

I rode west on 90 until I crossed a bridge over the Amistad N.R.A and noticed a little campground on the Amistad Reservoir just below the bridge. It looked pretty empty and clean and so I made a U-turn at the other side of the bridge and went down to the campground on the long, windy road that dead-ended there. It was a self-serve site with nobody there. I picked a spot and dropped my panniers, put money in the payment box, and made my way back to the convenient store that I had just passed. I topped Mabel off with gas and went looking for some beer and something to make for dinner. I was looking for something local but had no luck. In the beer fridges was nothing but the usual. I picked up the best of the worst and a couple of bags of chips. It looked like dinner for the evening. When I walked outside I noticed a small, motley motel with a sign out front: "Burritos and Tacos"

"Sounds good!" I said to myself and crossed over. I went into the seemingly empty motel went in.

"Hola!" the smiling motel manager greeted me brightly.

"Hola! Burritos?"

"Si! Cuantas quieres?"

"Dos. No carne por favor."

"OK!"

We tried to speak a little more using his broken English and my terrible Spanish but ended up just smiling to each other.

"Mañana! Mañana desayunamos burritos!" he said.

"OK! Por la mañana. Adios!"

I took my bag of burritos and made my way back to the campground with my quick and surprisingly cheap dinner. Pulling into the campground I noticed a Harley that had arrived while I was out shopping. It had a small trailer that opened up into a tent-like structure and an older guy was sitting at the picnic table drinking a tall boy and looking out over the lake. Also, while I was setting up camp a truck pulling a large Streamline camper came in searching for the easiest place to back his rig in. About thirty minutes later he was backed in and had started to setup. I waved and they waved back. An older gentleman and his wife plus two small, old dogs. I was finishing my burritos and chomping on my chips when a third car rolled in with what looked like a younger couple. They parked a few spaces over. Picking up my second beer I made my way over to the Harley to take a look at the interesting setup he had.

"Hello." I called out, looking at the little trailer.

"Oh…Hey!" he answered.

"I noticed your rig when I came in. It looks interesting."

"Yea. I'm taking it back to California. I just bought it in Arkansas and decided to ride over and get it."

"That's very cool. Makes for a great ride."

"Exactly. You on the bike over there?" he asked.

"Yea, that's me. I'm starting a longer trip. I'd love to take a look at your new trailer."

"Sure!"

We walked over to the big Harley Bagger with the pup-tent trailer on the back of it.

"My name's David."

"Nice to meet you. I'm Mark"

David opened the little tent-trailer and I was surprised at the room it actually had. He explained his plans for the little camper and I answered questions about my trip. He had better beer and graciously offered me one and we stood talking bikes and drinking beer, a motorcycle tradition.

About that time the young guy from the car walked by on his way to the bathrooms.

"Hiya." He said, happily.

"Hey! How are you doin'? David and I answered.

"Great. Great. I'm Don. Hey listen, me an' Jennifer are gonna have a cook out and we have more than we'll ever eat. Why don't you guys drop by?!"

Don had a slight Canadian accent and so David and I just assumed that his hospitality was part of his culture. We talked about that as well after David left.

"Yea. We'll do that. Thanks!"

"No prob. Just come on over."

"We'll see you soon."

David and I continued our discussion about his trailer which soon grew into biker stories and a third beer. The sun was setting.

"Let me get my things in order, David. Are you planning on going over to…to Don's?"

"Yea. If you go."

"Yea. Let's go. I'll see you there in about a half hour?"

"Sounds good."

I walked towards my campground and saw the older couple sitting outside in their lawn chairs under their pull-out awning, the two dogs meandering around the camp ground, nose to the ground. I waved. They waved back and smiled.

At Don's campsite we met Jennifer. I had never seen as much stuff at a single campground.

"Wow! I'm impressed that you got all this stuff in that car!" I said as I walked up, smiling.

"Yea. Don likes his stuff." Jennifer answered as Don rolled several large sausages on the portable grill he had set up and going.

"We got burgers too! I brought a deep fryer but I haven't got that set up yet. If you want some fries let me know!"

David and I laughed and shook our heads.

"No thanks! I'm good." David answered.

"Have a seat!" Jennifer offered, pulling out two extra fold-out chairs from somewhere in the stacks of stuff sitting all over the campground.

They had a huge tent with two full size cots and a couple of lamps inside. And there were large coolers filled with beer and food sitting around as well.

"Where are you guys from?" David asked.

"Oh, well Jennifer is from Chicago and I'm from Toronto. My wife doesn't like camping and so Jennifer and I go."

Don and I looked at each other. We didn't want to be nosy.

"So, your wife is in Toronto and doesn't like camping? Where are you guys headed?"

"Ah, well. We don't really know. I like to drive and Jennifer likes to camp."

"That sounds great." I added.

"I like to camp, but all the stuff is Don's!" Jennifer added, smiling.

Don pulled a few sausages off the grill and Jennifer hurriedly set up a spot on the table with ketchup, mayo, mustard, relish, fresh cut onions, cucumbers and a few family-sized bags of chips and hot sauce.

"There's beer in that fridge over there, the blue one. Or Coke if you'd rather, in the one over there. I'll have the queso warm in a minute."

Jennifer pointed at the two coolers.

"Help yourself! We've got plenty!" Don chimed in.

It was dark and the mosquitoes were starting to swarm. Don noticed our swatting and put his large tongs down and ran over to the car, pulling out three electric mosquito lamps and set them up at each corner of the campsite and plugged them into a little generator sitting behind one of the boxes.

"You've got everything!" I laughed.

"We got what we need for sure!" he answered, hurriedly walking back over to the grill to manage the hamburgers he had started.

"Make room for some burgers, guys!"

We all talked for a while and David and I forced ourselves to eat a hotdog. Don and Jennifer were friendly, talkative, gracious hosts and were full of questions about motorcycle travel. As it was getting late, Don and I excused ourselves and thanked our hosts for a wonderful night and made our way back to our own spots. At my campsite David stopped.

"Mark. You're heading west tomorrow, right?"

"Yea. I'm heading to Big Bend."

"Would you mind if I tagged along? It's a long road and I'm not sure about the gas situation. My bagger doesn't get great gas mileage, especially with that trailer. It would just make me feel better."

"Of course! I get up pretty early."

"No problem. I'll leave when you want."

"Great. We can play it by ear, but I'll see you in the morning?"

"Yes! Alright. Sounds good. Good night!"

"Goodnight. Enjoy that 'fancy' trailer of yours!" I said with a chuckle, walking towards my own campsite and my old tent.

"I will! Don't you worry."

3.4

I was up early, just before sunrise and was enjoying my first cup of coffee and writing in my journal when I heard David rustling around. It sounded like he was packing earnestly so I walked over with my coffee.

"Hey! Good morning."

"I'll be ready in no time." He said assuredly, quickly packing.

"There's no hurry. This is my first cup of coffee and I have a French press full of it to get through. You good?"

"Yea, but thanks."

"No hurry. Take your time. We'll make it."

I walked back to my campsite to finish my own ritual: coffee, writing, waiting for sunrise, and then a methodic packing up of the campsite. It was a ritual that I had come to enjoy. I heard David's big Harley start up and it appeared as I was putting on my jacket.

"Perfect timing!" I said, looking up at him as he shut the big machine off. It was quite the rig. A big, red bagger with a trailer in tow.

"I try." Don smiled.

"I was looking for gas stations between here and your turn-off to Big Bend. I'm pretty sure the one I was hoping for is closed. The only one I'm sure about is the one where your turn off is. It'll be close for me."

"You'll make it." I assured him.

I led us out of the campground and on to Hwy 90. Once we were out of the Del Rio area the landscape reverted back to its natural, desert state. The heat rose steadily throughout the morning as we rolled down the small highway. The trip wasn't that long, about 180 miles or so, but David was worried. The big Harley's didn't get good gas mileage on a good day, much less with a trailer. My old '97 Dyna would go about 175 miles before I had to switch it to reserve. I understood Don's worries. Mabel, however, had no problem. I had averaged almost 300 miles on a tank of gas so far. We had gassed up in Del Rio and went by the old hotel and bought a few breakfast burritos from the very excited host before we had left. On our way to Marathon I passed an interesting dirt road and made a mental note. In Marathon itself we pulled into the only gas station that we had seen on the trip. David had been right, the only other station had been closed for quite some time. He rode directly over to a pump and fed his big machine. I did the same with Mabel. I wanted to explore the dirt road I had passed and as a rule I liked to tank up at most opportunities anyway. We went in to see what they had to eat.

"It got pretty low. I got worried there towards the end. I'll admit it."

"Yea. It's never a good feeling to have to worry about fuel. As fun as bikes are they're equally no fun if you have to push them."

David laughed. The place had a decent but greasy little restaurant where we ordered big, greasy burritos. We chomped on them and shared road stories when I noticed that Don was packing a pistol. It took the wind out of our comradery for me, at least. I'm not against guns but I don't understand why people felt the need to carry them all of the time.

"So, what do you do?" I asked.

"I'm a fireman, or at least I was. I still am but only part time. I getting ready to retire."

"Alright. That explains the fancy tent-trailer. Do you think your wife will come with you?"

David chuckled, "She's not the camping type, even in this luxury trailer. I've got plans for it, though. Maybe she will when I'm through?"

I took a bite of my burrito and a sip of coffee. I really didn't want to broach the subject, but I had to ask. I couldn't help it.

"I noticed you wearing a gun. I'm just curious. Why?"

David smiled as if he had been waiting for me to ask.

"Well, we're down here by the border and out in the middle of nowhere. I like to be ready."

I wanted to say "Ready for what?", but kept the snarky comment to myself.

"Yea, I understand that. But I'll have to say, in all the travels that I've done I've never felt the need to carry a gun nor have I had the need to carry one. I carry a few knives but mostly for camping. Never a gun."

"No?!" Don exclaimed, almost surprised. "Man, I wouldn't do that. You never know when you'll need one."

"Well, I've never needed one, and don't think I ever will. I have nothing against them, but I just think they bring more trouble than they're worth. I think it's a mentality, maybe."

David ate his burrito in silence for a few minutes.

"A mentality? What do you mean?"

I sipped my coffee.

"I think a gun is giving in to fear rather than fighting it. I'd rather not do that."

I thought a moment. I didn't want to get into a political or social argument at a gas station in Marathon Texas. And anyway, I didn't think that David was the type to change his mind. Maybe I wasn't either? Perhaps if we had known each other better?

"If I carried a gun, I feel like I'd be looking for trouble rather than trying to circumvent it. I think a gun gives you the illusion of safety. Kinda like a car. And that's why I love motorcycles. There is no illusion. They're just dangerous. There's no getting around it."

"I see your point, but we live in the world we live in and I don't trust people that much."

"You see, you don't have to with a gun. I think guns give us this idea that trust is an option. That's my problem with them. I have to trust people to an extent, at least. I don't want to live in a society where I feel the need to carry a weapon."

"You already do." Don exclaimed, losing a little patience.

"No. That's not true. I've never carried a gun and never have felt the need to."

"Maybe you've never been in a situation where you needed one." He interjected.

"I'm not sure such a situation exists out here."

Don shook his head in disagreement.

"Well…" I interjected, before we could continue the conversation.

"I saw a dirt road about ten miles back back. I think I'm going to see if it takes me to Big Bend. You good with the gas situation?"

"Yea, thanks. Alright." David answered. "I appreciate you riding with me."

"No problem. No problem at all. It was nice to have met you. Good luck and maybe you can talk your wife into luxury camping with you in that big trailer." I said, trying to lighten the mood.

"I don't think I will ever swing that." He replied, smiling a bit.

"Never know. Anyway. Good luck, be safe and have fun."

"Same to you!" David replied, and we went our separate ways.

3.5

I was alone again. The way I liked it. I mounted Mabel and pushed the starter switch and as usual, she fired right up. I made my way back until I found the turn-off for the dirt road and stopped. It was pretty hot at this point, so I made sure I had water in my pack. I did and so started down the mystery road. It was dusty and rough, full of ruts and rocks. It meandered through dry, tough desert and Mabel and I took it slow crossing dry creek beds and picking our way through the deep ruts. About fifteen miles in I came across what looked like an old abandoned farm. The only structure left standing intact was a small windmill with the blades still slowly turning. The leftovers of buildings, wood, and metal, lay strewn about.

TWO WHEELS AND A TENT

"A sign of optimistic hope." I thought to myself as I stared up at the rusted-out blades squeaking away.

"I think you're an optimist if you think this road will lead to the park!" Mabel chided.

I heard something rustle in the bushes and suddenly a Havalina ran across the road. I had seen the pigs before and knew that where there was one there were probably more. So, I waited. Sure enough, three others appeared briefly following the lead of the first. Back on Mabel I crossed another dried-out, rocky stream bed and made my way up the narrowing and gradually rougher road, scooting by rocks, roots and two-feet deep ruts. It was tough but beautiful nature. I was hoping to make it all the way to Big Bend, hitting 385 at the end of the dirt road and cutting off quite a bit of the long road that led down to the park. 385 was the main road leading to the park and if the map was right, the dirt road I was on would hit the road about half way to the entrance. About forty-five minutes later I came to a gate with a lock. The first thing I noticed was a big sign with a sloppy, hand-written message hanging across the front of the gate. I couldn't imagine who it was for, given that the road was obviously rarely travelled. Also, according to the map it was a public road. Nevertheless, the sign read:

"If you don't support Trump, then turn around or be ready to defend yourself. You're not welcome here."

I shook my head not only at the idiocy of such statements, but also because I had travelled about twenty-five miles for nothing.

"What a dumbass!" I thought.

"Well, not for nothing." Mabel reminded me.

"It was fun." She added.

"You're absolutely right!" I said as I wrangled her across the deep ruts to get turned around.

And indeed, it was fun. Even backwards. Back on the main route I stopped again at the same gas station I had left David at. I got gas and rode the long straight road into Big Bend National Park. When I finally arrived at the entrance there was a ranger with a small table set up.

"Hello!"

"Hi." I answered. "I'm looking to camp tonight."

"Well, no luck here. Nothing's open. But you can go down to the main office and maybe they'll know more than I do?"

"Thanks. I think I will check."

"Well, this is no good." I thought to myself as I walked back to Mabel.

"The road will be pretty. Let's go!" she answered.

"Wow. That's surprising! I thought there would be plenty of camping." I continued thinking.

"Everybody always does." Mabel retorted.

"I'll take my chances. I don't want to ride all the way back to the gas station. And anyway I didn't see much else."

"I agree." Mabel revved.

I rode towards the main office deep in the park on a beautiful road that twisted and curved through the ever more breathtaking nature, taking my time and enjoying the scenery. I was in no hurry thinking that if it didn't work out in the park, I would find a place to stealth-camp. At the office I parked among the crowd of cars and saw large tables set up out front with lots of tourists milling around, many asking questions and even more looking confused. Staring at the scene, I didn't see much hope in getting a camping spot in the park that night. Finally at the table I asked the ranger about camping.

"Nope. Sorry. There's nothing available." He hurriedly replied, starting to turn towards the next person in line.

"Nothing?! I don't need electricity. I just need water and place to pitch a tent."

"Oh." He said sounding surprised, pausing and turning around. He looked down at a large map taped to the table top.

"Well, there's primitive camping down at the border but it's a rough road to get to it."

Noticing my riding attire, he looked over at Mabel, the only bike in the parking lot.

"Can that thing go off road?"

"She has before. Anyway, primitive camping sounds good to me."

"Oh, in that case, there's plenty. Nothing's booked out there at all."

"And water?"

"You can get water here if you have something to carry it in."

"I do. Is there a place I can get water other than here?"

"Yea. There's a campground on the south side. Depending on where you camp it would be 20 to 40 minutes for you to get to it though."

"Alright!" I answered, excitedly, "That'll work!"

"Well, do you want to do that?"

"Absolutely. Thanks!"

"How many nights?" he continued.

"Let's do two nights!" and then thought about it. "I can add another if I choose, can't I?"

"Out there? There won't be a problem."

"Great!"

I paid the ranger the pittance for the campsite and filled my water container up as well as my Camelbak. I had the foresight to stop and get food that morning because I was planning on staying at the park, and so I was ready and willing for whatever came.

He gave me a map of the park and pointed me in the direction of the dirt road and I continued following the paved path through the park towards the southern end. The nature down in that part of Texas was rough and ready. Heat, rock, and sand mixed waiting to make a stew of heartache for someone not prepared. I couldn't imagine having to traverse it two hundred years ago as I twisted around the beautiful park roads leading to the far, southwest corner. They did it on horses and in wagons. I was comfortably doing it on Mabel. I was told to look for a campground and then turn left on River Road,

"It's a dirt road" he had said, "It goes along the length of the park along the Rio Grande River."

I stopped at the campground entrance and double checked my water situation just to make sure. I was good. I decided to check out the campground before riding down River Road, and I found the water spigot. It was the only water source on this side of the park and full open it was a slow trickle. But my water container was full for now so I headed back to a dirt road and stopped. I assumed it was River Road and sat eyeing the whitish, dry gravel ahead of me. I didn't have any idea how far the campsite would be so I just started. At first it was gravel with baby-heads here and there, nothing big, but the further Mabel and I rode the sandier it became. About 3 miles in the sand got deep and I found myself goosing Mabel to get through, trying to keep the front wheel from "bulldozing" and keeping both my legs splayed out just in case. I could feel the loaded bike sinking in the sand as I gave her more gas. The back tire wobbled back and forth slightly in the sand as it dug its way through the deep, loose powder. Mabel did great but I was a little nervous. As I rode through the desert I realized that there were really no "campsites" per say so I went a few miles more and just started looking for any spot that was doable. I found one and pulled off what was now a makeshift road.

We stopped for the day and I found a rock to put under Mabel's kickstand in order to keep her from falling over in the hot, dry and very loose gravel. She was glad to get rid of the panniers for a bit though, and I pitched the tent in the shadiest section I could find, under some sage brush. I went for short walks through the desert that afternoon, and ate chips, dried strawberries and tortillas for dinner. I watched as a few golden eagles soared high over the desert. I saw three cars the entire day, all 4x4's, and two the next day. I didn't have beer but I felt like I had the entire desert to myself. I took a hot nap late in the day and woke up as dusk set in. I didn't put the rainfly up and woke during the night to the darkest and starriest night I'd seen in a long time. I looked over at Mabel and she was gleaming in the moonlight, even in her dusty condition. She looked happy in her natural setting.

"Goodnight Mabel." I said aloud and turned over falling asleep to the sound of the rustling desert around me.

"Yes, it is." She answered.

Early morning in the desert was a beautiful thing. No sound except the slight rustling of the brush around me. But it was already warm and was only 6:30 am. Up and coffee made, I stood and looked out over the rough desert hilltops and out over the jagged horizon that surrounded me. Mabel stood serene in her confidence, awaiting the day's adventure. I ate some instant oatmeal, half-cooked, and downed the coffee I had made while looking out over an empty and beautiful vista. I was going to explore the park today. First, Mabel and I continued down the rough and sandy road exploring the desert. Then we twisted around the roads of the park exploring where they went and making note of possible hikes along the way, of which the map showed many. We also ventured out beyond the borders of the park.

"That might be a place." I said to Mabel, glancing over at a trailhead as she purred around the sharp corner, me managing her throttle. We couldn't go too fast in the park.

After a few hours of exploring roads both in and just outside the park we went back searching for the hikes I'd noted. I did three short walks through the desert, all under three miles a piece, until the heat drove me back to my simple camp in the desert. Stopping by the campground where the water spigot was, I filled my Camelbak up, having had the foresight to take it with me. It went slowly as the water trickled in. Then Mabel and I headed down River Road battling the deep, hot sand again. Without bags Mabel had no problems at all and we even played in the loose sand. I swung her back tire one way and then another dodging ruts and baby heads along the way. Back at camp nothing had changed and when I shut Mabel's motor off there was total silence. My panniers were sitting by the tent where I'd left them. Having nothing I needed to do, I unpacked my kitchen pannier to see if I could repack it a bit more efficiently; more out of boredom than anything.

I made coffee, took a nap, went for a few short walks, lubed Mabel's chain and tightened it a bit, studied the map and made tentative plans for tomorrow. We were heading out but I didn't know where yet. All in all, it was a perfect day.

"West my son. West!" I said aloud as I pondered the big, paper map I always had with me on long rides. Dusk came and we went to sleep early, waking every now and again to desert sounds and yelping coyotes.

3.6

"Today is going to be a riding day!" I told Mabel.

I packed up my things, loaded her down and headed out on Park Route 12 towards Gano Springs where I made a wrong turn on Ross Maxwell Dr, headed back to Panther Junction and ended up on Maverick Road, another dirt road but fairly graded and

heading the wrong direction. I turned around, headed north on 180 until I realized that I wanted to ride 170. I turned around again and still couldn't find 170. I was sitting in front of a house hoping for cell service for GPS and looking for a short cut on my big map, to the ever-evasive 170 when three dogs came running out. It was 9:30 in the morning.

"Hey pooches!" I said, lowering a hand, palm down for them to sniff. They weren't interested, though, and kept barking at me.

Then a young man came walking up with a huge hat on, a flowered shirt and huge, worn-out cargo shorts. He had a beer in one hand and a cellphone in the other. He looked like what people referred to as a "parrot-head", those adamant fans of being wasted in "Margaritaville".

"Hey man. You lost?" he asked in a friendly manner.

I thought about the question a second.

"Well, I'm looking for 170 and hoping I could get there from here.

"You'll have to turn… 'Hey! Shut up'…you'll have to turn around and go back. This dead-ends."

"Oh, OK. That's what I was wondering."

"Yea." He agreed and looked down at the three now silent dogs.

"You been at the park?" he asked taking a swig of beer.

"Yea. I stayed two nights. It's really peaceful there."

"Yea it is."

He paused again.

"Hey man! You wanna beer?"

I declined the offer, thanked him for his help, and turned around as he and his dogs walked back to his small house. I paused for a second, considering taking him up on his offer. I'm sure there would have been a story to tell. But thought the better of it.

I finally found Hwy 170, wondering how I'd missed it at all, and rode west through the nicely twisted rollercoaster of the road. It's rolling demeanor made for a relaxing ride on the border of Mexico. The Rio Grande was to my left and beautiful mountains and forests were to my right. I came to a poor border town, Presidio, where I saw a couple that had broken down. He was under the car and she was standing beside it on her phone. I slowed a bit but they paid me no attention. Then Hwy 67 and we were heading north towards Marfa, a little artsy town in the middle of nothing west Texas. In town I met the school teachers in their camper rig that I'd waved to briefly back at the campground in Del Rio. I didn't know what to expect with Marfa but what I got was a small, up and coming 'hipster' town full of art and big hopes for the future. I hadn't ridden very far, but I was in the mood for a cheap motel and a bar for the night in order to check out all the weirdness in town, but no such luck.

"There's an art show and most everywhere is booked up." The young lady who owned a local motel told me apologetically.

"A friend of mine has a great, old hotel in Van Horn, about eighty miles north of here if you're going that way."

"I can check it out. What's the name of it?"

"El Capitan. It's a bit pricey, but it's really cool!"

"What's pricey?"

"Well…" she wavered, "I don't know, but it's more than mine."

"I'll keep it in mind. Right now, I'm looking for the Prada store."

Marfa had a tiny Prada store, a gimmick, with shoes in it. It say in the middle of nowhere and I had to check it out.

She smiled.

"It's west on 90. It's towards Van Horn in fact. You can't miss it."

So, off we went, Mabel and I. And soon we found that the friendly lady was right. It was hard to miss. There on the side of Hwy 90, a lonely, dusty one lane road sat a sparkling, white Prada store. We pulled over and parked in the back where I started some water boiling for coffee. I was going to have lunch there.

"Why not?!" I thought.

Inside were rows of shoes perfectly set on shelves. The little building could have been a little store, but it wasn't. It was built by the town of Marfa as a sculpture and has since become a great marketing tool for the town as well. I had my look around and went to the back where my water was boiling when I noticed all the locks hanging on the fencing around the store. I made coffee, walked around looking at the store and the locks. Afterwards, on the ground looking at the map, I realized I had missed a great chance to ride Hwy 170 up the border of Texas to Candelaria. I needed to have plenty of gas for it though as it looked like it dead-ended.

"Next time!" I promised Mabel.

The break was short and Mabel and I were soon on our way to Van Horn.

El Capitan stood like the captain of a sinking ship. It was an architectural beauty that stood in a dying town. But the Captain stood proud. I went in and found out that my Marfa friend wasn't lying. It was pricey. But one look at the hand-tiled, Spanish themed open bar and the beautiful courtyard and I was hooked. I later found out it was original to the old hotel, the bar that is. I dished out the cash for a room and after dumping my top case and tank bag headed directly for the bar downstairs. The hotel had been built in the 1930's and had retained its early century feel. The architect, Henry Trost, was evidently influenced by Frank Lloyd Wright. But the crown jewel was the amazing bar. I sat at the colorful, tiled tavern and instantly the bartender came up to me.

"Local beer?" I asked.

"Yes. We have a few."

"Let's start with one of those and an appetizer. You choose."

"Do you like…"

"I like anything you bring me." I smiled.

"OK!"

There were a few men lounging around the other side of the bar. They looked like tourists or workers, but were not dressed like the typical construction workers or tourists for that matter. I found out they were engineers for Jeff Bezos' pet rocket project that was evidently not far off. I fell into conversation with one of them. Let's call him Joe.

"Yea. I'm an engineer for Mr. Bezos. It's just up the road you know."

"How long are you here?"

"I've been here for two months and I have two more to go. I love it here and I want to move." He said, thanking the waitress for his meal.

"Oh, where do you live now?"

"I've got a wife and a kid in the Pittsburgh area. She won't move though. Her family…"

"Yea. I get that. So, how's it like, working for that kind of a project? What do you do there by the way? You told me you're an engineer."

"I'm basically an electrical engineer. But, I'm kinda all over the place. He gets parts brought in on trucks and we sift through them, trying to find things we can use."

"Wow!" I said, wondering at that idea and taking a sip of my great beer. "How does that work?"

The waitress brought up my first appetizer. It looked great and I dug in, famished.

"Well, it takes some time to find out what we have and then it takes some time to find out what we can do with it all. There's not really a set plan, just a goal."

"We're talking about a rocket, right?" I looked up, surprised.

He smiled. "Yea. It's kinda fun. He's got the funds and doesn't mind us fooling around a little, as long as we get it done."

"That sounds pretty exciting, but it also sounds kinda dangerous. So, if you don't know what you have and you don't know how things are supposed to go together, and you have this goal, how does it all work out? How do you know if you're doing it right?"

"That's the thing. You don't. It's all a big experiment."

"Experiment?!" I exclaimed, "That's quite the experiment! You want a bite of this? It's great!"

Joe chuckled, "No thanks. Yea, but it makes life exciting."

"So, what happens if you mess up? How do know what's going to work and what's not going to work?"

"Well..." Joe began, "Things are pretty loose there. A lot of the time I'm just putting things together and figuring it out as I go. I work mostly with the electrical stuff of course. There are a lot of engineers involved doing other things." He pointed at a table of guys drinking and eating dinner.

"How do you know if you make a mistake?"

"Well, if I make a mistake, there'll be nothing but a big crater where I stood. If I'm still around, I haven't made a mistake."

I hadn't planned on staying at a motel, much less an expensive one like El Capitan, but for some reason a comfortable old bed was what was needed to soothe my traveler's soul and the big old bed at El Capitan did just the trick. Especially after three or four beers with Joe and an excellent meal. The shower I took right before loading my top pannier and heading downstairs to load Mabel didn't hurt either. Mabel and I were headed north to look for aliens and we found them too. On the way there I searched for Bezos' little pet rocket project but never saw it. I did, however, find a hefty side wind that kept Mable and I on our toes. We stopped at the Guadalupe Mountains Park to see about camping. We puttered around the park looking for a possible campsite but hurriedly found that every nook and cranny was taken. The place was packed and had a frenetic feel with as many campers and cars as rocks and trees. And we weren't the only ones hunting a possible place to camp as there were several cars doing the same. Mabel and I felt like predators on the hunt, and had no time for that. So, off we went to Carlsbad Caverns. I turned in but thought the better of it when I saw two large buses pulling in behind me. It felt off so we gave up on that idea as well. We were reminded why we rarely visited touristed areas. It was early though, and I was in no hurry so I pointed Mabel towards Carlsbad, a dusty, spread-out little town that felt very rough around the edges. It was just north of us. I found a great little diner, The Carlsbad Diner where I had scrambled eggs and green hatch chili with ample amounts of coffee. It was delicious. I filled Mabel up at the gas station nearby with her favorite meal, premium gasoline. Afterwards we headed towards Roswell.

Just outside of Roswell New Mexico were large, wooden signs of green spaceships that welcomed you to the little, dry town of UFO fame. We rode to the main drag and slowly felt Roswell out. I really wanted to like it. It was really trying hard. I wanted it to be a little hipster place with a snarky, cynical-hipster-UFO feel, almost making fun of itself. Instead, Roswell was a little town that had not done much for itself since the big UFO scare in the 50's that had put on the map. Less cynical-hipster, it felt more conspiratorial. It had numerous shops on main street, all accommodating the UFO notion as well as a shabby looking museum. Everything except for a few cool coffee shops was cheap, old and worn out with faded UFO signs sitting out front. I did peruse the UFO museum for a hefty ticket cost. It claimed it was "historical" and presented "real" UFO sightings as proof. There were some pretty poorly integrated art confabs with cheap paper mâché aliens standing around. As I stood reading the ample literature on aliens visiting earth, I heard a screech and turned around. With the help of a few smoke machines the paper mâché aliens had "come to life" for a few seconds. I got a good laugh and went to the great little coffee shop nearby to stock up on coffee for my moto-kitchen.

Even though it was a little early I was feeling lazy, and started looking around for another motel. I was partial to the old, fifties-style motels, my rule being that they must be clean and neat; they must be safe for both Mabel and myself, and they must be reasonably priced. I'd much rather stay at one of those little mom and pop joints than at one of the major, over-priced chains, as clean and neat as they might consistently be. And so, after a quick expresso and my coffee beans to go, Mabel and I were off looking for a place to hang out and spend time in Roswell, maybe at the coffee shop writing. There wasn't much to choose from, and to find anything we had to go to the sprawling outskirts of town among the fast food and liquor stores. Finally, I settled on the Crane Inn. It was questionable, but close to our prerequisites. It had the look. I was met by a friendly enough woman, but even then, I had already begun to doubt my decision. It was cheap though and so I gave in.

The room looked fine upon entering, but immediately I smelled the pungent odor of cheap incense.

"I might have to sleep with the door open." I thought.

"Maybe that's a sign that we need to camp!" Mabel added. I didn't listen.

I unpacked Mabel and decided to ride around Roswell, luggage free.

"Let's camp." I could hear Mabel say as we made our way back to the downtown area, "This is not what we want."

"There has to be more to town than that!" I told Mabel, disregarding her skepticism again.

"Let's check it out."

She continued being doubtful, and she ended up being right.

Not long after we'd left, we were back at the motel, having f0und nothing much of interest. As I was taking my helmet off, I noticed an old man banging around a beat-up car a few doors down. At first, I thought he was doing something to his own car but soon realized that he was breaking into the car and paying me no attention at all while doing so. Then, I noticed another beater on the other side of the parking lot with two flat tires. It had been there for a while. I stood and stared for too long and then looked around the place and noticed that this was truly a dump of the doubtful kind and no place for Mabel.

"I tried to tell you!" she chided.

My mind made up, I packed Mabel and pulled out the map to search for nearby camp grounds.

"We're in luck Mabel. There's a state park not too far away."

"I told you so.", she repeated, "Don't you know that I'm always right?!"

It was getting a bit late at this point but I had food for a quick dinner if I needed. I knew one thing. I wasn't staying here. The incense in the room should have been the tell-tale sign. It alone would make it impossible to sleep. So off to the Bottomless Lake State Park we went.

About twenty minutes later we were turning into what seemed to be an empty park. At the entrance was a sign that pointed towards tent sites and so we followed the course. I had my pick. There was no one around. I found a nice, secluded spot and set up camp, readying myself for a star-filled night and didn't even plan on putting the rain fly on.

"This is much, much better." I said. Mable agreed, sitting on her center stand.

"I'll just eat the $40 room."

I set out to hike the Bluff trail and by the time I was returning to the trailhead a blustery wind had picked up and dark clouds were quickly rolling in out of nowhere. I looked west.

"There must be a fire." I thought out loud.

The horizon was incredibly hazy and getting darker. By the time I came to the trailhead I realized that it wasn't smoke that I was looking at. It was a dust storm of a magnitude I had never seen. I ran back to the campsite hoping to beat the storm and frantically tried to cover things up as best I could. However, the wind picked up out of nowhere and almost instantly. The rainfly was almost impossible to hook up as it whipped around in the wind and dirt. I finally got the rainfly on but it was too late. I climbed in my only respite, the tent, and it was full of powdery dirt and filling up more every second as the wind and dust whirled around the entire park like a demon. I realized I had my kitchen set up outside on the table and donned my helmet to protect myself from the whirling powder-like dust, and went out to try to save what I could. Mabel stood brave against the whipped-up dust but the storm pulled the tent up, stakes and all and sent it blowing into the tree beside the site. The stove and pot were on the ground and the tent was stuck in a tree, sideways. I ran over and pulled the tent out of the branches and staked it back in the ground and got back in just to hold it down. Thankfully I had not taken out my sleeping bag or my underlay yet although they were in the tent when it was blown into the tree.

The storm raged and I sat in the dirt-filled tent watching helplessly as the wind blew buckets of powdery dust on and in everything I owned, blowing continually under the rainfly and through the mesh under-tent. I continued to batten everything down the best I could but there was very little I could do other than cover my nose and mouth with the kitchen towel I had. I had to wait it out while dirt filled the tent minute by minute. An hour later it was sunshine and blue skies. I peeked out of the tent fly nervously. I hadn't heard a thump, but I would not have been surprised to find Mabel on her side. She wasn't, thankfully. She had stood like a queen but was filthy. And so was everything else I owned. Everything. Everything was covered with a thick coat of powdery, white dirt. I stepped out of the tent, took the rainfly off, and dumped what felt like a few pounds of dirt out of the tent. I gathered up my poor kitchen stuff and brushed off the table and set it all back up. It was as if the dirt had found every nook, cranny and crevice to blow into. I felt like I had crawled through the desert on my belly. I cleaned everything I could with my little dish towel and waited until well after nightfall to take my sleeping bag out. I left the rain fly on and set out at the table waiting for another storm to come out of the night. It never did. It was a beautiful, starry night.

Around 10:30 I crawled into the tent albeit hesitantly. The night air was cool and the bugs chirped peacefully. It was as if nothing had happened. And even after all of that, I was sure it was better than that dump of a motel I had paid for.

The night at the campsite had been a night of sporadic sleep. The wind would gently rattle the tent and thoughts of the dust storm would rattle my brain, waking me up instantly. I was glad that I had left the rainfly on. Not just because of the dust storm but also because it had gotten a bit cool during the night. I zipped up my sleeping bag and pulled the drawstring tight around my head. I was up around six. I and everything I owned was still filthy.

"But I have a shower!" I thought out loud, realizing that I still had access to the crappy motel room.

I hurriedly packed Mabel up and headed back to town and to the motel. The old, broken car was still there, now with a broken window, but the parking lot was empty and silent. It was still early, so I didn't worry about Mabel too much. Anyway, I wouldn't be long. It was just a shower. I took a long, hot shower and almost had to hold my breath for the incense. What would the maid think? Shower and no sleep? Afterwards, I made coffee out front and unpacked Mabel, taking all of my panniers off and emptying them, brushing and cleaning everything out. It would be my only chance for a while as I was heading for the mountains soon.

"You second-guessed yourself." Mabel said.

"I know. I know. I went against my better judgement."

"You went against my better judgement! We had a game plan for the day, you know."

"You're right. I didn't follow it. I got lazy."

"You forgot, again, that I am almost always right." She said, irritated.

"You said 'almost'." I reminded her. I could imagine her rolling her headlights.

I thought Roswell was what I wanted. It wasn't and it cost me forty dollars plus the ten for the campsite. It cost me riding around at dusk looking for a place to camp, grief, energy and stress. Even after several more camping trips this still happened every once in while.

"Not if you listened to me."

"I know, I know. You know best Mabel. You know best."

3.7

After cleaning things up, I was off, just wanting to get out of Roswell. But first I wanted breakfast and I found it. I had a great plate of huevos rancheros and lots of coffee at Martins Capital Grill, a wonderful little out of the way place. Finished, I went out to Mabel and saw that there were a group of Harley's revving their engines up and getting ready for a morning cruise.

"Don't worry about them, Mabel. You're just as much a bike as they are, more if you ask me."

"I'm not worried." She answered confidently. "Are we ready to go yet, or are we just going to sit here and compare ourselves to others?"

"You're in a mood!" I reprimanded.

"Well, it was a rough night."

We headed out on Route 246 and I thought of that great Supertramp song. There's a verse in it that goes:

You never see what you wanna see
Forever playing to the gallery
You take the long way home
Take the long way home

"Take the long way home…take the long way home." I sang as I headed out on the little road, leaving Roswell, literally in the dust.

"Take the long way home…take the long way home…" Mabel joined in.

In no time and with almost zero traffic we were in Ruidoso, a town that again beckoned me to stay a night.

"No! Not this time." Mabel reprimanded me.

"I'm not. I'm not."

"Let's do some miles instead!"

The road from Ruidoso to Cloudcroft was beautiful, reminding me of the many gorgeous, twisty rides in Colorado. The smell of pinion, lemon, pepper, pine, and cinnamon all came wafting into my helmet and put a smile on my face. Mabel was having fun on the mild twisties, leaning first to one side and then to the other.

"They'll be no chicken-strips on me!" she revved.

We made Cloudcroft, a one-street, one-block long town of tourists and tourist attractions. There were already crowds milling about and staring into the numerous shops and restaurants. We moseyed through downtown and then onward. It was still cool and Mabel and I had roads to ride. First to Hwy 130 which would hit Hwy 24 looping around.

"You seem to be showing off, Mabel!"

Even with all the weight on the back of her she was handling great, almost like a sport bike. We explored the area, both smiling and enjoying the beautiful weather and the fun roads. Stopping in Pinion at the only store in town, in fact the only thing in town, I picked up supplies. I had eyed some stealth camping opportunities and wanted to be ready. Two generous women ran the place, smiling and friendly.

"You look happy! Having fun?" one of them asked.

"I'm on a motorcycle and it's a beautiful day. There's no way not to be happy!"

They smiled. I'm sure they'd seen my look before. Pinion offered ample off-road opportunities and Mabel and I tried a few before searching out more paved roads. We climbed a steep and rocky road just to find a great, flat place filled with the carcasses and bones of deer. It stunk.

"Hunters!" I mumbled.

"There's more. Let's go look for them." Mabel reminded me.

We road back to Cloudcroft taking some dirt roads and found a perfect little spot to set up camp. It was in the middle of nothing and it was free. We stopped and stood silently to get a feel for the spot.

"I told you."

"Yes, you did. I know I need to be a little more patient."

The site was a free campsite in the State Forest. There was one other car there on the far side that had made camp. It didn't look to be a problem and so I started my camp ritual. The other camper was a lone lady with an old dog. She waved as I set up camp.

"Hi!"

"Hey. How are you." I answered.

"Great."

We fell into conversation about the time a third car, a Prius rode in and to the last campsite on the far end of the tiny campground, across a little bridge. Joan was living in her car and while we talked informed me that she had four degrees, one being in anthropology and another being in something she called "Feminine environmentalism".

"I have to ask, what is 'feminine environmentalism'?" I interrupted the free-style, thought- monologue that had been being delivered for the past few minutes.

Joan looked at me a little irritated, about me interrupting or about me not knowing what 'feminine environmentalism' was, I didn't know which? She was explaining the concept in detail when the other girl came up and introduced herself. She was young and full of laughs and smiles.

"I did a stint with Ameri-core and now I'm just travelling around. How about you?" the young girl started, looking at me. Joan now gave up on continuing her lecture and interjected another topic instead.

"I live in my car. You want a tour? It's pretty cool."

Joan was a talker for sure. The young girl looked at me as if to ask what she did wrong. I smiled and then she shrugged her shoulders. We listened and followed Joan around as she pulled one thing after another out of the over-stuffed Honda Civic. Joan's dog meandered around camp and started towards my camp and Joan stopped mid-sentence and walked over to the dog to get him back.

"Don't worry about him. He's not going to hurt anything!" I assured her.

"He's deaf" she informed us, bringing the friendly pooch back to the car.

The young girl and I started to walk towards our respective campsites thinking that the tour was over.

"We're not finished. There's more to show." Joan assured, beckoning us back to the car.

The young girl and I looked at each other again, now with a silent understanding. It was getting dark and it was getting cold. After a few more minutes, I interrupted Joan.

"Well, I'm going to call it a day! I have writing to do and dinner to make. Thanks for the tour"

"Oh…OK. Goodnight. You know, *I've* written four books!" Joan added.

I smiled at the young lady as I made my getaway. Joan kept talking to the young girl for a few minutes more. Then everything fell quiet.

Lounging around a beautiful campsite in the mountains with a simple dinner cooking and sipping on a beer is one of those beautiful things in life. I was leaning up against a log sitting on my porch that I had commandeered from the tent.

"You think there'll be a dust storm tonight?" I asked Mabel.

"I don't think so. At least I hope not. But you need to lube my chain. We've been riding dirt today."

"You're right."

I got up and did a quick check and lubed the chain. It was already cooling down as we were almost 8000 ft up in the state park but I felt refreshed after the day's ride. Riding nice, small roads and enjoying the nature clears the mind and feeds the soul. Beer helped washed down Joans one-woman monologue.

"We haven't found a rhythm yet." I said to Mabel.

"No. But it'll come. You know how it works."

"Sometimes travel seems like a guilty pleasure of mine." I thought to myself, taking a swig of beer and picking up my journal.

"You need to get over that."

I could hear Helle's voice reprimand me almost instantly.

"She's right, you know." Mabel added.

I finished my beer, ate my simple rice dinner, put Mabel to bed, and then crawled in my sleeping bag. It was getting dark and it was already cold.

"This is life." I thought to myself, "This is what it's about."

The next morning, the only thing that mattered was getting warm. I knew I was camping in the mountains but the cold, morning air was still a surprise. I had learned from previous trips that the secret was to rip the band aid off quickly and just deal with the cold. I always kept my shirt in the sleeping bag with me though, better wrinkled than cold. But unless you were a yoga professional getting it on in the sleeping bag was near impossible. So, off came the band aid. I unzipped and shook myself into my hurriedly cooling shirt and then into some freezing pants. My advice to anyone that asked was to sleep in your socks, but I hadn't followed my advice that night. It was all over pretty quickly but I had my motorcycle jacket and my inner jacket slung all over the place. I had woken up cold earlier in the dark, and pulled my riding clothes over the sleeping bag hoping it would help. I even used my "pillow", the inner jacket of the riding jacket to cover myself up.

Coffee first, instant oatmeal, and then I started packing. The tent had dew all over it but the sun was shining in the far corner of the campsite, so I hung the rainfly and the inner layer upside down on a branch and let the sun do its job. The two women were not up yet and so I had the place to myself. I love mornings when camping. They were quiet and the stove made a gentle hissing noise that was somehow relaxing. The coffee even tasted better and usually I didn't need more than one mug. There was an eagerness that pushed.

"Get a move on. Daylight is burning." I could hear Mabel say.

Soon I had her panniers on and was warming up the motor a little bit while I donned my gloves and helmet, always putting them on in the wrong order and making my life a little difficult. I spent the day zooming around twisties and stopping for photo ops. Hwy 152 was exhilarating! There was ample tight turns and no time for relaxing. Any sight-seeing had to be done when Mabel was parked, which wasn't that often. I went through the Gila National Forest, beautiful and pristine. All the campsites were free in New Mexico State Parks and I took advantage of them. They weren't all pretty and nice, and some weren't well kept, but it was camping. After a full day of twisting around mountain roads and exploring dirt paths I found a promising one and rode in. There were a few small campers set up and I spotted a hill leading to another section of the site and made my way up the rutted, dirt road. That's when I met Pablo and Michael and their families. They were the nemesis of Joan, the talkative Phd.

There were two women sitting in the jacked up pick-up trucks on their phones and there were three kids playing down by the small creek which was down a steep hill in front of the sites. I rode up and instantly noticed large coolers sitting on the tailgate of one of the big trucks. I also noticed that both Pablo and Michael, whom I hadn't met at this point, were decked out in full military camo and both had large pistols strapped to their waists. I decided to find somewhere else and turned around carefully on the dirt incline. I made it a little way down the hill towards the campers and remembered I didn't have any water, and that there were no water spigots at these camp sites. I decided to hit up the military-looking guys for a little water.

"Excuse me." I started, as I turned Mabel off, "Do you guys happen to have any extra water? Don't need a…"

"No problem! We have plenty. We're about to leave anyway, if you want this spot." the bigger of the two men, started.

"Are you sure?!"

"Of course!" He said, instantly pulling a large watercooler off the stanchion on the truck.

"Let's get you filled up."

I handed him my water jug.

"Do you want some food? We've got a bunch of steaks."

"Wow!", I started, "that's not necessary…"

"No problem. We have to carry all this shit back anyway."

"Well…OK. But just one. I don't have any way of carrying more than I can eat."

"You sure. It'll last."

"No, no. That's, that's fine."

Michael grabbed a huge steak out of the cooler and handed it to me.

"Are you guys hunting up here?"

"No. no. We're just fuckin' around. We've been here for two days and 'they' are ready to go." He said, motioning towards the women in the front of the truck.

"Hey. You want some smoke? We've got a ton."

"Well…" I started.

"I noticed the pistols. I know you guys aren't hunting with those unless you're a great shot."

"Oh.", Michael started, "These are for bears." He smiled.

"Bears?!" Are there bears here?" I didn't think there were, but I wasn't worried. I had spent a lot of time camping in Colorado where there were actually bears.

"Fuck ya! Lots of those bastards. We just carry these for protection." Michael answered, pulling out two tightly twisted, big joints.

"Hey man. You want some beer? We got a lot left over, and some chips too!" Pablo added, closing up my water container.

"I don't want to take you guy's food!" I said, amazed at their hospitality.

"Dude, no problem. We know how it is. And you can't have much on that thing." Pablo motioned to Mabel, sitting quietly and almost smiling.

We continued talking as they packed their gear up. They asked me about my trip and the usual questions that motorcycle riders get. In no time they were packed and offered me more steak.

"Man. This a great site. You'll want to stay here longer than one night."

"Watch for the bears!" Michael added with a smile on his face.

"I will. And thanks!"

Soon they were pulling out, kids and all and honked a 'good-bye'. The site was up on a top of a small hill at the bottom of a larger mountain. It was by itself except for a small campsite some fifty yards away. These two campsites had their own bathroom building because they were so isolated.

"This is a great spot, Mabel. We may stay more than one night."

I rounded up some kindling and some firewood for the huge steak and opened one of the bags of chips and one of the six beers they had left me. I found a flattish rock and threw it in the middle of the fire, piling some wood on top of it. I pulled one of the three tightly wound joints up and lit it in the campfire. It smelled like hops. When the fire was down to embers, I cleaned the rock up as best I could and threw the steak on it. I always had salt and pepper with me, so I had added those to the meat. It instantly started sizzling. I sat back and listened to the meat sizzle, and drank my beer.

I was on my third beer and full of steak when Bob and Bill came riding up on their KTM's. They were decked out for dirt and both men had full riding gear on. I decided to be neighborly and walked over after they had settled in.

"Hey! I noticed the bikes. Are you guys doing the BDR?"

"Oh, hey. Yea. Some of it anyway."

"My name's Mark I'm the black bike up the hill."

"My name's Bob, and this is Bill." Bob motioned to the half-naked man changing into shorts.

TWO WHEELS AND A TENT

"Want a beer?"

"Sure." I answered, thinking about the three I had already finished.

Bob was a tall thin guy that seemed serious and determined. Bill stood up and instantly smiled. He was what I called 'portly'. Bob still had his riding pants on and Bill stood up revealing extremely white 'chicken legs' in some loose-fitting shorts that flopped under his huge belly.

"I'm Bill"

"Yes. I'm Mark."

Bob flipped open one of his hardcase panniers and I started laughing out loud in disbelief.

"You guys have your priorities for sure!"

The whole pannier was a cooler and it was full of beer.

"Yes! We do." Bill said, opening his first can.

Bob moved around the site, busily getting ready to cook, or reorganize. He was nice but he was a much more serious man than Bill seemed to be. We talked about their bikes and touring. All motorcyclists have stories and enjoy telling them.

"Yea," Bill started when I asked, "Our wives like us to leave the house for a few months a year and so we do this. We've been doing this for a number of years, at least since we've retired."

"What do you do?"

Bob started, never sitting down, but taking a long swigs of beer.

"I was an accountant at a construction company."

Bill interjected.

"I worked heavy machinery for thirty years, mostly big backhoes."

"That's can be an art." I said, "My father-in-law is an artist with most machinery and roughshod tools."

"Yea. That's true. I think it's an art too. I really enjoyed it."

Bill grimaced.

"I hated accounting."

We talked for a while before I bid Bob and Bill farewell to let them enjoy their dinner after promising I would come by in the morning and share a cup of coffee. We weren't quite done recounting motorcycle stories.

"I get up pretty early."

"That's fine. If you see us, come one down. If not, then great travels and nice to meet you!" Bob said, shaking my hand but never really standing still. Bill, always smiling, shook my hand slow and methodically.

"Well..." he said, speaking much slower than Bob, "When you see your father-in-law, say 'hello'. And be careful out there. Bob likes to ride a lot faster than I do, but I manage to keep up." Bill said, smiling big and taking swig of his second beer.

"If I don't see you guys, be careful and have fun!"

"Alright. Goodnight."

The next morning, I woke right before daybreak and lay in the tent waiting for signs of light. It came in the form of a bluish-grey hue and I started my morning ritual. Drinking coffee, I kept an eye on movement from Bob and Bill's site down at the bottom of the hill, but there was none. I ate some peanut butter crackers for breakfast and started packing. Suddenly, I stopped, deciding to stay at the camp another night.

While I was putting my panniers on the picnic table and having a second cup of coffee, Bob and Bill had come out and were packing up. I stopped on my way down to the bathroom.

"You staying another night?" Bill asked, seeing the tent still up and no panniers on Mabel.

"Yea. I studied the map last night and saw there were some nice-looking riding possibilities around here."

"Good idea! You know, you said your folks were in Missouri. There are wonderful roads in the Arkansas Ozarks!"

"Yes, there are!" Bob added, sitting and putting on his riding pants quickly. "You could ride the roads there for a long time and never get bored."

"I've never ridden that area, but I've been planning on it."

"You'll really love 'em"

"You guys heading out I see."

"Yep. We hope to make about 150 miles today. It'll be all dirt though."

"One day I would like to try a BDR."

"Take someone with you when you do." Bob interjected. I noticed that he said "when".

We shared a cup of coffee and by the time it was cold they were packed up and I was ready to start exploring the area. We said our good-byes, and well wishes and parted ways.

The morning was cold but I was bundled up in long-johns and my long sleeve, lightweight sweater under my riding gear. I had my big winter gauntlets on too. I was ready. Out on the road Mabel and I made our way to Gila and Silver City. I took 152 with its high cliffs and twists and turns. The sun made artwork out of the trees, the cliffs and the road. I had decided to go to the Gila Cliff dwellings. Arriving well ahead of any crowds I parked Mabel and bought a ticket. Walking through the cave-like dwellings, I amazed at the structures and especially the thought of the people, the Mogollons, who had lived there for centuries before leaving them. The hike through the Gila Cliff dwellings was great too. When I got back to Mabel, the parking lot had a few cars in it, and when I was heading back out to 152 a few more were heading up to the park. I had no plans so I just turned and followed the road. Seeing a big snake in the middle of the little road, I stopped and moved it to the side knowing it would be hit if I didn't. I saw a little jaunt, State Rd. 15 and took it on a whim. It was magnificent and I looped around and made it to Silver City around lunch time. Silver City was a very small, clean town that was doing its best to scrape by. I found a distillery that doubled as a restaurant. It looked promising and I stepped in. The sign said "Seat yourself" so I did. I waited, and waited some more but no one ever came. I got tired of waiting and walked out, riding around a bit until I got cell service. I found a place, Las Cantinas, off a dirt road and gave it a shot. The food was great as was the service.

I explored more roads, most of which were wonderful, for most of the afternoon before stopping for beer and food for the night. I found 152 again and rode in the opposite direction. It was funny with these kinds of roads. They were almost like new roads riding them in the opposite directions. It was almost like a road dons new clothing. I hit the sweet spots just after passing 61 and leaned Mabel over letting her play. We dipped and dived past the high cliffs and turned into the long drops that took my stomach up into my throat at times. The valleys below were beautifully decked out in oranges and reds. In the shadows the colors were hues of blue and grey. New Mexico was truly an amazing place in the mountains. Down below it was dry, high-plains desert but the parks throughout the state were Colorado-like, forested and beautiful offering the rider ample opportunities. I took my time and took breaks on the turn-offs admiring the wonderful nature before making my way back to camp around 4pm.

I turned into camp after enjoying every twisty turn I could find and it seemed that I had the place to myself. Parking Mabel, I pulled out my hammock and found some trees to hang it in and pulled out a beer. I laid there listening to the wind constantly gush and whoosh through the forest. It was always nice to take a day and enjoy the local roads. It was nice to be able to feel time and taste life. I let the late afternoon tick by at its own pace. No one ever came, that I saw. And when I was hungry, I ate. I was relaxed in a rare way. Truly relaxed, and not feeding the guilt that always seemed to creep up. I felt it come and go, not being able to get a grasp on my mind. These trips were not what I would call vacations, but they have times when they were much better than when we intentionally tried entertain ourselves. I wasn't busy. I had plans, but not too many. I had found that if you listened, you'd know what you needed to do and when. I was practicing that.

Two wheels and a tent could remind you of the wasted time we spend in front of screens while beautiful places like this one sit and wait. Without the modern, so-called conveniences boredom was allowed to play. There was no entertainment except the roads and the searching for twisties and scenery. I thought about all this while I swung lackadaisically in my hammock.

"Last night my entertainment was the stars, Bill and Bob, and my thoughts."

"We have more to do. There are endless numbers of roads." Mabel added.

"I know. I like the idea that the world holds beautiful curves of paved goodness out there, just waiting for your two wheels and my chapped smile."

3.8

Night came quickly and I was in bed early. When camping, darkness usually meant sleep. I checked my cellphone. It was 9:45 but I didn't have cell service. I wondered what Pablo's and Michael's wives were doing on their cellphones earlier? With that thought, I crawled into the tent and zipped up. It was already getting cold.

In no time the temperature seemed to drop drastically so I zipped up tight in the sleeping bag and was soon asleep only to be woke up again. I heard leaves rustling near the tent and now lay there, still as I could, wondering what it might be and the chances of it leaving on its own.

"There it went again." I thought. And again.

There was certainly something out there.

"I shouldn't have done the steak on the fire. Animals can smell that!" I thought. Michael's smile came to mind when he had told me about bears. The rustling repeated. It sounded like there were more than one.

"But bears don't travel in packs!"

I lay trying to think of animals that travelled in packs, and able to make the noises that I had heard, but with no luck. Finally, I unzipped my sleeping bag quietly, grabbed my knife and headlamp and fared the cold night air in my underwear and camp shoes. I turned the headlamp off, thinking I would spook whatever it was out there, and made my way to Mabel. The thought was that at least I could take cover behind her if whatever it was, attacked. The only thing I could think of were coyotes or wolves but it didn't sound right. I started her up and instantly her bright headlights lit up dozens of red spots that appeared about twenty feet from the tent, staring right at me. The noise stopped for a few seconds and then the red dots turned, looking like they were staring at the ground. The rustling noise continued. I was dumfounded for a bit but it finally dawned on me.

"They're cattle!" I said out loud.

"And lots of them too!" Mabel followed.

I turned her off and let my eyes adjust to the darkness. It was a herd of cattle meandering through the campsite.

"It must be an open range here." I thought, waiting for my eyes to adjust to the pitch-black darkness a little more.

"I don't want them trampling me in my tent. I better wait until they're gone."

But they stopped. A few minutes later I walked slowly towards them with my headlamp to get them to start moving again, when a large Bull appeared. He wasn't afraid of me, and had stopped and was now staring directly at me in the dark. I backed up slowly and waited some more. I wouldn't win a fight with a jealous bull. About thirty minutes and numerous cows and calves later I felt it safe enough to return to the tent. By that time, I was freezing.

Afterwards sleep was sporadic as I lay and listened for more visitors. For some reason, perhaps because I was aware, the more I lay awake the colder I got. Finally, just before daybreak I gave up and got up, made a cup of coffee and tried to plan the day. It looked cloudy, almost dreary and even though the grey skies gave the surrounding nature a beautiful blue hue I was too tired and cold to pay attention. After packing Mabel up, I decided to make it back down to Silver City to get gas and find a coffee shop. More coffee was obviously needed. When I got to the gas station I opened up the tank bag to grab my wallet. It wasn't there. I rummaged through the stuffed tank bag, not too worried, but with no luck.

"OK." I thought. I stood and tried to go through the morning.

"Could it have fallen off the bike, out of the bag?"

Now I was worried! I didn't see how, though. I started rummaging through the top case. Nothing. At this point my worry turned a little panicky.

"It's always, always in the tank bag!" I said aloud.

Back on Mabel I backtracked slowly, scanning the road for anything that resembled a black wallet. Nothing.

"Well, I have cash." I thought, remembering my daily carry pouch. Then it dawned on me. I hadn't checked the Camelbak. Pulling over I opened the backpack up and there it was! Disaster averted but I felt I had aged a few years.

Relieved, gassed up, and a cup of coffee in my hand, I sat outside the gas station looking up at the skies. North? It looked like rain. South, and down towards Arizona? Hot! I decided to take my chances and head north. After the coffee I found 152 for a third time and enjoyed its twists and curves, always seeming to renew themselves to me. Surrounded by scrub brush and red/brown hills and grey cliffs the mountains of New Mexico always smelled like pinion and pine, a lovely and inviting smell.

"You're sewing your oats this morning, Mabel."

"It's a great road. What do you want me to say?" she answered as she leaned into the tight curve.

As 152 flattened out and led out to a mesa the wind picked up. It continued to pick up as black clouds loomed in front of me. Dark and blustery, unfriendly, they continued to gather until the wind was simply horrific. A sidewind that caused Mabel and I to be whipped back and forth. At times I felt like the tires were sliding sideways on the windy, mountain road. The temperature dropped quickly too, a sign of bad weather anywhere, and I stopped and donned all of my cold weather gear. I was still cold. We had been riding for hours at this point.

"We'll be needing gas pretty soon." Mabel reminded me.

"This is neither the time or the place." I answered, keeping an eye on the weather.

"It will be."

The wind never let up and as a rode over a high peak I noticed that the dark skies were dumping rain just ahead. I stopped and considered my options. There weren't many. I was equally screwed no matter what I decided.

"Onward!" I said with faint courage.

"This is the adventure too." Mabel said, almost snarky.

I continued to climb wonderful switchbacks up towards the mountain pass slowing because of the horrendous wind. Then phase 2 started. It started hailing on us. Suddenly I noticed I had a smile on my face. I had the helmet visor up as I usually did and felt the hail pricking my smiling smile. Down went the visor.

"I feel alive!" I yelled surprising Mabel and even myself. And I was alive!

Further north and up the mountain the temperatures dropped. The cold became relentless and knife-like. I entered the Apache National Forest and the hail turned to hard, cold rain. Phase 3. The wind threw the drops like rocks at Mabel and I. I could almost hear the drops pinging off the gas tank which, I remembered, was getting emptier all the time. Mabel typically had wonderful fuel mileage, but the load and the wind was taking its toll. Finally, I made the peak and stopped. It was cold. It was pouring down rain and I was in the middle of nowhere. Grant was miles away and it was simply beautiful! Parked on a pull-out I looked out over the grey and white mountains half covered in clouds and foggy with a down-pour.

"We can probably make it, if I go slow."

"Probably." Mabel added.

I was nervous but happy. My phone was useless here and I stood on the beautiful peak not able to make a decision.

"Well, we can't just sit here!" Mabel reminded me.

"A gas station can be just around the corner or a hundred miles away." I said nervously.

"There's only one way to find out." Mabel added.

I started her up and decided to forge forward. About forty-five minutes later I spotted a small grouping of buildings. I looked down and the "Get gas now!" light was blinking.

"You are the luckiest man I know." Mabel said.

A small restaurant, an even smaller motel and…a gas station!

The little group of buildings sat at a sharp corner almost cut into the mountain side. It reminded me of my rides in West Virginia, a beautiful motorcycling state. As I stood reminiscing and filling Mabel up, phase 4 started. At first, I thought myself lucky, as the rain began subsiding. And then I noticed that it wasn't subsiding, but changing into snow. It began snowing on me as I stood filling Mabel up. I couldn't do anything but laugh.

"Well, let's make the best of it." I said.

After filling up, the snow stopped and the sun started shining. I rode to Malpais to see the clay cliffs. I stood in awe of nature as I usually did on these trips when it started hailing again. I took off down the mountain and the hail returned almost out of nowhere. Then, about thirty minutes later, it changed to a cold rain. The rain continued for some time. My hands were soaked, even though I had the leather winter gauntlets on.

"Should have brought rubber gloves." Mabel reminded me.

"Thanks for nothing!"

"No problem. I'm here to help."

I followed traffic down the narrow mountain road, fighting a cold, wet mist. Finally, the little road dumped out onto the freeway and for once I was actually glad to be on a freeway. It was a welcoming sight, but at the same time totally out of place. I took the freeway and barreled past ugly fast-food franchises and truck stops, getting wetter every mile. The adventure would have to be put on hold. There was no way I was going to camp tonight, not wet. I would camp in the rain but setting up in the rain and being wet already pretty much sealed the deal for a hotel. I was already disappointed with the thought. Albuquerque never really appeared. It sort of widened until the beauty of New Mexico began to disappear as the cement virus overtook everything. The scenery seemed to become beige. I stopped at a noisy truck stop to gather myself. Sante Fe was my goal but I realized it wasn't happening today. Tonight would have to be a motel to dry out and perhaps wash some clothes in the bathtub, a little trick I had learned some years back. The room was overpriced but clean. It had a particular smell of cheapness but the price did not mirror that. After warming up a bit and getting some clothes washed and some dry ones on, I ventured outside. It was a typical freeway motel, drab and lifeless. It pretended to be what it wasn't. Nothing looked promising as I glanced over at Mabel sitting forlornly in the wet parking lot.

"I feel the same." I said, quietly and under my breath.

I knew she stood dreaming of mountain roads. That's where we both came alive. But all that would have to wait. Right now, I was in search of a place to eat.

"Why not?!" I thought to myself, "I'm here and I've got to eat."

I spotted a plain looking little restaurant across the busy intersection. It was beside a dying truck stop. A larger one had taken all the business up the road, closer to the highway. It was an Italian restaurant. The waitress was prompt and friendly, a good sign. I sat alone waiting for my food and spotted a young lady sitting alone, silently. I could tell she was lonely. Not just here, but in general. So, I talked.

"Does it always rain, sleet and hail in one day around here?" I started.

At first, she didn't realize I was talking to her. Then she looked startled when she did finally realize it.

"Oh! Oh yea. Weather in New Mexico can be strange."

"Are you from around here?"

"Yes, yes…I come here at least once a week. The food is good and they're pretty friendly."

I found out that she fostered dogs and had adopted several. I always respect that sort of person and told her so.

"Are you travelling?"

"Yes. I'm on a motorcycle tour."

"Wow! That sounds interesting!"

"It can be. Today certainly was."

We continued talking even after our meals came. An older couple beside us chimed in and we all sat and talked. Salads came to the older couple's table.

"My salad was supposed to have walnuts." The older lady said.

"It does." The waiter pointed to the nuts.

"Yes, but that's not enough."

"I'll fix it." The waiter replied blankly, and walked back to the kitchen.

With that, I thought about my day in the mountains, being cold and wet and not having a plan. Camping and dirt and oil, and all the things that come from living outside and being on a motorcycle. I thought about how wonderful crappy instant oatmeal tasted on a cold morning and the smell of a wet fire. I thought about the mosquitoes, and cattle grazing through my campground, and how it was all still so worth it. I didn't know what to say.

Back at the hotel I wrote in my journal as I usually did.

"Today was a day of decisions, of acceptance, of realizations about life. I need these days. I need this travel, on a motorcycle, to remind me that I am alive; that I am a person and that there are things in this world that are worth

doing. For some reason, I find happiness on two wheels, with a tent in my pannier and no plan."

See the curve ahead.

It's to the left.

Veer just slightly…slightly to the right, not much

Catch the solid yellow stripe just right and…

Start leaning, in your mind at first

Then the bike

Don't be afraid

Lean and watch the curve of the line

There's no time for mistakes so pay attention

Follow the yellow line and look for the white line

Think, almost feel the bike over towards it

Don't let off the throttle and don't turn your head

Don't give it more, not yet

Think your way to the white line

See the curve ahead

It's to the right…

I woke up early, but in a hotel room. The sheets were nice and warm and as usual there were too many pillows. I wrapped the warm sheets around my head and rolled over. It was still dark. I knew that outside it would be cold and the day met my expectations when I finally stepped out of bed and packed my top pannier. I had a feeling that today would be a day of waiting rather than riding. I knew that, but I didn't want to wait in Albuquerque. I drank the weak motel room coffee and took a shower (one of the luxuries that I actually do miss when camping). I planned on finding a coffee shop to get a good strong cup on my way to I didn't know where. I would try to hunt down a good breakfast place. It was more difficult than I expected. What I did manage to find was a mediocre bagel with a package of cream cheese and a single, poor egg that had been beaten into a glop that was unrecognizable. I forced the quick and dirty meal down in the parking lot. The coffee was so bad I didn't finish it. Ah! The life of a motorcycle adventurist!

As I stood there looking down at my big map trying to figure out a way to beat the eminent weather in the area, I looked up and noticed more dark and foreboding clouds coming up out of the south. I needed to get going…somewhere. The highway was quickest and really the only way to get out of the city and so I talked Mabel into riding the slab of cement for a while, towards the north. Boring but effective, or so I thought. Five or so miles north of Albuquerque I was sitting in traffic for over an hour. I *was* on a motorcycle and *did* consider just running alongside of all the cars or just riding through the big ditch at the side of the long scar of a highway, but I didn't want to be *"that* guy". And so, I waited along with the rest of the cars. I felt the wind change from warmish to cool and looked behind me as I watched the oncoming storm catch up easily. I considered putting on my rain gear just in case, but it was just warm enough to make having it on miserable, and just cool enough to make me nervous. I didn't feel any better looking towards Sante Fe up in the mountains. Up there were even more angry looking bags of misery just waiting for me. At least I presumed so.

It continued getting colder and colder and finally the traffic began to move, slowly. I sat on Mabel, riding along slowly in first gear and fuming at my predicament. I had a feeling that there would either be a very wet night in a tent, or another night in a hotel in my near future. My boots were still wet from the "fun" weather the previous day had thrown at me, so were my winter gloves. Although I didn't want to admit it, it was my feet getting soaked that made my mind up. I didn't mind hardship, but wet and misery was not my choice, and luckily I had a choice.

"This is fun!" Mabel said, cynically.

"Hey! Your feet aren't wet." I answered.

Sante Fe is nestled, almost secretly, in the mountains. A hidden little town, growing fast, and as hard as it might be to believe I got lost trying to find it. I knew it was right off the highway somewhere, but where that somewhere was, was alluding me. It kept getting colder and when I stopped in a newly developed suburb it started raining...hard. Cold and rain. Rain and cold. They had been the theme for the past few days.

"This is getting irritating!" I said out loud to no one in particular.

"Remember, we're having fun." Mabel reminded me. I almost chuckling.

Because I was irritated, I couldn't make a decision and so I stood there with big drops of rain beginning to fall on me, in a suburb, looking blankly down at a map that was getting wet. I needed to do something, and fast. It pained me to get yet another hotel, but that's what I was going to do. I felt it even before I decided to do it. I found a cheaper one and luckily (for once) I had cell service.

I found myself on Cerrello Ave which was packed with cars. The rain was now coming down consistently. I had donned my raingear and was wet anyway because now I sweating. I just needed to find the place. That's all I cared about. It was early but I didn't care about that either. The hotel seemed almost empty but it was nicer than the previous one. It was still a hotel though. The room was on the bottom floor and had a sliding glass door and even a little rock patio that led straight out to the parking lot. So, I parked Mabel directly behind the room and brought in all the panniers. Afterwards, I went and got a quick bite to eat and three local brews to take back to the room. I spent the day planning possible routes and watching weather reports on my phone. My rule was to ride in rain, but not leave in rain. I had all my stuff, camping stuff and all, spread out all over the floor of the room and spent the afternoon drinking beer and perusing maps, and fantasizing about twisty roads and dry camping spots. Hotels were not adventure, or were they?

"Well, if I'm on an adventure, then they are part of adventure." I thought to myself.

I wrote in my journal and thought about that question.

"There is an analogy using highways, to the way we live our lives. Highways are easy, well-worn paths down the middle of life. They invite mediocrity and mediocrity invites all sorts of things that we think we want but truly do not need. Highways have a pretense about them, somehow. It's presumed that highways are what everyone wants and so everyone simply drives on them. They are exciting only because of speed and the necessity of sharing them with so many other drivers. Highways are vehicular consumerism, an invitation to commodify everything. They ask no questions and expect no answers other than 'How much?' and 'How many?' Highways are point A to point B; don't pass go and don't collect anything, especially memories. Bland, fake, and self-righteous."

There was more. I was in a mood.

"Hotels sell themselves on comfort and ease, much in the same way that highways do. But somehow, they are uncomfortable and do not put anyone at ease. Hotels try to substitute a basic need of all humans: a home. But as a substitute they are nothing more than capitalism in a building. I'll sleep in a consumeristic bed and I'll write on a plastic table made to emulate wood and warmth. And I will be comfortable. Hotels are easy but they are not alive like the woods. They are environmentally controlled, but not wild like the mountains. Hotels are the unnatural persuading us that it is the most natural thing in the world."

Yes. Today had been disappointing. The stores, the highway and now the hotel. While I ate my takeout and brushed my teeth in the clean sink, I looked forward to the complication that camping brought to such mundane tasks as cooking a meal and using the bathroom. While staying at hotels these things, these every day occurrences that most people never paid attention to, myself included, reminded me of the importance of actually living life.

"Camp?!" people have said, looking at me in disbelief, "Why?!"

"In a tent?!" others would say with disdain in their voice.

Staying at a hotel was like travelling by car; it was boring but safe. As comfortable as I was, I realized that a hotel was easy but it was not living. Comfortable yes, but unnecessary consumption. Life is dirty and hotels and highways cleaned it up and bleached it out. Adventure tended to create switchbacks and twisted roads unravelling through forests and deserts; analogies for life. Highways cut a swath, bulldozing everything. They gouged themselves through rock; connection through consumption. I wrote one more thing in my journal before falling asleep in my comfortable, clean, hotel room:

"A highway is fast food. A switchback is a gourmet meal."

I thought about my previous question.

"No. hotels are not part of adventure."

I closed my journal and turned off the light.

3.9

From the nice hotel room to the parking lot filled with sunshine. It was early in Sante Fe. The skies were blue and it was sunny and even a bit warm. This was a far cry from the past two days of being rained on, hailed, and snowed on, in a single day! But the weather and hotels hadn't beaten out the sense of adventure that I had in my heart. Then I noticed that there wasn't even a breeze, no relentless sidewinds, something that I often noticed in the mornings in a tent. It had been a nice quiet night in a comfy bed, but the hotel life wasn't me. I really felt like I belonged in a tent out in the wilderness with Mabel parked close. The relentless rain had been a game-changer, though. I'm not sure there's enough gear to make camping in the rain fun.

"Let's find some nice roads." I said to Mabel.

We headed north on 285, not necessarily a highway, but a big road. It jutted off of the mammoth slab of cement called I-25. Soon I found my road. 502 was an unassuming strip of asphalt that soon turned twisty enough for some morning excitement. It started up the mountain and soon turned into a gently rolling road leading to Highway 4.

"This is going to be a beautiful day!" I said, as I made the sharp turn onto 4.

Hwy 4 was a beautiful, meandering road through the mountains near Los Alamos. I thought of the ugly history in this area, the military, Robert Oppenheimer, and the atom bomb.

"You know, he used to ride horses. Probably through these mountains." I told Mabel and myself.

I started passing trailheads and decided to stop for a short hike. I strapped my Camelbak on and was on my way. The trail was dusty and flat but I enjoyed picking the leaves of an abundant bush and rubbing them in my hands. The scent was wonderous. It was like a peppery lemon antique store. I hiked a few miles through the high desert and found a spot to sit and enjoy an energy bar; I always had a few in my Camelbak for just such occasions. After a quick rest I headed back to the bike noticing the forks in the path that I hadn't noticed on my way in. I turned a corner, though, and saw the handlebars of Mabel. Loaded up I continued down Hwy 4 twisting and turning in the switchbacks. It had warmed up a little but not much, and in the short straightaways I enjoyed the scenery for a bit before hitting another sharp curve. All around were conifer forests with red cliff faces and grey canyons in the background. I passed an interesting dirt road and made a U-turn. 289 ended up being motorcycle paradise.

It was a wide dirt road that led to a hidden gem of a dispersed campground. I came to a parking area and shut off Mabel's engine. It was still. It was quiet and I enjoyed the view over the large expansive meadow. The place was heavy with peace and quiet, and resplendent with mountain beauty. I sat on a large log and took it all in before deciding to have some coffee. Water boiled I poured it over the grounds in the cup. Sipping coffee I leaned back and let the sun warm my face.

"I can't leave this place. Not right now." I thought. I looked down the wide road and noticed some smaller dirt roads that forked out into the mountains.

"And there's exploring to be done!" Mabel added.

I had only ridden about ninety miles but decided to stay and find a camp spot. I packed up Mabel and headed down a narrow, winding dirt road and found a perfect little gem of a camping spot about seven miles down a rough and craggy fire road. It was set in a small valley between two small mountains with tall, slender pines covering them. I unloaded the panniers and headed off to explore the other surrounding dirt roads. Just outside of the dispersed camping area the road got steep and rutted. I carefully rode in or beside the ruts, at times falling into them and giving Mabel gas to keep her upright. I noticed the destruction of the surrounding hills, once forested. There had been a fire sometime in the past. I always hated seeing it. About twelve miles of weaving between ruts and baby-heads, I spotted an even narrower dirt path leading out into a meadow with tall, desert grass. I took it. The path was even steeper than the one I'd left and I found myself leaning over the tank a bit and carefully giving Mabel gas in order to keep the back tire from spinning. Her V-twin motor had good torque and did well climbing the rocky road. I didn't do so well staying out of the deep ruts in the road though. At times I had to splay my legs out on the sides of the sometimes 3 ft deep trenches to keep my feet from getting pinched in the dirt walls and keep Mabel from scraping them as well. This was definitely 4x4 territory. Suddenly a dear darted in front of me. Then another, and another. I stopped and watched as eight or nine deer darted across the road. I was ready to turn around but was looking for a good place to do it. The good place didn't come and so I waited until I found a shallow rut. I rocked Mabel back and forth until I had her turned down hill. I only dropped her once and she didn't fall completely over, leaning rather, on her footpeg against the wall of the trench I was in.

I continued exploring the dirt roads in the area and found another trailhead and did another short hike through the burned-out forest. The Aspens were starting to come back though. The trail ended at a hilltop looking out over a magnificent green valley, a stark contrast to the burned-out forest. I sat a while and sipped water out of the camelback and then took a nap. I woke peacefully and made my way back to Mabel, waiting patiently under the Aspens.

"It's time to find some water." I told her as I strapped the Camelbak onto the seat.

Stopping by the campground I picked up my collapsible water jug and went looking for a creek or a river, something. About seven miles down Hwy 4 I found a little turn off that had a fish symbol on it. It was brown like a park sign and so I turned in. Sure enough, a little creek gurgled near a small landing. It was fast flowing which was good and so I pulled my handy water filter/pump out and filled my collapsible jug. I was set. Back at the campsite with plenty of water I made yet more coffee and set up my hammock. I fell asleep listening to my audiobook. The sun warmed me even though I was about 8800 ft up. I basked in the luxury of silence, nature and coffee.

I was getting hungry. I gathered firewood to supplement the neatly stacked and split wood someone had left. Walking around I found plenty of dry wood and made a sizeable stack to leave a little for the next camper. I pulled out my homemade fire-starting globs (beeswax with sawdust) and set one in the middle of some kindling and lit the pile with my flint and steel starter. Soon I had a little fire going. Now I was starving having eaten only a few flour tortillas left over from some I bought a few days earlier and the energy bar. I had eaten all of my grape tomatoes but I had some bread and peanut butter as well as a bell pepper. Of course, I always had instant oatmeal. I made it work.

"Mabel!" I said aloud, "This, Mabel, is living. This is where I belong. This is me!"

"Well, as long as it's not raining." She snarked.

The tent set up, I was sitting in front of the fire, watching campfire "TV" when I noticed the cold.

"It's gonna be a bit cold tonight."

"I think so too." Mabel said.

Thirty minutes later it was dark and I was in the tent. The sun was still up, but the hills around the valley shaded the little site from any light, and from any heat. That night in the perfect campsite, I froze. I donned my long underwear and kept my socks on before going to bed, but during the night I had to get up and put on every stitch of clothing I had and clamor back into the sleeping bag, only to wake up an hour later, frozen again. I took my gloved hands out of the sleeping bag and carefully pulled my riding jacket and my riding pants over the sleeping bag and got an hour or so more sleep before I felt the cold again. I rolled around all night, with one or another part, and most of the time most my entire body cold. My sleeping bag was a three-season bag and this was not one of those seasons.

After a fitful night of battling the cold, I finally gave up and unzipped the sleeping bag and wrapped it around me, but only after putting on all of my riding gear. It was about 4am.

"This is getting weird." I thought. "I guess the worst-case scenario is that I get up and ride to lower ground. Or just start Mabel up and warm myself next to her motor?"

Those were not great options. I was frozen and riding wouldn't be any warmer and the thought of myself huddled against a little running motor wasn't much better. I forced myself to unglove my cold hands and dug around in the firepit for embers. Smoke appeared and I carefully blew into the ash seeing a faint, orange glow. It smoked more and more.

"Where are you? Where are you!" I demanded.

I blew again and saw a small orange glow in the dark of the morning, about an inch down. I smiled. About fifteen minutes later I had kindling started and was slowly feeding the small fire until it could sustain itself. While it built up heat, I moved Mabel close to the fire and started her up. Letting the engine warm up I put my gloved hands first on the exhaust pipe until they were too hot, and then on the cylinder heads. I bounced back and forth from Mabel to the fire until the fire was good and settled.

"Thanks!" I said to Mabel.

"What would you do without me?"

"I wouldn't be here, for one thing." I answered, snidely.

I made and downed three cups of coffee and ate four packages of gooey instant oatmeal and never got further than three feet away from the fire. The sun finally came up, but not on my little campsite. It was still severely cold. I didn't wait. I packed in the blue-grey shadows and snuffed out the fire as Mabel sat idling. Soon I was riding down the dirt road when the sun finally hit my face. I smiled. It had been a lovely place, a freezing night, and a learning experience.

"I won't be camping in any valleys any time soon."

"It was better than a hotel room." Mabel smiled as she revved up and we continued down Hwy 4.

"Yes, it was." I agreed.

I always like travelling with water so I stopped to fill my Camelbak up and to pour the extra water back into the stream.

Once all done, I sped down the beautiful, gently rolling road and headed to Bloomfield on Hwy 550. It was a two-lane job that rambled through the hills of New Mexico. I stopped in Cuba for a rest.

"Not much of a place." I said to Mabel.

"It's got fuel and food. And a food truck! What else do you want?"

I ate lunch at the little food truck next to the truck stop and continued down 550, which seemed long and drawn out. Finally reaching Bloomfield, a rough oasis, primarily a pitstop for the many natural gas and fracking workers in the area, I stopped at the little grocery store for supplies, and forgot beer. Continuing, I made my way towards 64 and then to 536. 536 was great riding and headed up to Navajo Lake State Park. I entered the park and realized it was mostly geared towards RV's. I saw a park ranger rolling around on a golf cart and stopped him.

"Hi! Do you have any tent sites?"

"Yes. They're down thatta way. They're all empty but you'll need to reserve online."

"Online?"

"Yep. It's all done thata way now."

"I understand. So down this road and to the left…"

"Yep. You'll see em' up on the hill to your right."

I rode up to four pitiful tent sites. They had great views but were horrible for tents. There wasn't a flat spot on any of them and they were covered with rocks. And I would have to ride down the hill to the other side of the park for the bathroom. They were obviously an afterthought. I pulled out my phone and started trying to find the website. My cell service wasn't great, but I finally found the site and realized that most RV spots were taken. All but two.

"The tent sites aren't looking too promising." I said to Mabel.

"What do you want from me? I'm just a bike."

I met the rolling ranger again and stopped.

"Did you find them?"

"Yea. I think I found a few sites down here a bit closer to the bathrooms and water."

"They'll be more expensive."

"I figured that. Online?"

"Online" he answered and punched the little golfcart in gear and sped off. I wasn't his problem.

When I looked back at the phone there was only one site that showed "available". I took it without knowing where it was or what it was. After riding around a little in the maze of RV's I found D52, my home for the night. It was a tiny little paved spot in between four big campers. I hurriedly threw down my tent among the mansions on wheels and got back on Mabel to do some riding and to find some beer. I'd be camping in the RV suburbs, but at least I'd have something refreshing to sip on. First, I took 511 and did a loop on some beautifully winding roads hugging canyon walls. It ran just under Hwy 550, and then found 173, an alternative route, to Bloomfield to find some good beer. I left the road to Aztec unridden, keeping it for the next morning's exit from the site. In Bloomfield I found a four-pack of some local beer and then made my way back to my tiny spot among the behemoths. That's when I met Lou, my camping neighbor. Lou was an older guy, my senior by about fifteen years or so, that walked with a working man's lilt. He was thin with a slight gut and his companion, Gus, was a two-year old black hunting dog that always seemed to be smiling and adored Lou. Lou had a full head of hair but it had greyed long ago, and he had a listful look in his eyes. As I sat enjoying my first beer and heating water for some rice he came sauntering up. Gus met me first. He jumped up on my lap with his front legs and a few licks to the face later we were best friends.

"Gus!" Lou demanded.

"It's OK. I've got one and I miss her!"

Lou acknowledged that he understood as Gus stood on his hind legs and licked me, tail wagging.

"I'm Lou. I'm next door." He started. I noticed the big pot he had in his hands.

"I went fishing this morning and caught a lot more than I expected. Gus usually doesn't take to people like that." He pondered watching Gus lay his head in my lap.

He set the pot on the table and opened it. It was full of fried filets and French fries.

"You like fish?"

"I certainly do! You don't need to give me any of your food. Keep it for yourself and…" I paused, looking at the dog.

"Gus."

"And Gus…"

"No, no. I've eaten all I can and anyway it won't be as good tomorrow. If you don't like it, that's fine."

"No, I love it! Thank you!! Want to sit down and have a beer?"

"I've got some in the camper. I'll go get it and be back." He replied, turning towards his camper, Gus in tow.

He came back with a Budweiser in his hand and Gus at his side. He sat a bottle of ketchup on the table.

"How long you out for?"

"Probably about a month. I don't know yet."

Lou nodded. He told me he was a builder and he loved to fish. He was from New Mexico and knew the lakes around the area.

"They're damming up the lakes and we're running out of water. It's a damned shame to me. There's too many people moving in and too many bureaucrats with their fingers in our pie."

Lou took a sip of his beer and I listened and chomped fresh caught fish and french-fries.

"There's still some nice lakes around here though, with plenty of fish."

"Are you married?" I asked.

"I was. For a long time. She died a few years back and a friend of mine found Gus here. He's been with me since he's been a pup."

"He's a great dog!"

"Young, and full of piss and vinegar. But he's a good dog."

I laughed.

"Yea. I love fishin' but I don't like what's happening in this state…"

Lou went on, hinting his disgust with Biden and what he called "the Democrats". I held my tongue and Lou was careful as well. I guessed because he didn't want to ruin a nice evening and we didn't know each other. He kept complaining and wisping contemplative thoughts about fishing. His mood bobbed up and down; first happy and then irritated, like a cork in the water. I played devil's advocate and we laughed at crude jokes and blue comments.

"And there's those damned Mexicans and 'natives'…" Lou continued. I held my tongue and tried to eat fish at the same time.

Lou went on more frustrated than angry, bobbing up and down with his mood. I played more devil's advocate and we laughed some more. I think we'd come to an understanding that we probably didn't agree on politics but decided that our company was more important. Gus lay contentedly on the cement pad beside Lou, half sleeping, disinterested in politics or fishing or even the fish I was gulping down hungrily. He was perfectly happy with his life. Lou asked questions about the motorcycle and touring, and we continued to laugh more. It made us both feel good. Under it all, Lou was good people and two beers later we said goodnight.

"I have enough of them. I'm here for three weeks!" he said, leaving an extra beer on the table.

"I'll just leave the fish with you. Eat what you want. I don't know what time or if you're leaving tomorrow, but if you want, come by for a cup of coffee…"

"I leave pretty early."

"I'm up early. There's no pressure." He hurriedly added, "Just if you want to."

"OK! I'll see you in the morning." I smiled.

I climbed into my tent on the hard cement pad and put my earplugs in as there was music playing a few pads down. I lay in my bag as the night cooled and realized I didn't even know what time it was. When camping, darkness usually meant sleep. I pulled my phone out. It was 8:45 on a Saturday. I hadn't even realized it was the weekend. Weekends can be a bit difficult. On weekends I usually like to find stealthy places to camp but this time I hadn't paid attention. I like peace and quiet over parties and beer. State Parks were usually wonderful places to camp but could get kind of busy on weekends. I fell asleep with visions of winding roads through canyons and forests and was up early the next morning warming up water for coffee when Lou walked over with a big cup of coffee in his hands.

"Thought you might need some of this. There's more over there if you feel like it."

Then he walked back to his big camper. It was camper that Lou pulled behind a big pickup. They'd both had seen some miles, or at least some days in campgrounds. I took him up on his invitation and walked over, turning my own water off. Knocking on the door Gus gave a quick bark and Lou answered.

"Come on in!"

I walked in. We talked about fishing and touring and life in campgrounds. After three or four cups of coffee, Gus started throwing his leash around.

"Well, it looks like you're being summoned to your morning duties."

"Yea. It looks that way." Lou said, taking up Gus' leash.

"Thanks for the coffee, and the fish! It was a wonderful surprise. Here's your pot."

"Thanks. No problem. Be careful out there." "

You ought to pack a fishing pole." He added.

I smiled and shook his hand again before walking over to Mabel, half-packed up and patiently waiting to explore some roads.

3.10

I was on my way to 4-Corners, the point where New Mexico, Utah, Colorado and Arizona met. It was more out of curiosity than it being an important or even meaningful place for me. I'd been there before and not gone to the monument. More importantly it was a place that I would make a decision concerning the future of this trip; whether or not to continue riding west or head back east.

"Don't worry about it now." Mabel said, "Let's just go there and see how we feel."

"Good plan!" I agreed.

I was close to the Colorado border, a state that I had left much too early and mistakenly. It was a sore point and I hadn't been back since leaving my beloved home there. It hurt to think about the mistake I had made, and the thought of returning simply dug up those memories. I knew I had to face those memories though. I headed off towards 4-Corners with this in mind, if for no other reason than to give me time to think about a plan. The ride out to the arbitrary point was tedious and cold. Quite honestly, it wasn't worth it. The road was straight and busy with traffic, especially when I hit Shiprock. I continued west of Shiprock where the traffic fell off but so did the scenery. In Teec Nos Pos I headed north on 160 and then hit 560 to the 4 Corners monument. It was closed and I found myself standing in the middle of nowhere now for no apparent reason. I pulled out my map and started to make plans. I must have stood there for thirty minutes. I couldn't make my mind up, a tell-tale sign of sorts. So, I made coffee and sat in the dust next to Mabel.

"You know what you want." She said, "Just make the decision. I can't do it for you. I'm just a motorcycle!"

"I know, but Colorado…"

"I know, I know. I'm from Colorado too and I miss it. Just man up!" she demanded.

"You're right." I said, giving in to the inevitable.

I considered taking 63 south. It had some dirt sections and then I could head back up 191 towards Colorado, but I had experienced the area in north-eastern Arizona and while it was beautiful it was not so friendly, at least not in my experience. Of course, I could just head down to Chambers and the Interstate.

"Interstate?!" Mabel exclaimed.

"You're right. You're right…again."

"Why are you trying to stay out of the state that you love?" she asked.

"I don't know! I have wonderful memories of living there, and horrible memories of leaving it."

"The past is the past. These trips are about now. You know what you want to do. Do it!" Mabel exclaimed, almost getting exasperated.

Then I thought of Bears Ears in Utah and then riding down to the North Rim of the Grand Canyon, a ride I had missed previously. To my utter surprise, I had cell service and found out that the North Rim was closed until May 15th, which was several weeks away. That made my mind up; it was almost fate! I decided that I would take 160 to Cortez and then through Durango, circling back to the mountains around Taos. There were gorgeous rides in that area, some that I had done and some that I hadn't, but that's how it was with these trips.

"Let's go!" Mabel said impatiently.

And just like that I was in Colorado. Immediately the landscape was familiar. The smells were of Colorado. The roads were bright and interesting and rambled excitedly through pine forests with rocks jutting out of mountainsides almost magically. It was beautiful and I was saddened by it all as I had expected. I was sad that I had left. I was sad because for years all of this was in my backyard. I was sad because I felt instantly at home here and knew that I would never live here again. And as the joy of the road ran through me like electricity, as I leaned into corner after corner inhaling the fragrance that can only be found in Colorado, sadness dipped into the soul of my being with each mile. This was paradise to me and felt like hell. I passed through the little town of Cortez with its typical Colorado-downtown. Even when I reached Durango, a place that I had not been impressed with previously, I felt sad that I had left. The mountains, the small mountain towns, the smells, the feel…it was all here and it had all once been mine, at least in my head. I noticed dirt fire roads that I knew would lead to campsites but I didn't have enough water. But I also knew that I didn't have the wherewithal to camp in Colorado.

"Water! Water is a problem in Colorado." I thought to myself.

"I know but that's not why you left." Mabel answered.

"I know." I agreed.

I took the fire roads anyway, enjoying the dirt and scenery, letting Mabel's back tire slide around corners a little, giving her gas and having fun. I stopped at one of the many free campsites along the route, and at one had coffee. I wanted to camp.

"No water." Mabel reminded me, "and we're higher up than you were in New Mexico. You'll freeze again."

So off I went, heading back to the main route and to Pagosa Springs where I started heading south towards New Mexico. As I passed the state line I felt Colorado disappear into my past yet again, but at least now I knew I'd be back. I tore the band aid off, as it were and felt better.

I came to Monero and started looking for place to fill up my water jug for camping that night. There wasn't much there but I found a small, abandoned campsite and tried my luck.

"The water's still on!" I said aloud in surprise when I pulled the handle and water came gushing out.

I filled my jug up and strapped it to my seat. Chama didn't look promising but there were some State Parks fairly close. I chose El Vado. I stood on a small, empty corner and stared down at my map for a route to the park when a beat-up truck pulled up and stopped.

"You OK?" the two young, tattooed men asked.

"Hey! Yes. I'm just plotting a route.

"Alright man! Just checkin'." they said and gave me a thumbs up.

A few minutes later an old Nissan truck pulled up with an old, overly wrinkled man in it. He was thin and skeleton like.

"You lost?" he asked.

"Oh Hi! Not really, just plotting a route. But thanks!"

"Where you wanna go?" he asked.

"I'm looking to camp at El Vado but don't know. Is it nice?"

"Yea. Lots of fish if you like that sort of thing."

He sat and stared, waiting for another question. I had none.

"Just turn around and go down this road here for bout…twenty mile, and then you'll see a little road to the left. Take that."

"OK! Thanks. I didn't know if this was the road to the park or not."

"It is. It's nice. Nice ridin' too. I used to ride…but that's been a long time ago."

"Oh yea! You ever want to get back on a bike?"

"Always, but I'm too old now. I'm not up for it."

"I understand. I always say: know your limits. Thanks for the help!"

"No problem." He answered, and drove off.

As I was packing my map and drinking some water another car stopped.

"You OK?"

"Hi! Yes, but thanks for stopping! I'm on my way to El Vado State Park."

"It's back thattaway. Just take…"

The young lady gave me directions to the park. I didn't have the heart to tell her I had already been told the way.

I saw three cars in the thirty-minute break and all three stopped to make sure I was OK. I was thankful and gratified. People can be nice.

El Vado was a large, spread-out park with open campsites dotting the landscape. I chose one farthest away from what I thought would be the popular area if anyone did happen to show up. Parking Mabel, I walked over to the little covered picnic table and laid down on it to take a nap. There were no trees so I couldn't set up my hammock. About thirty minutes later a truck pulled up and four young people got out and started setting up camp at the nearest campsite across the small, dirt road. I would be lying if I said I wasn't disappointed. But I went back to sleep, at least for a while. The site wasn't perfect for camping. It was on a hill and I knew I'd find myself rolling to one side of the tent constantly that night. So, I got up and looked around for another site and found a flatter one a few sites over. I didn't think the young people would be a problem but I felt weird just packing up and moving again. I walked over.

"Hey!" I said, "I'm Mark, the guy with the bike over there."

They had all their gear out and were cooking and drinking beer. They were fishermen as they had several poles laying in the back of their trucks.

"Hey!" they answered and turned.

"I'm going to move over a few sites and just wanted to let you know that I wasn't moving because of you. I'm moving because there's not a good spot to set up my tent."

"Oh…" he looked a little surprised, "That's no problem. Hey do you wanna beer before you go?"

His friend went and pulled a beer out of one of three coolers opening it up before I could answer.

"Sure he does! What kind of question is that?!" the young man smiled and held out a cold can of beer.

"I guess I'll have a beer. Thanks!" I smiled.

We sat and talked for a little. They all worked and lived right there in the area and were enjoying a rare long weekend.

"It's the weekend!" I exclaimed, forgetting about that point again.

We all laughed.

"We've got some deer meat and we're making a stew. You want some, stick around."

"That sounds great, but I've got some stuff that I need to cook. I appreciate it though.

"Well, if you need another beer come on over."

"I really appreciate it!" I said, finishing my beer and thanking them again.

I made my way over to my old campsite and finished carrying my gear to the new site. Before long I was set up and sat watching the sun go down over a beautiful lake. I smelled the deer stew from my table and decided to walk over with my bag of chips and the local brews that I'd bought earlier.

"You know what! I'd love some of that stew. I can smell it from my campsite!"

"Alright!", the young man cooking exclaimed and motioned me sit down.

I sat and we enjoyed each other's company for a few hours before I walked back over to my tent and crawled in for the night.

"Happy fishing!" I called, and said goodbye.

Motorcycle trips are odd beasts. On the one hand they're adventurous and fun and on the other hand they're places where the past meets the future, where memories are drudged up; a fantasyland that actually exists. They have all the emotions in them: doubt, happiness, sadness, exhilaration and boredom, and contentedness as well. You miss your loved-ones and you lose your will to go back home. It's all very strange and exciting all at the same time. And even though you might want to continue, you find that sometimes you don't want to find the will to do so. Home starts beckoning. I picked up my phone and called my wife. Sounding surprised she answered.

"Well hey there!"

"What's going on?!"

"Not much, just sitting here knitting."

I smiled.

"How do you feel about meeting me at my folks house?" I asked.

"Oh. OK! When were you thinking?"

We figured out the logistics and decided that I'd call the day before I thought I'd be there. After a peaceful night's sleep I woke up for the first time on the trip, in a warm tent. The sun was shining into the open flap of the tent and onto the sleeping bag. I took my time to get up. I wasn't in a hurry and there was something about knowing, at least a little, about what you're going to do that is relaxing. Later, I started my ritual. After three weeks of travel, rituals had become settled. I'd become a "one large mug of coffee guy" in the mornings and I had learned to relax enough to sit and enjoy them before starting to pack up. Sometimes I ate breakfast and sometimes I didn't. I had come to enjoy sitting and looking at Mabel basking in the early morning sunrises.

"Don't rush too much. I'm enjoying this." She seemed to say.

Packed up and throwing out the coffee grounds, I started Mabel and was soon on my way back to the park road. It was a wonderfully lonesome road, paved but a little rough; it wound around enough to make it interesting but not so technical as to have to miss the scenery. I turned south on 84 and soon found a gas station. From my Iron Butt ride, I'd taken on the habit of filling up even if I really didn't need to. Mabel was pretty miserly on gas, but I had a call to make. I got coffee at the small station and a Danish just because.

"Hey! This is me."

"Hey you! I didn't expect you to call so early. It's Sunday."

"Yea. I found that out yesterday."

We talked for a while but I could hear that she had the typical "Sunday jitters" that we both got when we were home.

"I'm thinking about another week out in Arizona. It might be hot, so I don't know."

"I *miss* you." She said.

"I miss you too!"

"I thought you were going to head to Malden?"

"I am, but I thought about a short jaunt to Arizona."

She didn't say anything, but I could tell she wasn't thrilled about the idea. She had been more than fair. I was being flaky and I knew it, and I could hear she wanted to see me. I wanted to see her too.

"Or not. You know what! I think I'll just start heading to Malden. I can meet you there in… about a week. How about that?!"

"That sounds good!"

We talked for a bit more.

"Well, I'd better get going. I have places to be." I said, laughing a little.

"OK. Be careful. I love you!"

"Me too."

I finished my Danish and hopped on Mabel. I took Hwy 64 through the Carson National Forest, a beautiful road that meandered through northern New Mexico to what I would come to call the "magical loop". In Taos I took 522 north to 38 and that back to 64. There were options after that, both dirt and paved, but I circled around back to Taos. Twists and turns kept me on my toes and I practiced "keeping my line". I was slowly learning not to tense up and instead roll with the road. It was beginning to talk to me a little, and so was Mabel.

"Lean a little on the outside. I know it feels weird, but it works." She would say.

"Don't brake and don't let off the throttle too much. You'll be surprised!" she would add.

"Downshift before the turn, but not too early and let's have fun out of the curve!" she would smile.

I learned to listen to both her and my body and before long was taking the turns much smoother and faster. This was fun! I entered Taos at the end of a thrilling ride. Taos was nice enough but too touristed and too busy. What had once been a quiet, unassuming small town in the foothills was now a noisy, dirty place with too many people and too much traffic. It was a tourist haven filled with touristy, consumer goods. I rode around as much as I could trying to give it a chance, but soon tired of the hustle and bustle. The streets were crowded and the sidewalks were jammed with mooing tourists. I decided to find a place for lunch and met a young man who noticed my motorcycle attire.

"What do you ride?" he asked.

"A Suzuki V-Strom 650"

"I used to ride, but not anymore."

"Why not?!"

"Well, I've got a family."

I had heard this excuse numerous times and it was always disappointing.

"You from around here?"

"Yea. Not far."

"Do you have any suggestions for good roads? I'd like to get out of Taos after this."

"Yea, yea! I do."

"Do you know any nice camping areas?" I continued.

"Yea. There's lots off of Five...uh...I think 570"

We continued talking and finished lunch but I was ready to get out of town. I followed 518 south, assuming it was what the young man was talking about, it was beautiful but had a lot of slow cars. I felt bad passing them, but always felt irritated (for no reason) when they would rob me of twists and turns. On a motorcycle it can often feel like a car is going 5 mph even though they're going the speed limit. I found the Rio Grande River at some point and noticed the many campsites alongside it. There were also signs of plenty of "river people" too, and so I passed. I finally took a dirt road to try my luck and found a little spot a few miles up. The road was dusty but the site was set about 100 yards into the forest. I maneuvered Mabel into the forest and made camp. The day had been filled with beautiful riding, wonderful nature, and lots of fun. Who could ask for anything more?! I ate an energy bar and a package of oatmeal for dinner, saving as much water as possible for coffee the next morning. The bugs weren't too bad and by 8pm I knew it was going to be a cool night and so hunkered down and read a book with my headlamp until I fell asleep and woke up a few hours later with the book on my chest and the headlamp still shining. I put them down and lay wondering at the stars before falling back to sleep.

I was living a life that most people couldn't even imagine and felt myself lucky. Mabel made life better in every way. Motorcycles in general were more exciting, more conducive to exploring, and quicker and easier to get in and out of places. Riding a motorcycle I smelled every smell, both good and bad, and felt all the weather that I rode through. I couldn't lie to myself and I didn't have time to "just relax" and "put it on cruise control". A motorcycle forced me to use my head, to think. I often thought of all the people I'd met and that I knew who would shake their heads at the thought of riding a bike.

"I couldn't ride that thing. It's too dangerous."

"I'm too old for a tent. And why camp when you've got a perfectly good house?"

"It's nothing but a donor-cycle."

"I've got a family…I don't see the point…it's stupid…it's uncomfortable…"

And yet, ironically it gave me so much life. I would always answer such comments the same.

"And yet I keep riding them."

This morning was sunny with blue skies and I had high hopes for a perfect day. I decided to take the time to have a few cups of coffee and some of my instant oatmeal and I was off. I was looking for backways to explore and found 576, a steep dirt road that supposedly dumped out onto 275 at some point. The road ended up being rough but had good, sharp switchbacks to practice my sharp turns in dirt. I climbed the steep road for quite some time before reaching the top and 275. From the peak I could see my future, and it was going to be very wet. Dark clouds hung everywhere, heavy and foreboding. I had climbed through blackness and didn't realize it until I reached this pinnacle. I didn't know where the weather had come from, but it looked like it was here to stay for a while. On the top of the hill, I stopped and pulled out my map to ponder and pretend like I could somehow ride around the walls of clouds that now surrounded me. I would be heading slightly south and east and the universe grinned as I slowly realized that there was no away around the Nimbostratus barrier. With that in mind I decided to follow my original route which would take me high into the Carson National Forest. As I rode, the clouds started covering the surrounding mountains like thick, ominous blankets and the weather started cooling quickly, all signs that I knew very well.

"You can't do anything about the weather." Mabel reminded me, "Just enjoy the ride and put on your rain gear."

My route took me on the wonderful road 503, a hidden gem of narrow asphalt and sharp switchbacks. It was technical, winding around high cliff walls, and climbing steeply through the mountains. The switchbacks got seriously sharp and I wondered about gravel and rocks from the cliffs so began taking my time and enjoying the beautiful landscape around me as I looked up at the threatening nature above me. The road became even more technically demanding and become a dance.

"Keep the momentum but don't go so fast as to lose the turn."

"Keep it smooth and consistent, let me do what I do best." Mabel whispered.

The weather continued to worsen but I ignored it and continued to thrill myself on the road, taking the switchbacks as consistently and sharply leaned as possible. I would slow around questionable turns though, reminding myself of the motorcycle mantra:

"It's not if...it's when."

The tiny road led to tiny villages built almost into the cliffs themselves. Small, neat houses dotted the landscape, almost invisible. Little gardens and fences started lining the road. The villages were poor but truly beautiful, and well kept. The road continued meandering and switching back and forth to the point that I was starting to wonder if I had missed my turn. As I was wondering this, I came to 518. It was no wider than 503 but had less switchbacks and gentler, rolling turns with more small villages dotting the landscape. I continued taking it all in ignoring the inevitable weather. Soon I hit 76, a beautiful winding road that just begged for speed. I overtook three or four slow-moving cars and gave Mabel some gas. She sped forward as if trying to beat the weather. The temperature continued dropping quickly and I had already stopped and donned my raingear but was still a bit cool.

About twenty miles later 76 started getting really small and narrow as well as rougher until it came to a muddy fire road that had a big, yellow sign that seemed to chuckle at me.

"No Outlet" it read.

It had obviously rained there quite a bit already. I was in the middle of another little village, this one cleaner than the last few and each house having a little garden of flowers and vegetables. I spotted and older gentlemen and rode over to him, killing the engine.

"Excuse me…"

"Yes?"

"I'm not sure what road I'm looking for, I thought it was this one, 76."

"Yes. Uh…no. This isn't 76. You'll need to backtrack to town a bit. You'll see a small, red building. Turn right there."

"Great! Thanks so much. You've got a pretty little spot up here!"

"We think so. I wish good weather to you!" he said as I started Mabel up again waving goodbye. Famous last words.

I found my turn off which led to more perfect roads, narrow and twisty with beautiful scenery everywhere. I was looking at the plains out east now covered in a dark mist. I was obviously at some elevation having the view that I had. As I followed the roads admiring nature, it reminded me that it wasn't there for my enjoyment alone and started pelting me with small, pin-like hale.

"It is the mountains after all."

Mabel wasn't impressed.

I heard the small hale pinging off her tank and fairings.

Finding a little town with one gas station and one pump, I stopped and filled Mabel up, apologizing for my short-sighted comment earlier. Then, the hale stopped for a few minutes until it turned to thick cotton ball sized snowflakes.

"Nice!" I looked up and said to the universe, impressed.

After filling up I rode on through the snow. The road turned very steep as the snow started sticking to my windshield, my pants and to my helmet. Soon, I was wiping thick snow off my face shield. As I rode, I noticed that the snow would hit the road and melt. But then, after some time, it started sticking to the road more and more making motorcycle riding…interesting. I slowed down. I thought I might have missed another turn as the road kept climbing and climbing rather than descending as I had expected. I stopped and looked at the map. I was on the right track. The snow soon dissipated and I gained a little hope, if only for a little while.

It started hailing once more.

"Great turn. Tricky!" I yelled up at the universe, now getting a little nervous.

As miserable as the weather was, I was on a beautiful mountain peak. It was very high up because to my estimation, the temperatures were easily in the low thirties. Snow was sticking to everything around me now, including the roads which had slowly started turning white. I flipped from misery to elation as I rode through the majestic mountains and stared out over the plains far below, watching the snow quickly turning Mabel from black to white. Speed was out of the question. I did what any motorcyclist would do: I stopped to take in the amazing view. But after a few minutes of standing in freezing weather I mounted Mabel and gave her gas. We finally started descending and as the elevation lessened the snow turned to a hard, cold rain. Flipping Mabel back and forth through the mildly sharp turns I resigned myself to the cold and tried to ready myself for even more wet that I knew was coming. I held out hope for warm though. As I descended, I kept waiting for the weather to warm up a bit. It didn't and the rain started pounding me even harder.

"Nice touch!" I yelled up at the universe, now getting irritated at the weather.

The road straightened out. I was obviously at the end of the exciting bits and was now going to slog my way on a main road. Through the thick mist and ocean like drops of rain I spotted a pickup truck ahead of me. For the next forty-five minutes or more, I spent my time behind a slow-moving truck, unable to safely pass for fear of oncoming traffic that the downpour made difficult to see, and hydroplaning even if I could see oncoming traffic. Neither was good on a motorcycle. A few minutes later I moved my toes and could almost hear the sloshing sound of water in my boots. I'm not sure how long I followed that truck, but I passed him in a small town when the rain let up just slightly. By this time, I could feel my core temperature dropping. It wasn't a pleasant feeling. For the last fifty miles or so, I shook like a leaf and tried to compose myself enough to ride. There were not any options of stopping other than under gas station awnings and so I continued, shivering and shaking my way down the road. I hugged my waterlogged boots against Mabel's engine trying to warm up my freezing feet. And shook water out of my leather gauntlets one hand at a time, and stuck my left hand down in my crotch area to warm it up. The visor on my helmet which had been caked with snow was now blurry with rain. Luckily, I had a fog protector on the inside which was doing its job. On the bright side, the rain had washed all the bugs off Mabel, my jacket, and my visor.

"I...have...to...keep...positive..." I stuttered in my helmet. I finally came to the ugly but bustling Las Vegas New Mexico and stopped at the only motel I saw. It was crappy looking but I didn't care. When I rode into the parking lot it was in the thirties and still raining. My core temperature was way down, I could feel that. Parking Mabel I stumbled in, shivering, and asked for a room.

"I'll bet you're cold." The young, obese girl instantly said upon looking up from her phone.

I grimaced, not bothering to answer.

The room was cheap, ugly, and too expensive. I stripped down and turned the heater on full and set every piece of clothing I had on the vents, including my boots that I sat on a chair in front of the heater. I then shuddered into the bathroom and turned the shower on, full hot. When there was steam coming out from behind the shower curtain I stepped in and stood under the sweltering water for at least forty-five minutes. When I couldn't stand it anymore, I dried off and crawled into the bed under all the blankets and slept until I stopped shaking. I woke up hungry and walked over to the nearest little Italian restaurant and ate, drinking a few beers and watching as the sun peered from behind the last of the greyish clouds and a blue sky opened up across the broad, New Mexico horizon. I wrote in my journal after eating my meal.

"I have mixed feelings today. Motorcycle touring is full of surprises and tends to break the rules and stipulations that I set for it. No matter though, I am leaving it once again; on my way to familiar faces and people I love. This touring takes me away from the daily deluge of drudgery and doubt. It's as if it's magical. The sludge of the daily grind gets washed away bit by bit. Highways and hotels begin adding bits and pieces of the sludge back, even when they are necessary. I am lucky enough to have the option to come in from the rain, snow, sleet, and hail. I am lucky enough to face these things temporarily knowing that I can find shelter, if not soon then eventually. But perhaps it is this safety net that makes me love motorcycling as much as I do? Maybe it's because I give up the safety net, at least for a while. My ass is on the line all the time on a bike. There's no denying that. I'm looking at Mabel sitting across a broad, wide, boring strip of road in a parking lot. She seems out of place. She has patience for such things, though. I don't. But as long as there is a back road devoid of "all this", I guess I'll be OK."

My desert came and I devoured it, ordering another Guiness and thinking about the future.

3.11

That night I slept soundly under three blankets. Around midnight I woke up, finally warm, got up, and turned the heat off. Morning came quickly after a good night's sleep but when I looked out the window I saw that it had rained more the night and the dark, foreboding clouds were still hanging heavily in the sky. I studied the weather on my phone over the worst cup of coffee in the world in my crappy hotel room feeling sorry for myself. The weather report assured me that the clouds would be receding later that morning, and so I made another crappy cup of coffee and stared at Mabel in the parking lot standing stoically. Around 7:30 I felt human enough to start looking at the day's trip and by 8:30 I couldn't stand it anymore. Clouds be damned. My boots were dry enough, most of my clothes were dry, and most importantly I was warm.

"Let's do this thing!" I demanded to myself.

I loaded Mabel up in the cold, grey morning and rode over to the neighboring gas station to fill her up and get something to eat for myself. I looked up at their sign. It was 37 degrees.

"Well at least it's not raining." I said.

"Not yet." Mabel answered, cynically.

Las Vegas was 6000 ft up. Tucamcari was 4000 feet up. That sounded good to me. New Mexico had been great to me: wonderful roads, beautiful scenery and nice people but it had been cold, sometimes really cold, and now I was ready for some warmer weather. There were more roads to ride here, but they would have to wait for another time. After an energy bar and a huge cup of gas station coffee I was off. Heading down 104 it seemed I was riding away from the little bit of blue skies, that were peaking in from behind the dark clouds, and into ominous dark skies ahead. I was sure I would get rained on again and it was still cold. I wasn't looking forward to that prospect but now I had a place that I had to be.

"This is adventure!" I reminded myself.

I screamed down the straight and narrow road, cold wind be damned. I was heading south with some hope of sunshine. At least I was dropping elevation. I could feel that.

In Tucamcari I found a little diner on the famous Route 66, a vestige of its former self. The diner was still touting the old 50's flavor that Route 66 was famed for, so I went in not expecting much. But to my surprise the place was just what I needed. It was packed. The service was great, and the food was excellent. I stuffed myself with huge globs of syrupy French toast and gallons of strong coffee. I was warm, happy and full! A quick stop at a gas station and I was heading south on 209 and into Texas. 209 started as a straight road through eastern New Mexico but soon turned into gentle curves and some moderate twists when I hit 214. It was pretty, and easy riding. Clouds still hung around but they were fighting a losing battle with the sun. Out on the flat plains below me were nothing but blue skies, a welcomed sight. Before long the road straightened, really straightened out. That kind of straight road that is found all over the Midwest with flat plains stretching out endlessly. I stopped and took a picture.

"You look pretty on this road, Mabel."

"Aww. Go on!"

There was nothing and no one around for as far as the eye could see. There were windmills everywhere and after passing a few hundred I decided to turn down a dirt road and see how close I could get to one. A few miles down a dusty road and I was standing directly under the huge whooshing blades of a large, white windmill watching as they spun right above my head. It was…strange. I rode on passing sprawling west Texas ranches and took a farm road north towards Amarillo looking for Palo Duro Canyon. After passing over the interstate the landscape turned to flat plains again, no canyon in sight. Suddenly a huge, gaping maw appeared. There it was. I stopped to see about camping.

"Honey, we're full."

"Full!" I exclaimed, a little disappointed.

"Yessir. Every last one."

"I don't need much. Just a primitive site."

"Sweety, I'd love to help you but I just can't."

"Can I take a ride through the park anyway."

The big, smiling woman looked down, seeming disappointed.

"It'll cost ya $5. There's nothin' I can do." She said, actually feeling bad about asking for the money.

"That's fine." I smiled.

I gave her the money and moseyed through the beautiful, twisty roads in the park. I was searching for a stealthy place to spend the night but I was out of luck. There were rangers everywhere, people in every corner and open space. The lady hadn't been lying. So, it was on to Amarillo.

As I neared the small but ever-widening city of Amarillo I felt the need for some lunch and stopped Yellow Street for some food. They had a great selection of local beers.

"This is necessary. It's warm. I'm tired. That's my excuse and I'm sticking to it!" I exclaimed to Mabel.

"It's your trip." She said, seeming disappointed in my decision.

A cheap hotel was hurriedly found in the city's industrial area. No camping again, but I rode through the little industrial roads of Amarillo searching for breweries to get some evening refreshments for the room.

"We could have just ridden up to Lake Meredith." Mabel reminded me.

"Yes. We could have. And we could have been turned away and been looking for a place to stay while it got dark too."

I was having none of Mabel's smarminess.

That evening I sat on the floor of the hotel room perusing the map and writing in my journal. "Adventures tend to change.", I wrote. I was turning east from the west and heading to the Ozarks of Arkansas to explore those beautiful roads and then on to my folk's house in southeast Missouri. While the east didn't offer the beauty of the west, it did offer a different kind of ride. A quieter ride in a way. Straight roads through small towns. The Ozarks would offer wonderful roads, I knew, but different. I looked forward to some quiet camping, a few breweries along the way, but as I knew plans could change, most of the time they did, and I really didn't know what the future held.

The next day I had things to see. I started out looking for the Cadillac Ranch. A field of Cadillacs that had been buried nose first in the ground. I also found a small field of combines buried nose first. After an early morning of searching out half-buried, burnt-out vehicles I was hungry and ran across Youngbloods. It was an old-school diner in a suburban area of Amarillo. It was amazing that I ran into it at all, totally coincidental.

"It goes to show you that a little exploring can get you a lot!" Mabel reminded me, still disappointed in spending a night in a parking lot.

The food was fantastic and being from Texas myself, I enjoyed that old-school Texas vibe. Truly friendly even if you didn't always agree with their politics. That's what I'd grown up with. After a little more exploring I headed north towards Perryton and into Oklahoma. Oklahoma offered its own kind of southern scenery. Small towns, each one having a silo, a gas station and a post office and miles and miles of ranchland punctuated by orange-red cliffs. The road was as straight as an arrow and gusty winds pushed Mabel and I side to side, sometimes gently and sometimes not, one town after another. We passed one silo, one gas station, and one post office, one after another. We'd take some time to explore a town every once in a while, and sometimes we'd find an odd little landmark or a small store. It was relaxing in a way. Easy. Towards the middle of the afternoon, I noticed some dark clouds welling up and it was cooling down.

"Again!!" I exclaimed in my helmet, "I can't get a break!"

It was about time to start looking for a place to sleep anyway. I found a small sign that pointed towards a campground and turned. The site was a small place that looked nice enough but it was surrounded by trashy trailers and burned-out houses. I passed. About a half hour down the road I found another sign pointing towards another campground, down another mystery road. It was about eight miles down 38, a small road off of 11. I took a chance.

Riding into the Salt Plains Campground I noticed a few houses along the fence that separated the park from the group of houses. They seemed quiet. It also seemed like I was the only person in the campground. I rode around checking out campsites and looking for a ranger station but there was none. It was a well-kept park with plenty of sites. After a short ride around the place, I decided to be its only guest for the night and I found a great spot next to a lake and made camp. Cooking dinner I sat and looked out over the lake, writing in my journal. As I sat cooking and writing I was watching the ever more accumulating clouds group up on the horizon. I had a feeling that my tent would be tested, again. It was an old tent, about twelve years old, and had seen a lot of campsites. I had waterproofed the seams a couple of times over the years but the zippers were starting to give out. The mesh had several holes in it that I had patched with bicycle patches.

"It has character." Mabel said, "Just like me!"

"As long as it's waterproof," I answered, "it can have all the character it wants."

The first few drops hit the tent right after dark. Then a downpour. It was coming down in buckets as I lay on my sleeping bag listening to my book. Suddenly I heard a sickening thud. Immediately I knew what it was.

"Shit!!" I yelled, hurriedly getting up and putting on a raincoat over my underwear. I unzipped the tent and threw on my sandals. Running out into the rain with my headlamp dangling around my neck I saw Mabel laying on her side.

"Son of a bitch!!" I yelled, already feeling the cold rain run down my back. I cussed myself for not checking the ground.

"What an idiot!!" I reprimanded myself.

I put my back against the seat and grabbed the handlebars and the luggage rack and righted her. The thunder cracked suddenly giving me a start and I felt mud between my toes. I looked down and noticed that I had parked Mabel on a strip of road that the water ran down, river-like. I also noticed the busted turn signal.

"Well, this is just great!" Mabel said, answered by a flash of bright lightning.

I moved her up to higher ground and found a large, flat rock to put under the kickstand. The rain was not letting up and now I was wet, miserable, and pissed off.

Back in the tent the fun was not over. I dried myself off with my motorcycle jacket and the dish towel I had under the fly and hunkered down in the sleeping bag. Checking for cell service I was amazed to find I had a few bars. I lay searching for turn-signals for Mabel when I felt a cold drop of water hit my head. I won't repeat what I yelled up at the sky. My old tent was leaking and I was camped in a rain storm. There was nothing I could do, except wait for the rain to subside and hope for the best. It did subside about an hour later, and I went to sleep listening to coyotes, cattle and dogs. I woke around 4:30 with a start, thinking that I heard thunder, but there was none. The next morning was bright and sunny...and muddy. I stumbled out of the tent after a rough night's sleep and saw thirty or so geese on the lakeshore just below my campsite. I made coffee and watched as they milled around and ate grass, complaining to each other about the stranger that had obviously encroached on their feeding grounds. I looked over at Mabel's mangled turn signal and mumbled a cuss word.

There was a lot of straight to ride today. County Road 60 ran across northern Oklahoma to Neosho Missouri, but I had plans of turning a bit south to catch some Arkansas Ozark roads. I was surprised though. Oklahoma was really showing off. I hadn't expected much but I got great scenery with rolling hills and small towns dotting the place every thirty miles or so. But the wind gusted during the day, wreaking havoc on my "nice peaceful" ride scenario especially when the numerous big rigs passed going in the opposite direction. At times it was like being hit by a hammer. Just before I hit the Missouri state line the landscape started changing slightly, and by the time I hit the state line the plains had disappeared and forest had taken over. Just south of Siloam Springs I found a dandy of a road heading south, county road 16. County road 16 was a rollercoaster ride with turns and twists coming down off of hills and sharp curves pushing my stomach into my throat as we sped up hills from the shallow valley bottoms. 16 was made for high-speed excitement and Mabel and I took full advantage of it. It was stomach churning but all sorts of fun.

"Be careful! These are tricky!" Mabel warned me.

Finding a camping ground in the northwest corner of the Ozarks seemed surprisingly difficult at first. But as I would find out on later rides, Arkansas held its cards close to its chest. Get out of the sprawling, noisy city centers and it opened up to beauty and nature that rivaled the west in many ways. I found free camping in the Ozark St. Francis National Forest. It wasn't much but it was better than a hotel. I even enjoyed the moderate heat and ample bugs, at least for a while. I was heading down past Fayetteville, hoping to get through it as fast as possible and make some mountain roads my own. Soon the city traffic dissipated and I was heading towards the Boston Mountains. For those that don't know, the mid-south is box-turtle country and I saw several which I had to stop and save from the inevitable car or truck they were sure to meet. They were slow creatures and seemed stubbornly intent on resting in the middle of roads. Being reptiles, they used the heat off the asphalt to warm themselves. I had to stop and save three, but the fourth that I saw had been hit. She wasn't dead, however, which posed a problem. I tried to justify continuing, but I couldn't. I had to do what was right and end her misery.

"You know it's the right thing to do." Mabel gently reminded me.

So, I turned around and stopped. She was mortally wounded that was obvious, but she kept trying to pull her head in as I neared. I felt horrible. Mabel sat on at the side of the road waiting patiently, understanding that what I had to do was difficult. I walked into the nearby ditch and found a large rock. It was over quickly but I would be lying if I said I didn't shed a tear.

"This is pathetic!" I yelled in my helmet at no one in particular. "Just f#$* slow down!! Watch out!!! That's all it takes for f$**# sake." I yelled at no one in particular and aware of my hypocrisy.

"You feel better now?" Mabel asked as we entered the heart of the Ozarks and beautiful roads and even more beautiful scenery.

"Yes. Yes, I do!" I answered.

16 was an absolutely beautiful road, custom made for motorcycles and I was lucky, not seeing many cars at all. I wheeled around the sharp curves and enjoyed the rollercoaster hills.

"What's the hurry?" Mabel suddenly asked.

She had a point. I slowed down and remembered that motorcycle riding can be a perfect way to relax and take in nature as well as leaning into tight curves and switchbacks. I slowed and gave myself time to take in the beautiful nature around me. 16 wound through beautiful curves with slight berms built for speed and excitement. It wasn't as technical as some mountain roads but it was still necessary to pay attention even at slower speeds; it wasn't a highway. The hills and valleys would have your stomach visiting your throat every now and again for sure. I stopped in Nail Arkansas for gas and then turned around to visit a small road I'd noticed but passed, County Rd 21. It looked very promising until I ran into road construction. I u-turned and enjoyed the ride in the opposite direction. In Deer I took 7. It was a beautiful road, beautifully paved and curved like a Greek goddess. There were so many little roads that connected to one another. The Arkansas Ozarks could be a wonderful ride that would take several weeks. One paved brushstroke after another appeared and I took several, cussing the local traffic that had the audacity to drive the speed limit.

"Really?!" Mabel huffed...at me.

With so many beautiful curves passing lanes were a rarity, both a strength and a weakness of these lovely little roads. Several cars would pull over slightly to let me pass, evidently knowing the nature of most motorcyclists. I waved and thanked them only to get behind another. After a while I simply began overtaking slow cars any chance I got. I continued down 7, a road that I would classify as motorcycle nirvana and spent the four miles behind four incredibly slow-moving cars. I almost cried at the wasted opportunity, but turned around at its peak and rode it down again with a smile on my face. Afterwards, I found 14. 14 was gold-standard motorcycle riding as well. I was a kid in a candy store. All the roads! The roads!! It was so much that I felt I needed a break from slobbering over the asphalt. I found a little coffee shop where I met Andrew.

"Man, I miss my motorcycle." He started.

"Well," suddenly realizing he was talking to me, "It's time to get another one!"

"Wish I could. Wish I could. Where you headed?"

"I'm not sure. Right now, I'm just riding all of these gorgeous roads that you have around here."

"There's plenty of them. Hey! Have you ridden Push Mountain yet?"

"I might have. I don't know the names of the roads, just numbers."

"OH! You *have* to ride Push Mountain Road. I remember it when I had a bike. You'll love it!"

"Well, point me in the direction! I'd love to ride it."

"From Yellville…"

"Yellville?" I interrupted.

"Yea. That's where you're at."

"Oh…" I chuckled, almost wanting to yell "Thanks!".

Andrew gave me directions referring to landmarks and houses that I wasn't familiar with, so I pulled out my map and set it on the small table. I saw the familiar look in his eyes and the slight smile on his lips, all signs of a motorcyclist looking for roads on maps.

"I think it's this squiggly one here" he pointed at a B road in the middle of the map.

"Man, you'll love it if I remember correctly."

"I really appreciate it!" I said, picking up the tab for both our coffees.

"Thanks!"

And "squiggly" it was. 341 is now in my top five best roads. I found out at a tiny gas station that it was called "The Sidewinder" by the locals in the proximate area. It did not disappoint. I rode the whole thing twice smiling so much my cheeks hurt. The second time around I searched for possible campsites. There weren't many but there were several dirt roads leading into the forest.

"Take a look behind you." Mabel reminded me.

I did, and what I saw I didn't like. Black clouds and lots of them accumulating quickly. Unfortunately, my tent wasn't up for any amount of rain without me sleeping in a wet, soggy sleeping bag. I'd tried that once before and decided it wasn't worth it. I finished riding the wonder-road and stopped in Mountain Home to check the weather report. Rain was predicted and soon. I rode a bit further and stopped to decide what to do. Ultimately, I was going to meet Helle at my folk's house. I looked back west at the seemingly endless and beautiful roads and lush, green forest that I'd spent the morning in. I also noticed the mean, black clouds that were gathering up for a wet, rainy war, one that motorcyclists like myself would inevitably lose. I looked towards the east and there were blue skies. As I started Mabel up I watched the dark, thick clouds move in my direction and turned her towards Mammoth Springs towards Missouri. The Ozarks of southern Missouri are a continuation of the Arkansas Ozarks and while not as plentiful they still offered wonderful riding. MO 142 was a rollercoaster ride with soft turns on almost every hill making every minute an adjustment and a wonderful stomach-churning moment. I was getting hungry but it was only 3:45 in the afternoon.

"Why does that matter?" Mabel asked.

"Yea? Why does that matter?!"

I continued down the beautifully empty road until I saw the only place I'd seen since finding MO 142. Crumpies. I walked in, found a place at the bar to sit, an ordered. That's when I noticed a woman and her small daughter stopping at Mabel and staring at her as if she was an alien. The little girl stood with her hands firmly planted on her hips. Afterwards, they walked in and the woman walked up to me.

"Is that your motorcycle?"

"Yes…" I answered not really knowing where the conversation would lead.

"Well, my daughter has never seen one. That's why we were looking at it. I just thought what she said was really funny."

I was amazed that there was someone on the planet that had never seen a motorcycle.

"Yea? Well, I'm glad I could introduce her to motorcycles, but I'm not sure you'll be happy about it."

She smiled.

"No, no…that's not it." The lady laughed. "She saw the motorcycle and said 'Well! Isn't that something!'"

We both laughed and I walked over and introduced myself to the little girl who shook my hand and stared back at Mabel in the dirt parking lot, and then shook her head in disbelief once again.

After a wonderful lunch talking to friendly people, I made my way towards the bootheel of Missouri and as I rode east wide expansive fields slowly took over the forest. The twists and curves of the Ozarks slowly straightened out to farm roads. As I rode the sun was going down and it cast its rays over a beautiful field of small, yellow flowers that almost glowed. It was a picture moment. The nearer I got to my family's house the nearer I was to the end of my adventure. They weren't expecting me and before I pulled up I knew they would be out to dinner. Stopped and parked, I pulled out a rocking chair and sat in the driveway sipping on a beer I'd picked up a few days earlier. About a ½ hour later their car came rolling in and I raised my beer to welcome them home. Their car passed me and drove into the garage, and as I was getting up to go say hello the garage door started going down.

"They didn't see me!" I laughed out loud, "They didn't even see me!"

Helle would come in the next day and I considered pitching a tent in the front yard but thought the better of it. I was going to spend a week with my family regrouping and contemplating my travels and then would head home. That would be it. Adventures end. Endings are a part of adventures but we tend to forget that. I sat in the driveway and finished my beer and wrote in my journal.

"A motorcycle is most at home on backroads, leaning into turns and switchbacks, not sitting in a garage or chomping miles on a highway. It will do these things but will taunt the rider if the rider listens. These things, these motorcycles, are cumbersome when standing still. They are like a seal on a beach. But give them a one-lane, twisty road and they come alive, like a seal in the ocean. Motorcycles are often called 'death-machines' but really they are a chance to live. That 'thing' becomes more than the sum of its parts. It becomes a part of one's body and psyche if enough time is spent on it. Experience will open up avenues to adventure and a motorcycle opens up adventure to life."

Perhaps adventure never ended with a bang. Possibly that was because adventure never ends. Instead, it took breaks? Parked under the pergola I sat in a rocking chair and stared at Mabel. She seemed to be waiting for her next adventure as I paused our current adventure to fulfill obligations, visit family and be a part of a productive society all the while making plans for my next trip. I put my beer down and walked over to Mabel. Pulling my wrinkled, dirty map out of the top case, I noticed that it had become creased and mottled from weather and use, with lines drawn dutifully on top of routes that Mabel and I had taken.

"This is what a map should look like." I thought to myself.

I realized that if one took enough time for motorcycle adventures, areas six states wide would start looking like weekend trips.

"I've somehow become and adventurist." I thought, borrowing a word that I'd forgotten about; one I'd found on a past trip.

The adventurist didn't work for money. He worked for time. Cash was a commodity for gasoline and food, but time…time was priceless. We couldn't make more time, we could only watch as it rolled away. When on an adventure daily structure was defined by the process of camping, a cup of coffee and a glance at the day's route, and then riding and searching for road nirvana.

For now, though, a break; some time off the road. I'd wash Mabel and do some maintenance. I'd unload the panniers and clean them up, repacking them, trying to eke out the most space from them. I'd try not to waste time as I waited for my next adventure. I'd live in a house for a while and eat dinner off of a table. And every once in a while, I'd grin while I sat comfortably in the living room talking to my family. I'd grin because I knew what waited for me just outside the door.

A day trip through the Missouri Ozarks sounded good and so Mabel and I took off the next day, early. The northern section of the famous Arkansas Ozarks was beautiful and in Missouri the adventurist could determine their adventure using the alphabet. Good motorcycle roads in Missouri use letters as names with double letters (AA, BB) denoting an even more out of the way and often more interesting road. These roads were empty of tourists and often had your stomach tossing around in your body as you enjoyed twisties on hills and long rollercoaster straightaways. The scenery was not minimalistic like the west but full of forests and fields, and farms. But one had to be careful on the turns because often there'd be gravel spread over the road from a hard to see dirt driveway, or a wide tractor rumbling around in and out of neighboring fields. That being said, it was easy to find roads that quickly turned to gravel. Sometimes they'd lead to small creek crossings with a truck or two parked with a john-boat trailer hooked to it, the owners nowhere to be seen. Three main arteries ran through the Missouri Ozarks with numerous smaller roads making loops to and from them. It would take weeks to explore all the bi-ways and dirt roads. Mabel and I were exploring a few on our way to the nearby Ozarks when we stopped for gas. A large group of motorcyclists were gathered, having come from the hilly roads just north of us. We waved to each other out of politeness if anything. Onward to the hills of Missouri Mabel and I dipped and dived, leaned and twisted our way around for most of the day, taking dirt roads here and there that led to creeks and fields, forests and small farm houses. After a long day of smiles and exploring I made my back to my folk's house and rode in just after dark. My mom met me in the driveway.

"I was getting worried. Mark, I hate those things. I wish you wouldn't ride them. Dinner's ready."

That was my mom! Full of information, worry, and love.

"Well, hello to you too! No need to worry. I'm a careful rider. I usually slow down to around 60 on corners."

"Oh Mark! You're gonna kill yourself." She sighed, having given up on trying to change me.

"Come get something to eat."

I went in and enjoyed some fried catfish and a few beers.

In a few days I'd be riding home through the Arkansas Ozarks. It wouldn't be a long trip but I decided I might as well make something of the last leg of the adventure. I'd be home again soon. Not in a tent but back to my house with my little office in the suburbs. I'd sit comfortably and contemplate the last four weeks of my life. I might compare; I might plan. But I knew that the future was always up for grabs and full of mystery. I imagined that I'd have a cup of coffee in my hand, leaning back in my office chair. I'd be waiting for the next road to show itself on a map or in my head. The day came when Helle and I headed home, me on Mabel and Helle in her car. I'd meet her several days later as I was taking the long way home.

"I'm going home." I said to Helle, out of the blue.

"Yes you are. How does it feel?"

"It feels strange. I love our home but I also feel at home on the road, living off a motorcycle, in a tent."

"You're on your own there." She warned.

"I know."

"Be careful going home and I'll see you in a few days."

We kissed and an hour later I was heading out of the bootheel of Missouri and towards the Arkansas Ozarks. About fifty miles away the land started living again, being free from the industrial agriculture that pervaded the bootheel of Missouri. First slowly and then more and more.

"Let's go find some roads. These straight and narrows are boring." Mabel said as I sped up to far beyond the speed limit.

Mabel felt different packed up. I'd been riding her with no panniers for the past few days and now the load made Mabel feel a little cumbersome.

"How quickly we forget..." she taunted.

When we hit Pocahontas Arkansas, the hills began making long waves out of the blacktop. The trees slowly overtook the brown, plowed fields I'd been passing for what seemed forever.

I took a few interesting looking roads that seemed to always lead back to major arteries through the Ozarks after a few miles of beauty. The main arterial roads seemed like highways, those wasted opportunities in the name of efficiency and speed. There was a lot of truck traffic, and people in a hurry. I waited, looking for my first turn-off to escape. It came quick enough and with a downshift and a lean, Mabel and I were back in our element. This was the first time I was going to ride the backroads of Arkansas. I'd made dozens of trips through the state but on highways and in a car. I'd hated it every time. Arkansas cities are busy, loud places filled with too many cars and too many people. From the highway Arkansas seemed ugly. Filled with fast food and greed, dirty and unkept. But from the small backroads I was soon going to learn that Arkansas truly shined. It was another country, another world. It was already starting to show itself. The road started sweeping back and forth, beautifully technical and fluidly artistic. It was perfectly paved and there were bucolic farms set back in the hills, well kept, and unassuming. Every once in a while, a small general store would appear with a single gas pump where I would stop to get a quick bite or fill up. And without fail friendly people would say hello and stare politely with no meanness or fear in their eyes and ask questions. On every hill, around every curve and behind every tree there were the rolling Ozarks, green and lush with the beautifully paved, tiny black stripes of asphalt running through them. They were absent of billboards and cement and as hard as I tried and as much as I'd rather not admit, my abilities were not up to some of the roads. But there was always a smile on my lips.

I'd make mistakes, inadvertently pushing the back brake on and feeling the back tire slide, or missing a sharp turn on steep hills and braking hard, downshifting quickly. I'd downshift too late in fear and Mabel and I would miss the opportunity to dance around beautiful corners. I would stumble and she would stumble. I could feel her disappointment, and my own. I would creep around corners when I should have been leaning and giving her gas. I was botching a possible piece of art, beauty with balance and physics. I wasn't letting Mabel breath and I wasn't letting myself play. Persevering as the ribbon of blacktop rolled and undulated through the beautiful Arkansas hills, I finally started relaxing and let Mabel live her natural life in the curves. I leaned and let the tires do their work, still watching for gravel on the road where driveways and business entrances met it, but there were few of those out here. I searched for clean lines and swayed between the yellow and white markings of the road. Hours went by like this, only pausing three or four gallons at a time. I went from concern to contentment and became mesmerized by sharp turns and the purple-green cliffs that heaved around me. Finally, I got my mojo back. I saw a GS sneak behind me and we swayed back and forth through the turns until we hit a straight away and the big bike overtook Mabel and I. About a half hour later I saw the GS turn into a gas station and join the big group of bikes I'd seen earlier. Not needing gas, I rode on to a park a few miles down the road and stopped to make coffee and grab an energy bar. I was quickly back on the bike and heading to Mena Arkansas where I would spend my last night in the Ozarks before parking Mabel and getting used to the normalcy of not travelling. I soaked in the last roads just south of the interstate. They were beautiful but slowly became more and more serene, more peaceful, with views of the disappearing hills in my rearview mirrors.

I was soon riding through Waldron and knew that in forty minutes or so I'd be in Mena. I later found out that Mena had an interesting history with drugs and the CIA but at the time my expectations were low and I wasn't let down. I stopped and ate surprisingly good Mexican food and then searched for a place to sleep, finding ample opportunities for stealth camping in the tiny town. I eventually set up camp behind a closed down motel, but only after checking the area for less desirable aspects. I slept soundly, but alert. Arkansas had opened itself up to me and I was happy to have met its miles and miles of blacktop in its amazing mountains and rolling hills. There were numerous demanding rides and I was already planning a trip back. But at the time I knew my trip would formally end the next day. I knew this as I rode the little roads taking me back home. My tent of twelve years had finally given up the ghost. Things end. I had grown a little weary but these last three weeks had been a reminder that a nomadic life on a motorcycle was always there; just outside the door. All of this went through my head as I was riding. The landscape changed slowly from rolling, wooded hills to flat lands dotted with farms and divided by field rows. The road was somewhat curvy but the turns were softening. Traffic had started to build and so I took a turn to try to circumvent the inevitable. It helped but it also gave me a good look at the gathering black clouds on the horizon just north of me. I was hoping to beat the rain…again.

I hadn't been home in almost four weeks and it was time. I knew it. As I rode southwest the landscape flattened when I passed the colorful "Welcome to Texas" sign that I'd always liked. I had plans to stop in Paris Texas and snap a photo of Mabel with the gravestone of Jesus wearing cowboy boots, and did just that. The landscape became more and more familiar as I headed down roads that I'd ridden on day trips from my house. Forest turned to fields which turned to suburbs and strip malls. The nearer I got to Dallas the more construction there was everywhere, eating away at land that had once been beautiful prairies. The road widened and traffic became thick. The clouds were now catching up to me. I still had high hopes of beating the rain but the traffic stifled my faith. Big, fat drops of water began falling and so I reluctantly pulled over and donned my rain suit. By the time I had it on it was stormy. Suddenly I heard the sound of tires on rumble strips and stepped quickly behind Mabel as a car raced by seemingly paying no attention to me or anything else.

"Welcome to Dallas." I thought to myself.

I was back on Mabel in Dallas traffic, and now was in the middle of a downpour. I had about forty-five minutes before I reached home when I hit the massive interstate, Hwy 75, going south into Dallas and fought five lanes of traffic and a torrential downpour that made riding horrendous. Hydroplaning was a worry, but more than that was not being seen by the mass amounts of cars, which was a problem even in the best of weather.

Finally, I turned off the exit and was minutes away from the house, ending a four-week adventure. As I turned into the driveway the garage door went up and I was met by my smiling wife and our dog, Maggie. It was nice to be welcomed home. A kiss, a shower and a beer later I was sitting on our couch like I had never left at all.

A Note

There's no doubt about it. I felt a strange mix of happiness and sadness seeing Mabel parked in the garage. She sat there after weeks and 6500 miles of travel. The adventure was over and now she was patiently awaiting the next. The ending of any adventure is really a beginning for many touring motorcyclists, me included. One trip ends and plans for another begin. A trip on a motorcycle can be as simple or as complex as you'd like to make it. From solo-camping to five-star hotels. But I would suggest that riding alone offers a freedom that is rare. A feast can be a bowl of instant oatmeal and some coffee or a steak in an overpriced restaurant in Las Vegas. It's a matter of perspective and perspective is exactly what motorcycle touring changes.

The suburban house offers safety and familiarity but a motorcycle somehow seems out of place sitting in a suburban garage. Mabel waited graciously. I knew she offered chance and change, and I liked that idea. She let me blow the dust off my soul and clean the flakes of society that got stuck in the crevices of my life. She let me spread my wings a little. I know that motorcyclists come in many different forms and fashions, and that there are those that take unnecessary chances in order to feel alive. But danger, while being a component of motorcycle travel, is not necessary to feel alive. All that is really needed is a full tank of gas, a long, twisty road, and time. We all have so little time and it behooves us to remember that every now and again. Time does not stand still. Somewhere down in my being of beings I believe that sitting still is not a natural state. Otherwise, a motorcycle wouldn't need a kickstand and I wouldn't need a motorcycle.

Chapter 4

Arkansas

I decided to visit the Arkansas Ozarks on a short, three-day trip, and throw a visit to my family in for good measure. I wanted to explore the beautiful roads that I had ridden through some months ago and hopefully find a few new ones. I had a feeling that short visits to the Arkansas Ozarks were going to become regular rides for me.

"Are you ready to go, Mabel?!"

"I was just waiting for you!" she answered, as I clicked the panniers in place.

The trip, as all my trips, would start in the panic and insanity that made up city-traffic in a metropolis and so, as usual, I was planning an early start to try to beat the worst of it. North on 75 to 121 and to Bonham. I passed the beautiful little state park where I had visited many times and was tempted to stop again, but I had the Ozarks on my mind. Through Paris where the Texas Eiffel Tower and Jesus with Cowboy boots was located, I was headed to Oklahoma and on to Arkansas. The weather was beautiful and I had finally found some back roads to ease my aching soul. The noise of the city behind me and the beautiful countryside in front of me I was feeling free; I was feeling good. I came to a corner with a tiny brick church that sat in the shade and couldn't help myself: I stopped for a snack and some coffee. I also stopped to settle my nerves because ten minutes earlier I had come close to going off the road in a blaze of fire.

I wasn't riding too fast, but I was being stupid. On a motorcycle there is no time for day-dreaming, and that was exactly what I was doing. The road was just so pretty and the weather made everything look magical. I saw the corner coming up and didn't read it right. It was much sharper than I had thought. About the time I realized my mistake the melting tar on the road gave out from under me and Mabel and I were sliding on gooey tarmac and into the gravel shoulder. Luckily my moto-cross days from eons earlier kicked in. I let off the throttle slightly and kept off the brake, letting the tires slide on their own a little. Then, I gave it throttle and threw my left leg down, forward towards the front wheel which I kept turned slightly but not too much. I felt Mabel's back tire sliding around in the gravel looking for traction and then I felt her front tire start sliding out from under me. It was all I could do to not touch the front brake. Suddenly her front tire found traction and jerked she and I both straight up and almost over. I had left the scene during all of this and let little Moto-cross Mark take over. He slammed the throttle on, keeping Mabel going forward through the rough ditch that we now found ourselves in and gradually straightened out the front end, following an invisible line. We headed towards the road. Then, as if nothing ever happened, Mabel and I were cruising down the tiny road again.

The whole episode lasted seconds but in those seconds Moto-cross Mark's mind was laser-clear. Afterwards, when older Mark came back, he had a big smile on his face too.

"Well! That was interesting!" Mabel said as she shook the pea-gravel out of her tires.

"I'm not sure I'd use that adjective, but it was…it was fun!"

"Want to go back and do it again!?" Mabel chided.

"Not that fun!"

After coffee at the church we headed towards Nashville, Nashville Arkansas that is. From there we followed little roads, slower than usual, into Hot Springs and hit Hot Springs traffic. It seemed that all of Arkansas' cities, big and small, had horrendous traffic problems. I tried a little bi-way with no luck. It was jammed with fire trucks and police cars. I kept poking small roads until one wiggled and soon we found ourselves on the north side of Hot Springs.

"I think weather knows when we're out touring!" I said with disgust when I noticed the dark clouds gathering north of us.

"It seems that way, but let's camp. Let's take a chance!" Mabel suggested.

I agreed.

The rain had just started when we turned into a small, almost hidden campground in the Ouachita National Forest. It was sprinkling rainforest style: big, globby drops but not many of them. I set up quickly and started cooking tomatoes and rice when I noticed a man in the far corner of the campground. He seemed to have appeared out of nowhere and had nothing more than two white, plastic bags. It looked like he was trying to get a fire started but with no luck. I watched him as I waited for my meal to cook. He finally seemed to give up and sat under awning of the picnic area smoking a cigarette. Just afterwards several pickup trucks drove in and parked nearby. The man walked up to them and then back to the picnic area. The drivers sat in each their vehicles, parked next to one another and talked for about ten minutes and then left.

"OK…" I said, as I watched them drive off.

The old man was still sitting across the campground watching his failed attempt at a fire smoke. I ate, but had made too much so left the pot on the little table for later.

"Breakfast maybe?!" I thought to myself.

The rain had stopped but now it was hot and very humid and I was becoming wet from sweat. As much as I hated it, I was chased into the tent by mosquitoes and dozed off there until I was woke again by the sound of a diesel pickup truck. I couldn't hear what the two men were talking about, but I could hear that one of them almost never took a breath, talking "like a waterfall" as they say in Denmark.

It had cooled down once darkness came and so I tested the waters outside for bugs. It wasn't too bad and so I meandered out and sat at the table writing in my journal and wondering about the old guy across the way, still sitting there and smoking a cigarette, his two plastic bags by his side. There was a river nearby and so I ventured down and sat at the bank watching beavers or nutria, I couldn't tell. That's when I met Bobby. He was already sitting there. I hadn't noticed his car in the parking lot.

"Hi! Mind if I join you? I'm in the tent just up the hill."

"No! Not at all! I'm Bobby."

"Hi Bobby! I'm Mark. You from around here?"

"Yep. Hot Springs."

"Well, you've sure got pretty country here."

"I like it."

"What do you do in Hot Springs?"

"I work in a rubber band factory. I've worked there for twenty-two years."

"Wow!" I exclaimed, "I've never heard of a rubber band factory, but they've got to be made somewhere."

Bobby chuckled, "Yep, yep, they do."

"How are they made anyway? I guess I've never thought about it."

"I don't know. I just work a machine."

I let the thought of a man working at a factory for twenty-two years without understanding how the thing he'd spent twenty-two years making was made. But Bobby was amiable and seemed eager to talk.

As we were talking, we were suddenly startled by a voice. It was the man from across the campground.

"Hey. Can you give me a ride down the road?"

Bobby answered.

"No sir. I'm sorry. I'm staying the night."

The thin man turned to me.

"You the one with the bike?"

"Yes."

"Can you give me a ride? Just down the road a few miles."

"I can't risk you falling off, I'm sorry."

"I rode before. I won't fall off."

"Nope. I'm sorry."

Bobby and I sat silently for a minute, but the man continued standing there. I had gotten up to face him, not liking my back to a stranger.

"I'll tell you what. If you're hungry I can give you some food. I've got leftovers."

"That'd be nice."

I walked with the man up to my camp.

"You got a plate or something?"

"I got a cup in my bag." He answered, and went across and picked up one of the white plastic bags and brought it back to my tent. I emptied the rice and tomatoes into his cup.

"You can't give me a ride?!"

"No. I can't. I can't risk it."

He ate silently and I stood there until he turned and went back to his corner of the campground. About that time, Bobby came up the hill.

"Hey! I was headed back down."

Bobby came over and watched as the man sat eating the food I had given him.

"That man's no good. He's no good."

"I'm pretty sure he's homeless, but what in the hell is he doing all the way out here?!"

"I don't know, but he's no good." Bobby answered, looking in the man's direction.

That's when I noticed the little red car parked a few spaces over.

"That's your car?"

"Yep. That's it."

"Are you camping tonight?"

"I'm sleeping in the car. I've got work tomorrow morning early."

"In Hot Springs?"

"Yep. At the factory."

We said our goodnights and Bobby walked over to his little car and got in. I didn't see him again, and his car was gone the next morning before I got up. I watched the old man finish eating, deciding that I wasn't going to get in the tent until I knew what he was going to do. About a half-hour later he gathered his two plastic bags and started heading down the little, lonely road through the forest, in the dark.

I decided to make a long day of it, enjoying the Ozarks at a relaxed pace, but eventually making it to my family's house that evening. My mom was going in for an operation the next day and I wanted to be there for that. On the way I found some new roads, twisty and beautiful, and enjoyed some old asphalted friends as well. A bit later I started noticing my face hurting and realized that I had been smiling in my helmet, making my cheeks hurt. I was at my family's house a little after dark, catching my mom by surprise. She started crying, happy to see me, but I couldn't wipe that smile off my face. The chain on Mable had started making crunching noises, never a good sign, and so I found a motorcycle shop about an hour away. They had a chain and it was the right size, but it was too long. I bought it and cut a few links out of it and screwed the thing up in the process. I'd make it home, but I would have to replace the chain again.

My mom's operation was a day surgery and she was back home in no time. A few days later I left them in the driveway waving. I was taking the long way home again and looking for new roads in Arkansas on my way back. I would ride along and see an interesting turn-off and take it. It was one of the joys of motorcycling. Most of the tiny roads that joined the little road that I was on, made loops and joined the throughfare again a few miles down. I continued this and thought about how different Arkansas was when I was riding in the country. I had a lot of time to think until I was about an hour away from Texarkana. I had been watching storm clouds come and go all day, the weather changing from blue skies to grey, and back again. But this time I was looking at pitch black clouds that made a dark scar in the sky. It looked bad. I saw a few turn-offs and contemplated hurriedly setting up camp and hunkering down through the storm, but that "keep going" mentality took over.

"I'm just about an hour away from Texarkana. It would be stupid…" I thought.

"Are you sure?!" Mabel asked.

"We can just ride through. It won't be bad."

I was wrong. It was bad.

About thirty minutes later Mabel and I found ourselves in a massive, torrential downpour with gale-like winds whipping us and everything around us like rag dolls. In moments the road had inches of rain on it. I felt the tires give a few times and cautiously caught up with the only other vehicle on the road, a small car in front of me. I tried to keep in its tire tracks to lessen the possibility of hydroplaning. It helped a little but the tires couldn't keep up with the rain, even at the 10 mph we were crawling. I had to play it carefully as the car was sending sheets of water to both sides. It was terrifying.

Needless to say, I was drenched in minutes, even with raingear on. Everything and every part of my body, including my head in my helmet, was drenched. In Texarkana the rain continued pounding and the winds seemed almost hurricane like. I stopped at the first hotel I saw and got a room, parking Mabel under the awning by the front door. In the room I opened up the top case with trepidation, thinking that everything in it would be soaked, but by some miracle of engineering everything was dry. The next day the sun was shining and there were blue skies.

"I should have stopped and pitched my tent!" I thought, after a night in a dry bed. It was easy to be brave when you were comfortable.

In a few hours I was home and Mabel was safe in the garage and Helle was sitting patiently listened to motorcycle stories from my short trip.

"Did you have fun?!" she asked.

"Yes I did. Even with the rain!"

"Well, that's what counts!" she replied, getting up and refilling our drinks.

As she was playing bartender I sat in my favorite chair and found myself thinking about my next trip. I'd save that conversation for later though.

Chapter 5

Arkansas, Missouri, Nebraska, Iowa, South Dakota, Wyoming, Colorado

The day finally came when it was time to load Mabel up again and take off on another adventure. I kept the side panniers packed and stored with the kitchen and camping supplies in each, respectively, so all that was necessary to do was the scheduled maintenance on Mabel, and load the top case and the tank bag. I was really looking forward to the tour that I had planned. I had played with the idea living as a motorcycle adventurist, secretly of course because I knew my wife was not going to be party to such an idea. I had mentioned it in passing to her.

"You're on your own." She had answered without even looking up from her knitting.

"Aw, c'mon! I'd buy a bigger tent and even some thicker underlays." I'd replied with a smirk.

"You ought to go by your parents' house on your way up." She answered, dismissing my sardonic comment.

"I know. I've thought of that. I think I will." I answered.

That was how my western tour turned into a midwestern start.

The start of the trip was rough Midwest or not. In the days preceding the trip I had a lot on my mind. First, our parents were getting older and health issues were starting to pop up. Secondly, Texas was in the midst of an extreme heat wave and leaving Helle alone with our dogs was weighing a bit heavily on my conscious. Lastly, as a self-employed individual I was going to have to put my work plans on hold. On top of everything else, in the preceding days there had been some extra issues with Helle's family that had sucked a little air out of the trip from the get-go. I had been doubting the trip for a few weeks, even toying around with the idea of postponing it. But with the help of Helle I had decided that it wasn't necessary.

"I think you ought to go!" Helle assured me, "I'll be fine. Don't worry. There are more important things in life than working."

"Like family." I replied.

"Yes! Like family. But also just getting out of the mindset of working all of the time."

"I agree. But are you sure? I have some doubts."

"You'll feel better once you're on the road." She recommended.

"Just go Mark. Thing's will be fine!" Helle continued encouraging me.

The day I left it was hot. It was really hot! As mentioned, I was headed towards North Dakota by way of Missouri, having decided to go by my parent's house. I live in a metropolis; everything is cement and glass and so the first hour or so was highway. I fought the five-lane city traffic as long as I could and then exited to find the backway up to Texarkana. Following 121 I passed through Bonham, and then on to Paris, where Mabel and I had stopped before. In Idabel Oklahoma I followed 70 into Arkansas. I skirted the beautiful Ozarks and concentrated on keeping Mabel fueled up and myself hydrated. I had bought some riding pants and wore underwear under them in hopes of a cooler ride, but the heat was too much. My ass started hurting early on. Stopping at a small Mexican restaurant I ordered a quick lunch and drank about four glasses of iced-tea. The rest of the day, well it's easy to fill in the blanks. In Hot Springs I hit a fast and winding bi-way, B 270 and then hit the freeway, Highway 30. I felt like I had missed out on the Ozarks but I had decided to "just make Missouri" and then get on with the tour west. In Little Rock I got a hotel. I was so hot and the heat had sucked so much energy out of me the entire day that I didn't even care to complain about my laziness.

"I need to turn my attitude around or this trip is going to go nowhere." I told myself as I took off the top case.

"Give yourself a week." Mabel said.

"Yea. I need to get past this. I've looked forward to it for a long time."

"I know. But sometimes it happens."

I checked into the comfortable hotel and searched for beer and dinner and found both. Taking the beers back to the hotel I checked on Mabel.

"I'm fine!" she assured me.

Afterwards, I hunkered down in the hotel room and wrote in my journal.

"Something depends on this trip. I don't know what it is but it's important. It's a mystery. The world as I've known it seems to be changing drastically and yet I'm on a motorcycle tour, on Mabel. It all seems to make sense, somehow. But trouble is like a weed. You have to pull it when you see it, and be sure to get the roots. While the best laid plans might not get me very far, they're a start. Camp every time you can. Get out of your own head and ride the road in front of you. It's a sin not to use your time. Adventure is life."

I put the pen down, finished my second beer, brushed my teeth and ducked into the covers with my book and my notepad. A chapter or two and some YouTube and I was asleep. Not much of a day, but like I'd written, any plan is a start.

I was up early the next morning and drank a quick cup of coffee at the nearby gas station with a horrible protein bar that I ended up throwing away. I was in a hurry to get going and most importantly, get out of Little Rock. Helle and I had done the drive to my parent's house numerous times and I knew that until I hit the north side of Searcy that traffic was typically horrendous. But this morning I had the highway to myself.

"It *is* Sunday." Mabel reminded me as we scooted up the highway as fast as we pleased.

There were numerous ways to get to their house from Walnut Ridge and I took my favorite. It had some windy bits that snaked through some poor, dead agricultural towns. I also knew some "double-letter" roads in Missouri to take knowing from previous trips that they were the most interesting. I wasn't in a hurry as I was planning on staying the next day at my parents' house, spending time with them. Around 2pm I rounded their driveway and they sat under the carpark in their rocking chairs, waiting. That night in their living room we talked while the TV was on.

"I hate those things, Mark. You're gonna get killed!" my mom said, referring to Mabel. It was a recording that she repeated to me any time the topic of motorcycles was brought up.

"That's not the plan."

"Well…"

"Well, I like myself too much to get killed. And even if I do, I'll die with a smile on my face if I'm on a motorcycle." I teased.

"Don't say that, Mark!" she answered, disapprovingly.

"When are you leaving?" my stepfather asked.

"Day after tomorrow."

"Well! That's not long!" my mom interjected.

The next day was spent lazily sitting under the carport visiting my folks. It seemed like it had cooled down a little.

"What time are you leaving tomorrow?"

"Early as possible. I want to get a fresh start."

"You know you could stay a few days."

"I know! But I'll be back."

I turned my chair to stare at Mabel sitting right behind us under the awning, waiting.

"A WHOLE DAY out of my way just for YOU!" I teased my mom that night.

"I know. I know."

"A WHOLE DAY!" I repeated, smiling.

"Dinner's ready."

Around 5 am I was up and drinking coffee when my mom walked in asking the same thing she did every morning when I visited.

"What do you want for breakfast?"

"I'm drinking it." I said, pointing to my coffee cup.

By 5:45 I was saying good-bye to my folks, rolling out of the little town and heading north. I followed the Missouri Ozarks to Rolla Missouri riding some wonderfully twisty roads. I stopped for a snack and to gas up Mabel when I noticed the dark clouds just north of me. They were bad enough for me to pull out my rain-jacket and strap it to the seat for easy access. Ten minutes later, though, I was stopped again and putting it on while big dollops of water fell on me. Back on Mabel I battled the rain. First it came in spurts and then the blasts of water became closer and closer together until it was just raining, and raining hard. Thunder and lightning filled the skies as I beat a path from Booneville to Brookfield. I had had to stop several times to change my soaked socks to dry ones only to have the dry ones get soaked within thirty minutes.

"I'm wasting my time!" I thought.

Obviously, my waterproof boots weren't water proof anymore. In Chillicothe I stopped and considered my options. It was still raining as I stood under the gas station awning considering my next steps. I noticed beautiful, sunny skies some miles west of me, but south of me it was as black as night.

"I'm soaked!" I exclaimed to Mabel, disgusted.

"Don't look at me." She answered.

I stood as a cold wind started up, blowing the black clouds my way and forcing me to quickly put on my only sweater under the riding jacket. I passed by a sign for a state park and made a U-turn and stopped and considered camping.

"Your boots are soaked. It's probably going to rain all night, and you don't have any camp shoes." Mabel exclaimed, "And you don't have rain pants!" she continued.

"Dammit! I forgot my camp shoes and my rainpants?! But I've got a new tent I'd like to try out."

"It's up to you. If you like misery…"

"It's gonna be another hotel." I said, "But first I need to get a new rain suit and some camp shoes."

In a fit of optimism and forgetfulness, I had only brought an old rain jacket but it was much too big and blew up like a sail when riding. I found a hotel with an Applebee's nearby as well as a hardware store across the street and decided it was time to stop. It had rained the entire time I rode through Missouri. Every time I looked around I saw the promise of blue skies "just ahead", but I wasn't buying the blue-sky argument anymore. I bought a rain suit and some sandals and when I was walking back out to Mabel the rain started ever so slightly and then began to build again. By the time I made it back to the hotel to check in it was pouring down.

"You can park your bike under the patio on the side. It's close to your room." The hotel attendant offered.

"Thanks! I'll do that."

I walked out to Mabel and the rain had stopped again. But, by the time I had Mabel tucked away under the covered patio at the side of the hotel a few minutes later, an all-out thunderstorm was pounding the area. Rain was being blown in every direction. I walked to my room on the 2nd floor and took a hot shower and put my wet clothes in the nearby dryer. Dinner was at Applebee's with two margaritas. Walking back to the hotel the rain had subsided for the time being but the sky was still bluish black with a dab of beautiful blue and orange sky some miles west, taunting me.

"It's going to be like this?!" I thought to myself.

I was in bed early and pulled out my journal.

"This is not camping!" I wrote.

5.2

That night I was woke up by a loud clap of thunder and lay listening to the rain beat on the hotel window. Looking out, there was an ocean of rain falling from the sky. The parking lot light, much too bright, made everything look eerily hazy and green in the night. I lay back down and went to sleep, dry and glad I had listened to Mabel. When I woke up it was still raining but not as hard. I lay my map across the bed and looked at possible routes, drinking hotel-room coffee as it was too early for the hotel attendants to put coffee out downstairs. Around sunrise I went outside to check on Mabel. There was a big Harley bagger sitting next to her under the awning. Both bikes were wet. I took a hotel towel and started wiping Mabel down when the Harley rider came out to wipe his bike down.

"Hey!"

"How are you doing?"

"How far are you riding?" he asked.

"I'm not sure yet. Do you need a rain jacket? I'm leaving this one here. I got a new one."

I pointed at the old rain jacket laying across the bench.

"No thanks."

"Where're you headed?" I asked.

"Sturgis!"

Years ago, I toured as a musician and played pretty regularly in Deadwood South Dakota, close to Sturgis.

"That's now?!" I asked, surprised. I knew what it was and was heading in that general direction, but wasn't aware that it was going on that week.

"Yep. I thought maybe you were heading that way. I see adventure-types there too these days."

"Nope." I answered, "I might go through it."

"It starts this weekend. I rode from Colorado and am meeting some friends. We're gonna ride up together."

"Sounds fun! Sure you don't need the jacket?"

"No, but thanks. You should go up there if you've never been. It can be a hoot."

"I might."

I headed back upstairs to pack, hoping to beat the black clouds already on the horizon west of me.

Almost immediately upon starting down the road the weather turned ugly. It started raining. Hard at first and then off and on, hard and light, never really quitting. I headed towards Burlington Junction Missouri. The entirety of northwestern Missouri reminded me of the southeast bootheel of Missouri: commercial agriculture. That is, until I hit Maryville, when fields and fields of corn started showing up. It was everywhere, still green and tall. I thought of Nebraska. When I crossed into Iowa the rain let up and by the time I was in Clarinda there were blue skies and sunshine. Taking 71 north to County Road 2 I stopped at a little cemetery to make some coffee and take a look around. For the entirety of County Rd. 2 all I had seen were farms and fields and then out of nowhere, the cemetery. I pulled under the only tree, an old, gnarled oak, and shut off the motor. It was silent except for the gusty wind that blew through the old tree and around the gravestones. I started water boiling and took a walk around. There was something strange: there were dozens and dozens of children's graves from the middle to late 1800's. I knew there had to be an explanation but I didn't have it. I drank my coffee under the old tree and enjoyed the warm sunshine.

Back on Mabel the road entered Nebraska and led to Hwy 50. I had noticed a grouping of state parks on the map, just south of Omaha, and decided to try my luck. First, I found an almost totally empty campground with the exception of one RV that looked like it hadn't moved in quite some time. It was a little early, but all the rain had put me in the mood to call it a day. I sat in a "primitive site", a flat piece of land with a fire grate, and then noticed the long line of house trailers that sat on the parameter of the whole campground. I decided to look around. Back on 6 I rode towards Ashland, a cute little town, and got supplies and some beer.

"Well, what now?" Mabel asked.

"I don't know? I can't seem to make up my mind. So, now I'm in the mood for a nice hotel room. I'm getting soft!"

There was silence. As I stood in the parking lot of the gas station a little red-headed boy came up.

"Hey mister. Can you rev it up?"

"I can," I said, "but she's not that loud."

"OK!"

I started Mabel up and gave her a rev. The boy stood with his fishing pole looking astonished and perplexed, as well as a little disappointed.

"You're right. It's not loud, but it's pretty cool anyway. Is it fast?!"

A few of his friends came sauntering up.

"This is L0uis and David."

"Hi." They said, admiring Mabel.

"Hey guys! Looks like you've been fishing."

They all started talking at once.

"I'll bet you know a good place to eat around here!" I said, half-jokingly.

David suggested I went to the nearby bar.

"They have good food." He promised, "I go there a lot!"

I thought about that for a second. The boys couldn't have been over twelve years old.

Back on the road, I almost decided to ride into Lincoln but thought the better of it and ended up at Mahoney State Park, a small park not far from Highway 80. When I entered the park office, I was met by a redheaded woman who was all smiles.

"Well, hello!" the smiling, portly lady welcomed me.

"Hi. Do you have some campsites?"

"I believe we do!" she said, sparkling every word with excitement. She pulled out a park map.

"I don't need electricity. Just water."

"All of our sites are the same. They all have electricity and water. Now the orange ones are a little cheaper, and the blue ones are little more expensive." She said, pointing at the laminated card she had pulled out.

"Why don't you go find one first. Not all of our sites are so tent friendly." She added, noticing my motorcycle jacket and the helmet.

She was right, tent-friendly sites were rare. I found a doable campsite and after paying, set up my tent and made dinner. I had bought three local beers and some snacks with plans on doing some people watching. The park wasn't my favorite, but it wasn't that bad. I'd found that many state parks were set up near roads and highways, making them a bit noisy and this one was no different. The highway was nearby and made for a noisy night. The rain had held off but the weather service was promising showers later that evening. I sat drinking my beer and chomping on snacks, hoping for the best. I wrote in my journal while waiting for the possible rain.

"It's been a long, few days. Hard. Nebraska roads have already been long like the long rows of corn they shoot through. People are friendly but subdued, like the landscape they live in. I'm tired and my head is elsewhere. This park is noisy but I don't care. I feel I'm missing out on the trip that I'm in the middle of. It's turned into destination not travel. I'm out for experiences and find all of them vanilla and bland. It's disappointing and I'm confused as to what to do. I've done over a thousand miles in the past few days but they seemed dreary."

"This is going to be an interesting trip." I thought to myself.

It didn't rain; that is, until I started making coffee the next morning. Even though I sat in my tent making coffee while thinking about the prospects of packing a wet tent, I was in a good mood. I had spent the evening eating snacks, drinking beer, and watching families in the campsite have fun, their kids and pets running around carefree. But I couldn't procrastinate anymore. The morning was overcast and it was time to pack wet gear into dry bags, a chore that's never fun and never neat. Of course, I had to do this in the light, misty rain that had begun. I went ahead and put

on the rain suit and was on the road again heading into the heart of
Nebraska, in a steady rain now. I followed 92 west, a small road that
paralleled highway 80 with my newish rain suit which was working
like a charm. I ducked under my small windshield and found that by
putting my boots up on the pillion's foot pegs that my socks got
less wet. I kept shifting on the wet seat as my butt kept getting sore.
Soreness is part of motorcycle touring and I had found that the
secret was to shift my weight before my butt got too sore. 92 was a
straight shot to 281 where I stopped at Jim's Truckstop. My rainsuit
was working wonders but my hands and feet were soaked and cold.
Jim's was on the outskirts of St. Paul Nebraska at the corner of 281
and 92. It looked welcoming so I stopped. It was tiny but it was one
of those quickly disappearing places that weren't owned by a
corporation of one kind or another. It was a local mom-n-pop place
that served up old-fashion, midwestern fare. I walked in and the
whole placed hushed for a few seconds. It was like walking into a
saloon in those old western movies, but I was used to it. It was just
a typical thing in small towns in the Midwest. Most "tourists" didn't
come here much less stop at a place like Jim's. There were a lot of
local farmers and truckers sitting in booths talking to each other
and the other people that walked in and out of the place. I sat at the
bar and perused the tiny place. It was painted baby blue and had the
50's Naugahyde on all the seats and chairs which were made of
shiny steel. The tables were right out of Leave It to Beaver. I didn't
have to wait long before the waitress came to the bar. She didn't fit
the place. She had purple colored hair and was heavily tattooed.

"What can I get you?" she smiled.

"Coffee. Hot and black please! Oh, and water."

The tall, tattooed waitress smiled and in seconds had a cup of
coffee and a menu in front of me. She busily took care of her

patrons as she went to and from the kitchen. It seemed most of them knew her.

"Know what you want?" she stopped, dirty dishes stacked in her arms up to her neck.

"Yea. I'll take a grilled cheese and French fries, please."

"Alright!" she said, walking away and somehow managing to take the menu with her. A minute later she was back filling my coffee cup up.

"Where you headed?" a voice asked from behind me.

"Uh…I'm headed west."

"It's been raining a lot."

"Tell me about it! I've ridden in rain, basically from southeast Missouri."

When I turned around there was a heavy-set guy sitting at a table with an ironed, plaid shirt tucked into ironed, white-washed, over-sized jeans which were connected to his shoulders by blue straps. He sat pouring salt on his hamburger and his fries. So much so that I thought he'd forgotten he was salting his food. He finally looked up while he poured spoonful after spoonful of sugar in his black coffee.

"That doesn't make for good motorcycle riding!" he said, adding one more spoonful of sugar to his coffee and then stirring.

He paused.

"I kinda miss travel, but not enough to do it again."

"You have a bike?" I asked, surprised at the idea.

"Oh me?! No! I'm a truck driver. I've driven near thirty years but now I just haul grain locally around here. I'm home every night and kinda like it."

"Trucker?! Believe it or not, I used to drive trucks. Way back in the nineties."

When we talked all the diners seemed to hush up in order to ease drop a little. He smiled and we began sharing stories as truckers will do. The patrons in the restaurant must have heard enough trucker tales because they didn't listen long, choosing to continue talking amongst themselves, disregarding our "trucker-lies". As we talked my coffee cup magically continued to be full of hot coffee. I hardly noticed that she'd come by.

"You know what!" I stopped the waitress, "I'll bet that pie is homemade!"

"It is! Wanna a piece?"

"Yes I do! Just pick one and I'll eat it!"

"Anything?"

"Yep."

A minute later a big hunk of cherry pie was in front of me and she filled my coffee cup back up. The old trucker and I continued "lying" to each other.

On my way out I spotted a carboard box of green squash and cucumbers. A paper sign taped to it stated "Free" so I helped myself to a few pieces and paid the waitress for the meal, leaving a hefty tip for the excellent service. I stopped and said goodbye to the trucker as an old couple made their way to the door. I recognized them because they had pulled in and parked next to me when I was pulling all my rain gear off. We followed each other out. At my bike the old man started talking to me, holding the door to his small pickup open and his wife sitting in the passenger seat silently waiting.

"Where ya headed?"

"I think I'd like to make Alliance tonight. At least Halsey."

"Yep. Well, you could go and take 11 up north to 91. It'll hit Dunning and then Halsey just up the way. Course, you could just follow 92. It'll take you highway 2. It's a pretty road. I think 2 would be your best bet."

"Thanks! I think I'm going to stay the course and…"

"I used to ride. A long time ago. I liked to take the small roads. Now I don't know where you're headed but if you follow 92 all the way it'll hit a road…what was it…let's see…"

"I've got GPS. I think I'm going to stick to 2. That was the p…"

"Oh yea. It hits 61. You headed to Sturgis?"

"Maybe. If I do, I won't stay…"

"I was never much interested in Sturgis. Too many folks…kinda a circus now. It's for the young people I guess."

"Yea, I'm not much fo…"

"It used to not be so big. You know, it was started a hunerd years ago by a few fellas. Let's see now, I can't remember their names…"

"I might…"

"Now a lot of folks like it. I don't got anythin' against it. There's just a lot going on…"

"I'll probably…"

I gave up, stood and listened, and smiled. This was America. Friendly people trying to help, sharing experiences and taking interest in others. It would be good for all us to remember that every now and again.

5.3

I pulled out of the dirt parking lot full of grilled cheese, coffee, and pie. Stopping at the grill had reminded me that adventures were not just about twisty roads and excitement, but about people and places, and putting yourself into situations that opened up opportunities for stories around the campfire or even in books. I tried to keep this in mind as I looked west and saw the now inevitable black rain clouds. Even before I stopped at the gas station to fill Mabel up it had begun raining lightly. I put my rainsuit back on and resigned myself to being wet. A few miles down the road the rain started again, coming down hard with gusty winds. I leaned into the handlebars and put my feet on the pillion pegs, trying out my new rain-position. The rainsuit was doing its job but Mabel and I fought endless grain and cattle trucks roaring up and down 92 and pounding us with blasts of wind every time they raced by. For about 130 miles the rain didn't let up and neither did the sidewind or the eighteen wheelers.

"Well...what can I do?!" I thought.

"Nothing." Mabel answered as she got whipped sideways by yet another truck going in the opposite direction. I just hung on tight.

Just outside of Halsey the rain stopped and the sun came out. Just like that. Just like magic. And then, just like magic, it started warming up, and quickly. So much so I pulled off to the side of the road and took the rainsuit off, stuffing it in my top case. In Halsey I stopped at a little roadside park set up by the town, and unpacked the soaking tent. Laying it out in the grass to dry in the now baking hot sun, I scampered under a big tree and started making coffee. It had changed from grey, gusty, and wet to a humid and hot summertime day. I started shedding clothing quickly. By the time I was drinking coffee the tent-fly and inner-mesh had dried completely out. So, I turned the inner -tent over to dry the bottom out. Halsey was a tiny, tiny town with the nice, small park, a gas station and a makeshift grocery store. I thought about visiting the grocery store but I didn't really need anything. I took my time under the large tree, drinking my coffee and just enjoying a little peace and quiet, except for the occasional Harley that rattled through the town, presumably heading towards Sturgis. Soon I had the tent and my kitchen packed up. I was on my way, feeling a lot cooler without all the clothing.

It was amazing! For the last three or four days I'd fought rain, cloud after black cloud. And now, sunshine and blue skies, and heavy, humid heat! It was almost as if someone had just turned off a spigot in the sky and turned a large, gas heater on high. Not long after Thedford, 92 began to be surrounded by a blanket of beautiful yellow daisies and sunflowers. I had entered the Sand Hills of Nebraska. While the road wasn't twisty or exciting, it meandered through this beautiful area of the Midwest. Up and down out of valleys and crossing long swelling hills I enjoyed a fast ride with no traffic. The problem was: absolutely no campgrounds or places to camp. Most of the surrounding rolling hills were fenced off and used for livestock or just too open to stealth camp. Stopping for pictures every now and again (I had Helle's voice in my head: "Take pictures!") I spotted a church up on a hill. I had camped behind churches before. They were nice and quiet as long as it wasn't

Wednesday or Sunday. There was a guy mowing with a big zero turn mower. I turned in. He finished his row and turned the mower off and walked up to me.

"Hi. I'm looking for a place to camp and was wondering if I could camp here. I'll be out early tomorrow morning. I promise I won't leave a mess. I've got everything I need."

He stared at the green grass as if he thought he missed a spot and then turned.

"Well, I don't care at'ol but I just mow the grass here. I'm sure the church folks won't care, though. But, my sprinklers come on twice a day. Once at 5pm and again in the mornings around 6am. You might get wet."

"Oh!" I said, already making my mind up.

"Well, there's a place in the next town up the way. They've got a city park. You wouldn't have a problem there. They won't mind. Just the next town up."

"OK! Thanks. I'll check it out. I'm not in a hurry. I'm enjoying the scenery around here."

"Yea." he started, "It's nice."

He nodded his head and turned to continue his mowing. I got back on the road and made it to Whitman where I spotted a tiny campground with a single RV trailer in it. It was down in a small valley. I stopped and checked it out. It looked deserted. There was an old trailer at the entrance and everything was mowed but it didn't look like it had been used for quite some time. I took my time and sat under a little tree, pulling my map out, to wait and see if anyone came. I checked the water spigots on a few of the sites and was surprised to find they worked. I waited around fifteen minutes or so when suddenly a train came barreling past on the nearby tracks. It couldn't be seen from the campground but it was loud and as there were a few road crossings around he blew the deafening airhorn right at the campsite. Maybe this was the reason it was deserted? About fifteen minutes later a car came in looking around. Probably doing what I had done. They waved and drove off.

"I don't think so." I said to myself.

"It's still daylight. Let's look around." Mabel suggested.

About a half hour up the road I found a nice, empty fairground and decided to stop. I rode past the arena and to a building set up for shops that were probably used during the fair. There were picnic tables everywhere and a place to park behind a storage building that would be unseen from the road. There was nobody around and a cement pad to park Mabel on to boot. I turned her motor off and heard music emanating from a hill back behind the fairground. There were golfcarts out in the hills and young men whooping it up and drinking beer. They were playing golf on what looked like a makeshift golf course out in the field. Obviously, they were having a good time.

"Who would have thunk it?!" I said out loud.

"They'll be done at dusk." I thought, and so decided to hunker down.

About the time I got the tent up and was making dinner a farm truck came rolling up to an open-sided building just next to where I had sat all my gear. I thought for sure they were there because of me. I walked up to it upon seeing them getting out.

"Hi! I didn't know who to ask, but I was going to camp here tonight, if that was OK?"

A young, pretty woman was getting out followed by two young boys who upon hitting the ground ran off like puppies in separate directions.

"I wouldn't know who to ask either." She answered, paying no attention to her kids.

"I'm sure it's OK though. The fair's not til' next weekend."

"Great! I'll be gone by tomorrow morning."

"That's fine. We're just dropping some things off here."

About that time a lean cowboy with dark glasses got out of the truck and slowly sauntered towards the building, saying nothing. I walked back to the campsite and continued cooking. The couple stood talking for a few minutes then he backed the truck up to the fenced wall of the building and started trying to manhandle large, heavy mats off the back of the truck while she stood under the roof waiting to "catch" them. I sat eating my dinner. The lean man was trying to lift the mats, each weighing around 80 lbs. a piece, standing at the side of the truck, something I knew wasn't possible. So, I turned off the stove and walked over, crawling up on the back of the flatbed pickup truck I helped him the best I could.

"These are heavy!" I said, lifting an end over the fence and dropping it off to the lady who immediately moved out of the way.

"They are!" she replied. He didn't say anything.

There were twelve mats in all and by the time we were done I had worked up a sweat. He walked past me to the driver-side door.

"Thank you" he said quick and silently, in a short, gruff manner. Those were the only words I heard him speak.

I walked back to the table and sat down. They stood talking in a small field behind the building next to where I was camped. Then, he drove over to a larger building and pulled out a trailer full of portable livestock fencing and they started putting fencing together nearby. I walked over again.

"Is there something going on tomorrow? If so, I can get out of your hair."

"Oh no," the lady answered, "this is for next weekend."

I walked back to the picnic table and watched them assemble and disassemble livestock fencing while their boys ran around wildly, playing. In the background I heard the golfers and now heard cattle mooing. There were cattle out on their makeshift golf course! The whole thing was surreal. Here I was in the middle of what I thought was nowhere, not a house to be seen, and now there was all this activity going on. I smiled at the whole thing.

"Life in the country, I guess!"

After about an hour they were still hard at it but I noticed it had gotten considerably cooler. I was sitting behind a row of trees and couldn't see out west. So, I walked around the building and turning the corner I saw what I really didn't want to see: pitch black clouds with flat bottoms and lots of lightning west of me.

"Shit! They're following me!"

Walking back, I contemplated my options. Stay here and weather out what looked to be a serious storm coming this way. Or, make my way to the little motel I had passed about twenty miles back. I could ride towards the storm to the next town if there was a motel, but I didn't know if there was. I checked my phone. Miraculously I had cell service, but not much. Online I found a small motel in the next town, about ten miles towards the foreboding storm. I called.

"Hello…" the connection was scratchy.

"Yes."

"Do you have rooms for tonight?"

"There's a storm coming." The voice answered.

I paused and thought about why someone would say that.

"Yes. Do have any rooms available?"

"Yes. Where are you?"

"I'm on my…." And then I lost the connection.

My mind made up I hurriedly packed the tent and packed Mabel back up, chunked my dinner and made a beeline for Ellsworth, towards the coming storm. There were massive amounts of lightning and it looked like it was raining buckets in Alliance. I got a bit nervous as the storm really looked serious. I got more nervous when I pulled up to the little motel. To say it was a dump would be kind. I pulled into the dirt parking lot and noticed several derelict cars, some missing wheels and tires, and other pieces of rusty machinery in the parking lot. There were buckets of who knows what sitting in front of several of the rooms. It was literally connected to an auto chop shop just up the hill. I couldn't find the office and so decided to look in some of the rooms to see what I was in for.

"I'm not comfortable with this. With leaving you out here."

"Then don't!" Mabel said, almost starting her own engine.

I looked through the windows and into a few of the rooms. They were a mess. Unmade beds that looked dirty, and greasy looking green wallpaper. There was broken furniture in one of the rooms and another was just filled with boxes. I looked at the auto shop, the derelict cars and the trash strewn everywhere, and then saw the office in a small corner of the chop shop.

"Really?!" Mabel said, astounded that I hadn't pulled out of the place yet.

In the office there were car parts and stacks of pillows. There was an old desk covered with grease and clutter. There were piles of semi-clean sheets and an even larger pile of very dirty sheets back behind the desk, which was also covered with clutter and dirt.

"This is an auto repair hotel!" I said, immediately walking out of the office and towards Mabel.

The storm was closing in quickly now. The temperature had dropped and the edge of the ominous black clouds had reached the little motel. The wind was picking up. It wasn't looking good.

"No way!" I said.

"Yes! No way!" Mabel repeated, astounded.

I had two options. The fairground with the possibility of setting up a tent in the middle of a bad storm or back to Mullen in hopes that the Sandhill Motel would have a room. I called.

"Hi! Do you guys happen to have a room available?"

There was a pause.

"Yes. You're lucky because usually we're booked. A guy cancelled, and there's a lot of construction crews staying here. But we have a room with two queen beds."

"I'll take it!"

I got back on Mabel and made a beeline, backtracking about forty miles to Mullen. I wasn't happy about it, but the idea of setting up a tent in this storm was something I liked much less. I was now speeding down a beautiful road with a large, mean storm on my tail. I was doing…well, I was going fast, hoping to beat the rain.

5.4

Finally in Mullen with the storm almost on top of the little motel, I stood as the clerk booked a large group of construction workers into their rooms. She was friendly and talkative and looked much too tired for her age. There were scars all over her arms and she had the kind of suntan that was common on people that spend long days outside. She thanked the workers as they walked out, and then turned to me.

"Hello there!" she started.

"Hi! I just called about a room."

"Oh yea. You called earlier today, didn't you?"

"No, that wasn't me. I did just call though and you said you had one."

"We do. You're lucky because we're usually booked by now. A guy cancelled earlier and there's a lot of construction crews that stay here. But we have a room. It's nice and clean…"

I stood patiently, thinking about the coming storm as the young girl typed away at the computer, continually telling her story. She looked overworked and underpaid but somehow had kept her cheery attitude. About then a young man came in.

"I got the fridges put in. Just in time too!"

"Great. Did you get the one put in room 115?"

They stood talking while she held the key to my room. They were so close, both the key and the storm. It was now dark and menacing outside and I heard rumbling thunder and watched as huge swaths of lightning lit up the entire western sky.

"OK. You're in room 118. I hope you like it! Please, please let me know if there's anything I can do. My husband and me are here. Right across the parking lot is our trailer."

Do you guys own the motel?" I asked, suddenly realizing that it was probably their own place.

"Yes. We bought a few years ago. It's been a lot of work but we're finally getting it where we want it. We've done a lot of work on it but there's still a lot to be done. It's clean though. Don't worry about that!"

"I'm not worried at all. Thanks!"

She was explaining their hopes and wishes for their new business adventure to me as she handed me the key. Finally, I rode over to the room, unpacked my gear and then went back outside. The skies were black split by bright flashes of lightning every thirty seconds or so, but still no more than a few drops of rain. I rode to the nearby gas station, filled up and bought a four-pack of beer. Pulling a chair outside the room I enjoyed my makeshift dinner of Guiness and chips. Guys in work clothes were standing around talking, going to and from each other's rooms and visiting. I watched as the little motel came to life; storm be damned. A tall fellow stood talking to the young lady, beer in hand, while the young man installed the new refrigerator in the room.

"Let me know if there's any problems."

"It'll be fine!" the tall, friendly worker answered.

The young lady walked over to me.

"I hope the room is good?"

"It's great! Thanks."

The young man stood talking to a tall worker who had evidently stayed at the place a few times. When they walked off, he came over to my room.

"They're nice kids! They work hard. This is pretty nice hotel."

"I agree." I said, offering him a beer.

"No thanks. We've got two coolers of beer in the truck. We're climbing poles around here."

"Poles?" I repeated, a little confused.

"Yea. Telephone poles. It's going to be quite the storm tonight, though!"

"I think so, but we'll see."

"Yea, we'll see." He agreed, looking up at a dark sky somehow becoming ever darker.

That night it was "quite the storm". Thunder and lightning came in loud, boisterous spurts, and rain washed dirt down the gravel parking lot creating a gullies. I checked on Mabel later night to make sure she hadn't fallen over. She was weathering the heavy rains with patience. Everything good, I went back to bed. The next morning the whole parking lot was empty and silent. I was the last guest there and it was only 7am. The young girl came walking by with a cup of coffee as I sat outside the room making my own coffee with my camp stove.

"Strong coffee! I love strong coffee. It's hard to get around here, but we try."

I smiled, understanding.

"I don't know what I'd do without my morning coffee." I answered.

"Well, be careful out there!"

"I will. I really enjoyed my stay here."

"Thanks!" she smiled, "that means a lot. We work hard."

"I'll bet you do!"

I said goodbye to the little motel and headed west. It was cool and both Mabel and I were enjoying that, and the fact that it wasn't raining. We headed to Alliance with plans to turn north towards Sturgis. As pretty as they could be Nebraska's straight roads were wearing thin and I was ready to find some mountains and twisties. Turning north at Alliance I started noticing more and more Harleys. By the time I got to Windy Cave National Park the greying bikers were everywhere on every imaginable kind of cruiser. The park was a beautiful little park that offered some nice meandering roads through what was slowly becoming more mountainous scenery. Rock formations started taking over the miles and miles of prairie and cattle that I had been riding through. I had started the day off riding on a sunny but cool day and as I climbed in altitude it began cooling off even more. I was planning on hunting down some camping around Custer South Dakota but the closer I got to Sturgis the more I started wondering if that would be possible. What had started as a few greying Harley riders became larger and larger groups and then processions of surly looking old guys on gleaming cruisers with grimaces on their faces. In Custer there were hundreds of Harleys parked all along the road with leather-clad, "tough guys" walking around.

Usually when a motorcyclist passed another there was a congenial wave of understanding or just friendliness. Any motorcyclist knew that riding a two-wheeled fun machine was, at the end of the day, taking your life in your own hands and "the wave" was a nice way of letting each other know that our craziness was not just our own. However, those waves of understanding had long since turned to gruff looks of "I'm a badass" and "look at me". I grinned slightly in my helmet at the idea. Mabel just ignored them.

"The bikes aren't that way." She assured me.

I passed dozens of interesting types of motels from tee-pees to two-person log cabins that lined the road, all of which were packed with Harley Davidsons. I was still over an hour away from Sturgis and was now getting a little concerned about finding any place to stay, camping or otherwise. I took my time though, riding in the Black Forest mountains on beautifully technical roads and trying not to pay attention to my technique, enjoying riding carefree. However, traffic became slow, the roads becoming stuffed with gleaming cruisers. They were like large, loud flies at this point. After an hour or so of goofing around, albeit slowly, on twisties, I decided that if camping was in my future I'd better find a place, and fast. They had promised rain that night but I was going to try to battle it out in my new tent.

The closer I got to Sturgis the more packed it became with loud, shiny Harley cruisers. I rode up a rough, dirt road to consider stealth camping but found a 4x4 jeep with a couple and tent already set up. A few more tries up rough dirt roads with no luck other than rocks and forested hills, and I remembered a fancy campground that I had passed a few miles back and decided that it would be my best bet. I turned around and gave it a shot. Parking, I walked in.

"Hello. I'm hoping you have a spot somewhere for me throw a tent up."

"Oh yea. We do. They're $36"

I cringed at the price for a tent site, but smiled. It was after 3:30 pm and my options were quickly narrowing and he knew it. We both could hear the hundreds and hundreds of bikes cruising up and down the mountain road, their big V-twins echoing throughout the hills.

"That's fine." I said, trying to hide my dismay.

The portly old man rummaged around for some paperwork, disinterestedly, and pulled out some forms. I had cash on the counter. He swept it aside and had me sign a few things and directed me to site#4.

"It's nice. You'll like it." He promised.

The campsite was one of those extremely organized and well-kept sites that families with large trucks pulling even larger trailers frequented. The tent sites were empty except for a few. The place was big though, stretching out into the hills. I pulled up to #4. It was a huge grassy knoll with a picnic table sitting under an enormous tree. It was basically an open space in the middle of the campground. I set up and made coffee. Reading my book and watching as vehicles trickled into the place I sat and listened to the sound of big, V twin motors. An old, beat-up Dodge truck pulled in followed by a three-wheeled vehicle called a Slingshot. Riding it was a long-haired, full-bearded guy with a leather vest. They pulled into the spot just across the perfectly graded gravel road from my site. He was pulling a larger camp trailer behind the car-bike. As the man unhooked the small travel trailer from the bike and started setting up, the lady, who was driving the truck, went walking with a small, nervous looking little dog. I met her as she walked by.

"Hi. Is your dog friendly? I have a few at home that I'm missing."

"Oh yes!" she answered. "This is her first time out. She's a 'house' dog."

I thought about that statement and bent over to pet the little, curious dog. She looked to be an older dog.

"How old is she?"

"She's about 4 years old."

I stood up to say hello to the lady and noticed a big Hell's Angels tattoo covering one side of her face. We talked for a while and she went back to the site. I sat watching them set up their equipment. They had a second bike in the bed of the truck that they carefully backed out. It was quite the show to watch them set up the little camper, though. In doing so, they tipped the thing over once or twice, eliciting a little scream and then some laughter out of both of them. Over the next hour or so more and more vehicles trickled in, a lot of them stopping at the campsite with the car-bike and the camp trailer. More tents went up and more bikes parked in the grass. One older man backed his truck onto the slight incline to back his bike off the trailer and came to talk.

"How are you doing? Travelling far?"

"I hope."

"Going to Sturgis?"

"I might ride through just to see the circus. I've never been."

"It *is* a circus. I'll tell you that much. I drove in from Michigan."

"Wow! I'm assuming all of you guys are going to Sturgis?"

"Who us?!" he chuckled. "No. At least I'm not. No, we're a group of friends who have met here at that camp site for the past eleven years. We just spend the week together and ride around the hills. It's beautiful riding."

"I saw that today!" I added. "So, no Sturgis?"

"No. I'm done with that shit. I'm too old. Let the younger crowd have it."

I hadn't seen many of the "younger crowd" he alluded to, but I didn't say anything.

"We'll hang out here and drink some beer. They're a bunch of nice people. Well, I better move my truck out of the road before someone gets pissed off."

That evening the campsite had filled up with RV's and motorcyclists. There was a big family from Colorado camped at the site next to me. It was about thirty yards away but there were a lot of kids which made for a noisy evening. I walked over to the now burgeoning campsite of tents, cars and bikes across from me to say goodbye. The old man had a crowd and was telling a story so I waited. He looked up and stopped.

"I just wanted to say 'have fun'. I'm leaving early in the morning and didn't know if I'd see you guys."

"Thanks." The old man started. "I was in the middle of a story."

The lady stood up and said goodbye.

I apologized and walked off.

5.5

The next day started fine but...

The rain had started around 8pm the night before, driving everyone inside. I hunkered down with my eBook and listened to the rain tap dance on my tent. I hadn't worried because I had recently replaced my twelve-year old tent with this one. It was just one year old, and the same brand. It kept raining until midnight. As I lay there enjoying the book and the cool night, I thought a felt a drop. Then another. At first, I dismissed it. The tent was one year old after all. But then another and another. I spent the next hour or so in psychological turmoil until I finally gave up and draped my raincoat over my sleeping bag. I was furious and kept waking up every two hours thinking I'd felt another drop. At 5:30 I just pulled myself out of my sleeping bag and purveyed the damage. It wasn't bad but the tent was damp inside and out. I made coffee in the damp, blue morning and immediately started packing. I drank coffee and packed the sopping, failed tent into its bag. I was disgusted. Everything felt heavy. Soon people started waking up as I finished up packing the panniers. I put the last of the cases on the back of Mabel and suddenly she started tilting over. It was a slow nightmare as I watched her drop. There was nothing I could do but watch as she crunched to the ground. I heard gasps from people walking by going to the showers and they stopped.

"You need help?"

"Is there anything I can do?!"

About that time a guy from the big campsite came over and asked the same thing.

"I really appreciate it, but no. She's pretty light if I get the panniers off."

I walked around and grabbed the handlebars and the pannier carriers and lifted the bike up.

"Man, I couldn't have done that with my Harley."

I smiled.

"No. But Mab…this bike is quite a bit lighter than your Harley."

"Sorry!"

"No. Thanks for coming over! I really appreciate it!"

I surveyed the damage. The right front blinker had been demolished.

"Well, last year it was the left…" I thought to myself.

"Maybe you can get a matching one this time?" Mabel commented.

At that moment I had had it with my inexplicable attitude and my bizarre inability to make decisions. And I had had it with the rain. For almost a week I had ridden in rain every day. But I was determined to make to Sturgis to see the circus and then was planning to ride to Theodore Roosevelt National Park in North Dakota. I picked up the chunks of plastic, those that I could find, and threw them in the tank bag. Mabel started right up though and soon I was on silent and empty but wet twisties through the southern Black Hills of South Dakota heading towards Deadwood. In a past life, I toured as a musician, spending way too many days on the road and Deadwood was one of our regular stops. By the time I rolled into Deadwood loud V-twins had taken over the place. I stopped at my old stomping grounds to get a picture with Mabel but was shoed away by the parking police. They wouldn't even take a picture of me, much less let me take a picture of the tavern. I gave up and headed north. On the way I was almost run off the road by a cruiser not watching what he was doing. The road from Deadwood to Sturgis was crammed with cruisers, mostly Harleys, with riders varying in degrees of expertise and experience.

"You better be careful!" Mabel warned.

The closer I got to Sturgis the more crowded the roads were until I hit the outskirts of the little town. I was needing gas and so I pulled into the least busy gas station I could find. It still had twenty or thirty bikes mulling around though. I saw a free pump and started towards it but was hurriedly cut off by an old guy on an even older Softail. He had a long beard and overalls. He saw me.

"Go ahead." He motioned.

So, I did.

"This place is nuts." I said while filling Mabel's tank.

"Yea," he answered, "it can get pretty crazy. It used to not be this big but for the past twenty years or so it's gotten out of hand."

"I would say so. Where's the main drag?"

"You've never been?"

"No, and I'm just passing through now."

"It's straight ahead."

He then went on a jag about how so many are now trailering their bikes in and "acting tough" like "they'd just come off the road."

"Yea..." I smiled, not really caring one way or the other.

I finished pumping gas and made my way to the center of the circus. The day I arrived was the first day of the week-long rally but already the streets were teeming with middle-aged men and their wives all wearing black leather vests and waving around cellphones. There were booths and bars with scantily dressed women and bored looking men. There was every sort of motorcycle service imaginable and even more add-on gadget and chrome accessory shops offering every piece of un-needed motorcycle hardware ever made. I crawled behind hundreds of Harleys and stared at consumerism-gone-wild. I hadn't had breakfast and so I parked at the end of a lesser busy street to get a burrito at a place called Pop's Donuts.

The people were nice and the burrito was good, but way over-priced to the point of being ridiculous. The coffee alone was $5 for a Styrofoam cup of Folgers (I saw the can of coffee under the machine). But it was Sturgis. Finishing my burrito I decided to ride around a little and take in the sights. I found out that doing so in Sturgis was a slow process during the rally, even on the first day. Following the parade of Harleys, I watched as bored faces in booths stared down at cellphones and bikini-clad young girls gyrated to no one in particular as loud, classic rock blared. They would presumably do this for the whole week. The place had a very fake vibe about it, but it almost seemed to know it and didn't care. Everywhere were big, shiny Harleys with glum looking "tough guys" tilting back their heads and hanging on to their ape-hangers. I had had enough and made my way back to Mabel. As I was putting on my helmet I heard a voice.

"Hey! You're an adventure rider? I'm looking for some good riding pants…"

I turned around. I had never been called an "adventure rider", and tried my best to give the stranger the help he was needing.

"Are you staying here the whole week?" I asked.

"No! Just a few days. We got a tent in a guy's backyard not far from here. Me and couple of friends come here every year."

"Well, good luck and have fun!"

"You too. Be careful out there!"

I needed to try to fix the hanging and shattered blinker while I was in town. The light itself still worked so there was that. I had epoxy and duct tape but I needed super glue and so I was off to the hardware store that I'd passed on the outskirts of town. Right off the bat I found the backway in order to escape the insane traffic through downtown. Riding past houses with six or more tents set up in their front and back yards I dodged cars and other motorcyclists. After buying some super glue I stood in the parking lot and searched for the nearest park in town and found one. Riding to the park I again took the back way and noticed even more houses with signs out front: "Camp Here!". There were people who had set up tents on the side of the road and chairs on the curb, sitting and watching as the sea of motorcycles rolled by. Finding the park outside of town I stopped under a tree and started trying to repair the light. Using the super glue I glued each broke piece together one at a time and then wrapped the whole mess in electrical tape that I kept wrapped around a few wrenches under Mabel's seat. About an hour later it looked like…well it was fixed. While at the hardware store I had bought some water-proofing spray for my new, but leaky tent. It made me mad to think about it so I tried my best not to. While piecing the shattered turn signal together I had shed some of my warmer clothing. The afternoon was getting hot and humid, but by the time I had the light together it had begun raining again. I mounted my phone in its weather-proof pouch and then on the handlebar. It was almost dead so I plugged it in. I noticed that nothing happened. The phone wasn't charging. It was now pouring down buckets of rain.

"This is just fucking great!" I yelled in my helmet.

It had less than 5% battery so presumably it hadn't been charging for a while. I searched for an auto part store in town. They didn't have the plug-in, a USB charger I needed.

"For that kind of charger you'll probably have to go to a specialty store. Have you tried a motorcycle shop?"

"No, but that's a good idea. Is there one nearby?" I asked, instantly forgetting about the Sturgis rally, assuming I would have to walk the entire rally trying to find one booth with a specialized charger that wasn't chrome-plated.

"Closest one is down the highway in Spearfish."

"Thanks."

Outside the sky was black and grey, and emptying all the water in the world down on Sturgis. Making my way to the highway and fighting traffic and monsoon-type rain I saw the motorcycle dealer off the freeway. I walked in the shop, dripping wet, with my cable to see if I could test it.

"Sure!"

Finding an outlet and using my adapter, I found that it was dead.

"Do you have these cables?" I asked.

"No. We don't have those but they probably do down the road."

He gave me directions to the nearest superstore, which happened to be right across the highway. I rode in the pouring rain and bought a cable and tested it in the parking lot, in the pouring rain. The phone still didn't charge. A few profane words later I was back at the motorcycle shop where I bought a USB adapter for the phone that had LED lights to show the state of the battery. Out in the parking lot, again in the pouring rain, I tried it out. It started charging the phone and then quit while Mabel sat idling. A few more cuss words and I walked back in.

"You again?!" the salesman smiled, looking a little confused.

"Yea. I don't think this thing works. It charges for a little bit and then stops."

"Just a sec…"

He was helping a customer so I waited. Finished, he came over and I explained the "issue".

"Rev your motor up and see if it charges. The stator has to be charging the battery for it to charge the phone. It's a failsafe so you don't run down your battery."

"OH!! That's smar…" I started.

He smiled.

"Oh…son of a bitch! This thing's smarter than me!"

We both laughed.

Back outside in the rain I tested his claim. And it worked. Deciding to wait out the weather I went to find a coffee shop to plan my next move. The rain was now beating down on everything creating small rivers in the roads. It didn't seem to be letting up. By the time I found the coffee shop it was an utter cloudburst. The rainsuit was working great but Mabel, my feet and my hands were soaked. I parked Mabel at the curb in what seemed to be a river of water. It washed through her wheels as she sat there. I just shook my head.

"I'm really finished." I thought as I propped Mabel up on her center stand. She stayed silent.

In the coffee shop I ordered a double-shot Americano and ate pastry while silently raging at the weather. I searched weather patterns on my phone and checked out the several weather apps I had installed. They were all predicting three or four days of heavy rain in North and South Dakota, including Theodore Roosevelt National Park, my ultimate goal. The ten-day forecast had the storm circling around Montana and Idaho. On the weather app I couldn't even see the national park for the big, red glob that covered it.

"Jesus Christ!!" I yelled silently, making a nearby patron raise her head from her phone and look around.

I looked for routes through Montana. Rain, rain, and more rain. I fumed and ordered two more expressos and stared down at the map not knowing what to do. I was utterly defeated by the weather after running through hard rain for almost seven days. But it was more than that. It seemed like the universe was trying to tell me something. Maybe it wasn't time for my epic journey like the one I had planned on taking. There were some family things going on in my life. Not only that, but I felt like I was forcing the trip. I didn't feel like my place was here on the road. I loved travelling by motorcycle, but my mind seemed elsewhere. I spent the next hour pouring over the map and looking at weather and searching for alternative routes already knowing I had made up my mind. I noticed that it was sunny down in Colorado.

"That does it." I thought, "I'm done. South it is."

My epic journey to Montana and Oregon would have to wait.

5.6

The coffee had warmed me up but now it was time to fight the
rain all the way to Newcastle Wyoming, my next planned stop. I
held some hope, seeing the promise of blue skies west of me but at
this point that meant nothing. One thing I knew for sure: if I had
anything to do with it, the rest of the trip would be out of the rain.
Outside of Spearfish I turned south on 585, a beautiful little road
that led to 85 south. 85 was beautiful as well but straight. Luckily
the wet weather seemed to subside the more and more south I rode.
Watching as the landscape changed from dark grey to green and
yellow with dark blue clouds hanging over me, I pushed towards
the purplish-white sky ahead with hope building little by little. It felt
great to feel the wetness slowly start evaporating in the wind. I even
stopped and shed my rain suit. I made good time on good road and
was soon in Newcastle. Now the hunt was on to find a room and a
place to waterproof my tent. Newcastle was a busy little hub and
there were still a few Harleys here and there but I had left the
majority of V-twin noise behind me. The downtown was a small,
brick road with a few restaurants where a big group of leather-clad
people heading to Sturgis had stopped and were eating. I kept those
places in mind while I searched for a motel. On a fluke I found a
quaint place tucked back in the hills among what seemed to be
suburbs. It was a tiny motel nestled in a small forested suburb of
50's style ranch houses. When I walked in the room it immediately
reminded me of my grandmother's house. Not only that but it was
cheap and it was quiet. And most importantly it was dry. Outside, I
laid my tent in the grass to let it dry out as it was soaked from the
night before. Afterward, a ride to the little downtown for dinner
and then to pick up beer. At the little liquor store there were plenty
of local brews to choose from. I chose an IPA and made my way
back to the motel. As I turned in the parking lot I noticed about

five Harley's parked outside with all the riders still on them, most of them staring at their cellphones. I parked.

"How is this place?" one guy asked as I took off my helmet.

"I like it, but I just got here myself. The rooms are clean and it's quiet." I answered.

"You plan on camping out here?" another asked, noticing the tent laying in the grass.

"Well, I was but then I just broke down and paid for a room. I think it's full, though. At least that's what the guy said."

"We got reservations." was the answer.

A big Harley pulled in beside the tent laying in the grass. As they checked in and went to their respective rooms. I popped a beer open and took the tent and started setting it up in the parking lot, getting it ready to waterproof. A few minutes later the guy who parked beside the tent, a tall, grumpy looking guy, came out and stood by his big, blue bike and started staring at me. At first, I ignored him but he just stood there saying nothing.

"You want to borrow my tent?" I turned taking a sip of my beer.

He just looked at me and then walked to his room which happened to be right next to mine. After he left, I opened a second beer up and started spraying waterproofing all over the tent, something I had certainly not planned on having to do. I waited for an hour, sitting in a chair outside my room and when it was dry, I packed it up on Mabel. The grumpy guy didn't come back. That night I sat in my chair and watched as the Sturgis-pack (as I called them) sat out by the fire pit on the other side of the parking lot, pouring lighter fluid on wet wood and complaining about "subsidies going to alternative fuels…" Finishing my beer, I turned in. Around 1am I heard a loud slam of the door for the third time that night. It woke me up this time. The grumpy guy from earlier was evidently still grumpy. But I slept soundly after the door slamming stopped and woke up around 4am the next morning. The motel manager had already made coffee and had bagels, and had the cream cheese out. Impressed, I took a few bagels and drank about three cups of coffee as I stood thinking about my day and the grumpy guy slamming the door all night. I went back and finished packing Mabel and while I let her warm up I dummy-checked the room and slammed my door shut.

86 was straight and very scenic and so I let Mabel feel her oats a bit. I didn't see a single vehicle until I hit 26. Turning on 26 a battle with what had been a tail wind started. It whipped Mabel and I from side to side on the beautiful little road and in between eyeing corners I was watching as large, black storm clouds gathered on the horizon just south of me. I grimaced. 26 hit the highway and I stopped at a rest area for a break. As I was taking my helmet off a friendly, smiling guy came up and starting talking but not about anything in particular. The sort of thing that always made me nervous.

"Hey. This is a nice bike. Had it long?"

"I ride too. Great riding around here..." he continued.

It went on.

Mabel sat there filthy from weeks of rain and dirt roads. I started walking towards the restrooms and he followed.

"I like it." he continued.

"You ridin' far?" he asked.

"I don't know. Not far enough and too far?" I answered, continuing to walk towards the restrooms.

He laughed.

"Hey! We've got a booth over here. We're Christian bikers and we'd love to..." he started. There it was.

"That's nice, but I'm not interested." I cut him off.

"Oh...OK. That's fine. If you want, we've got some juice and snacks at the table. It's just right here." he pointed to a table set up in one of the covered picnic areas.

"Thanks." I left him and went to the rest room.

The friendly guy didn't accost me on my way out, which was surprising, and I shed my long underwear from under my riding pants, replacing them with shorts at another nearby covered picnic spot. Before long I was speeding down the highway. The gathering clouds had somehow disappeared and now it was a sunny day: blue skies and warm sunshine. I was glad about that but when I looked around, I found them, still gathering on the horizon. At the junction with 34 I headed southwest towards 287. The road was nice, fast and just a little curvy. Almost no traffic impeded us and it was very scenic. Things were looking up. When I hit Laramie, I turned onto 130 to head into a little wilderness, Medicine Bow National Forest. 130 was a little busy but the traffic had turned into RV's and off-road pickups, always a nice sign as it meant scenery and camping areas. Just before hitting Centennial, I turned onto 11. 11 really showed off. Mountains started and the road got technical with nice curves around mountainsides and high cliffs. There was a lot of tourist traffic but not so much as to slow us down. I leaned into the turns and enjoyed the slowly dropping temperatures as I gained altitude quickly. This was what I'd been looking for. After enjoying the wonderful mountain pass and making it to the peak, I turned around to explore a few of the whitish, gravel roads that had piqued my interest on the way up. Finding one that looked interesting I took a turn and found myself on a steep, twisty, and rocky road. I followed the road past a few rough looking and empty camp sites and continued until I hadn't seen one for some miles. The road dipped and started descending, hitting a small creek and then immediately ascending steeply again. Right at the peak of the rough little road was small camp site. It had a little fire circle and even some stacked wood. I stopped and sat in my little camp chair taking in the vast and empty mountainous forest that surrounded me. I had gone about twenty miles up the little dirt road and had enjoyed every foot of it. I started feeling a smile come across my face. I took a nap, woke up, and then laid back down in the tent after setting up camp. This was a spot that I was going to enjoy. Starting a fire and setting up my little camp I spent the evening staring into the orange crackling embers, the only sound I could hear.

The night was a bit rough. First the camp pillow went flat and then around 3am the wolves started howling. There were a lot of them, some of them sounded like they were pretty close. One howl and then another and then a group howl. I had camped in wilderness areas a lot and typically wasn't worried, but I unzipped my sleeping bag just enough to grab my camping knife that I always took with me in the tent…just in case. Then the cackling cacophony of coyotes started. It sounded like they were just outside the tent and I continued laying there waiting to hear footsteps. None came. I went back to sleep eventually waking up around 5:30. I stuck my head out of the sleeping bag and decided it was too cold, and slept until 6:30. It was still cold when I crawled out of the sleeping bag. After coffee and some instant oatmeal, I headed to the creek a few miles down with my water jug, filter, and my pillow. Dunking the pillow into the water looking for bubbles, I couldn't find a leak and gave up. Back at the campsite I got the fire going from the embers, left over from that night. Another cup of coffee and the hammock came out. I crawled in and dozed off for a few more hours. Lunch was a bagel with a tomato I had left over, and then back in the tent because of thunder.

"Fucking rain again!" I mumbled, zipping the tent up.

About a ½ hour later I realized it was not going to rain and crawled back out. There were blue skies and I realized that it had been a typical afternoon mountain shower just south of me, in Colorado. I stared at the tent and then at the skies.

"I wonder if it's going to be tested tonight?" I thought to myself, "I hope not."

I wrote in my journal:

"As I sit here somewhere in Medicine Bow National Forest off a dirt road called Little French Creek at a near perfect camp spot after enjoying an afternoon of superb riding I watched as rain clouds gathered south of me. It's quiet here, peaceful but for the occasional 4-wheel drive vehicle or dune buggy that passes by. I have the newly waterproofed tent set up. Today I took a lonesome highway through Ester Wyoming and into Medicine Bow up to Medicine Bow peak at 10,120 feet. Everything reminds me of Colorado and I will have to admit to shedding a tear in my helmet as I rode."

After my session with self-pity, I decided it was time for a ride. Unloading Mabel, I hopped on and took off. I careened down a little side road which led me up and around curves letting Mabel's rear wheel "play" a little. It curved around the edge of the mountain and gained altitude pretty steeply. Little camp spots started appearing, and looking around, the entire national park seemed visible. For the first time in days, I felt alive. My body and my mind started to wake up out a fog and shed the drudgery that this trip had become. Everything had a familiar pine scent that when I smelled it, I realized that I'd missed it. I started feeling the heaviness go away.

"I'm where I belong. In this wilderness watching rain clouds roll in." I said, smiling and letting Mabel do a controlled slide around a slight corner.

Mabel and I headed off down another rocky road in search of more adventure. Finding a few dirt road off-shoots that turned into double-tracks and then into gnarly single tracks we went as far as we could before being forced to turn around.

"I'm not a dirt bike!" Mabel complained.

As we bounced around on the rough trails through the dry mountain forest I started feeling more and more alive. Back at the camp I took my water filtration pump and rode down to the creek to fill my water jug up.

"I'm going to be eating camp meals for the next few days." I thought to myself.

Back at the camp I pulled out my food supplies. A few cans of beans, oatmeal, four cans of beer, a tomato, two bagels, a dried camp meal, some par-boiled rice, some cheese crackers, and of course, coffee. Perfect. I had the dried camp meal for lunch. For the rest of the afternoon, I sat in my little camp chair in front of the perfect campfire and watched the sun settle behind the mountain forests until it got chilly. I had only seen two cars come by the whole day. I noticed rain again, on the horizon just south of me but now didn't care. More hammock time then beer. I gathered some firewood and stacked it next to the fire ring. I did my daily reading, wrote in my journal, sat in my chair next to the fire, made a simple dinner of rice with tomatoes. I packed the hammock up and sat in my chair staring into the camp fire as the sun went down. I finished off the beers and waited for the cold and the dark to set in. The fire died down and I let the embers fade before covering the whole thing with dirt. Then lazily walked to the tent for another cold, wonderful night.

Life was good. Life was simple.

5.7

The morning came and I was up early. It was cold but my old sleeping bag had held its own against the crisp, mountain coolness again; on the verge of giving up, but stubbornly doing its job nevertheless. Up. Coffee. Packed. The ritual was set. The sunrise was beautiful and moving the chair out to the road gave me a better view of the rays crisscrossing the mountainous forest that surrounded me, and it let me sit in the sun. The first rays of morning sunshine hit the campsite about an hour later making the dew that covered Mabel glisten. Looking down at the long, winding dirt road below me I decided to follow it off the mountain to see where it would dump me out. Mabel had gas and so why not. It didn't disappoint. It followed the foothills of the mountain range for about forty miles and linked down into another dirt road where a primitive camp ground was located with several dozen spots, all open. On a secondary road we ran across free range cattle and pronghorns, watching as large eagles looked for prey on the prairies. Thirty or so miles later the dirt road widened and became well-graded. We were going through ranchland now passing over cattle grates regularly. About 1 ½ hours later we reached Encampment, a town that looked somehow like its name: barren and simple. We rode through Ryans Park, Riverside, and Savery until we hit the first paved road for over a hundred miles, in Dixon. We were on the Colorado border now. It had been a great scenic ride through Wyoming's beautiful countryside on dirt roads. A few miles before

Craig I looked up and saw...rain clouds; dark and heavy. Mabel and I stopped and I donned my rain suit. When we entered Craig it started downpouring. So much so I had to find a car wash to hide under while I waited for the rain and small hail to subside.

"This is getting really tiring!" I said to myself.

"You're on a motorcycle! What do you have to complain about?!" Mabel reminded me.

"You're right, and the forecast promises sun in Colorado!"

I searched around Craig for a diner, for a cup of coffee and a quick lunch, but there was nothing. It was a hub for oil and fracking trucks as well as construction workers of all ilk. They had no time for the likes of me or evidently coffee shops either. I finally gave up and rode back to the gas station where I had gotten gas earlier. While I sat out on the gas station patio it started raining again while I munched on my "diner" breakfast of coffee, pepperjack cheese and a cheap, old strudel. Finishing my fine cuisine, I waited the rain out, drinking coffee and pouring over maps. I looked east and the rain clouds were starting to head north now.

"I can beat them."

"Like you have the whole trip?" Mabel teased me.

40 was a good road, straight but it was Colorado. I considered taking the long way into Steamboat via 27 but was planning to try to get a hotel room in Steamboat proper and that could be tricky, as it was a heavily touristed town. Helle and I had taken long weekends in Steamboat, snow-shoeing, and we had eaten at Wynona's Diner and I wanted to try it out again. I had plans of going back and getting one of their scrumptious breakfasts the next day. There was camping around Steamboat but there were also a great deal of dark clouds lingering, and my tent had not been tested

since I water-proofed it. I didn't trust it anymore. I got the last available room at the Nordic Lodge and parked Mabel right next to my room, taking all my panniers up, unloading them, and then taking off for some riding in the mountains on a nearby loop: 27 to 131 and 134, and then back. I zoomed into and out of tight turns and leaned Mabel hard into the inside line of the road. She came alive without all the baggage, light and nimble. This was living! I went up Gore Pass and down again. Instead of doing the entire loop and riding the straight line from Hayden to Steamboat I turned around and took some dirt roads that led into mining territory, looping around back to 131. I took the whole ride again going the other way. Even the weather was accommodating. It was Colorado beautiful. I was getting used to the smile on my face again.

After stopping in Steamboat for groceries I rode back to the room to get ready to go out, find some local beer and even a burger! I was basically a vegetarian, but not tonight. My parking spot was still open and as I was parking Mabel a voice called me from above.

"Your bike?" a man, obviously from the Midwest, called down.

"As far as I know." I answered.

"That's my car right next to you. I ride. Let me come down."

"OK!"

He came down and shook my hand all the time eyeing Mabel just as all motorcyclists did when they met a new bike.

"Adventure rider, eh?"

"Well…"

"How's she do?"

"Oh, Mab…it's great! Handles well. Really light and basically trouble-free. I can't ask for more. I love her…uh it."

"Oh, by the way. I didn't back that in." he said, pointing to a tiny travel trailer hooked up to the small SUV parked next to me.

"I took er' off and pushed it. I'd like to say I did back er' in, but…"

"Well, I don't think you should have said anything. I was impressed"

He laughed.

We talked bikes and touring, and Sturgis. His wife, on the phone with her daughter, came over after hanging up.

"Hi! Sorry. Kids. He didn't back that in." she added, smiling.

"Well, he should have!" I kidded, grinning at him.

On my way up to my room I was behind an old couple slowly climbing the stairs. They moved over to let me by.

"I'm in no hurry. The party doesn't start til' 10 pm."

"Oh?" the lady turned and looked at me, noticing the motorcycle gear.

Her husband smiled.

"Are we invited?" he asked.

"Sure! There'll be women and lots of beer. I have a lot of motorcycle friends coming over. I hope you don't mind."

The lady said nothing, but turned and kept walking.

"No. Not at all. Women you say?" the old man grinned.

At the landing I stopped and unlocked the door to my room, right next to theirs. The woman glanced at me and walked into their room.

"10 o'clock!?" the old man asked again, smiling.

I smiled back.

"No, no. I'll be in bed by 10. I'm pretty boring."

"Oh? Well, I was looking forward to a party!" the old man said.

5.8

It was just as I remembered. Being early the streets were empty of wandering tourists and the little diner, Wynona's, had three or four locals in it. Ordering sweet potato hash and fried eggs, every fork full took me back to my times years ago, when we had lived in Colorado. I fell into a conversation with a couple of local guys that were eyeing Mabel parked outside. The usual questions and information about motorcycle touring and then we started talking about Steamboat.

"It's really changed since I've been gone. About ten years now!" I said, sipping on a newly refilled cup of coffee.

"Yea. It has gotten bigger. I think there's more tourists then even before." Todd answered.

"It used to be kind of a cool little town. Everyone knew everybody else, except for the tourists of course." he added.

"Now all of those condominiums are going up…" Steve said, almost rolling his eyes.

"and hotels…" Todd added.

"Yea, those too." Steve concurred.

The conversation was typical. Everywhere I had travelled there seemed to be construction in most towns. At least, towns that were close to cities or had something special to offer, like Steamboat.

"Well, it's not just Steamboat. It's everywhere." I assured them.

"I'll bet!"

"There's just too many people in general, I think."

"I would agree." I said, sipping my coffee.

We touched on politics and social issues, Colorado and the dreams that they had.

"I'd love to tour some. What would a bike like that run you, if you don't mind me asking?"

"Not as much as you might think. You can tour with what you've got, if you've got one. I like the Suzuki because you can find parts if you go way out, and the V-Strom is about as reliable of a bike as you can get! If you already camp and have the equipment you've won half the battle. There's been guys that took off with a few thousand dollars in their pockets and toured for ten years straight. It all depends on what you want and what you want to give up."

After a great conversation we finished our coffee just as the first few tourists started wandering in.

"Good luck and be careful!" they both said, as I shook their hands and thanked them for the pleasant morning.

I headed out of Steamboat and enjoyed a beautiful meandering road, Highway 40, into Kremlin where I stopped for coffee again (of course). Heading north a few miles I took another small, beautiful road full of twisties to 131 and turned south. From there, I hit highway 70 in Wolcott and filled up with gas, and then headed south a few miles not really knowing where I was at. I was looking for a tiny road with no luck, 10A. Stopping I pulled out the map to try to find the little dirt road I had run across but couldn't find it. I used my satellite GPS to try to find it.

"According to the GPS it might be Cotton Pass Road, but I'm not sure." I said to Mabel.

I looked up and saw a sign: "To Cotton Pass Road".

"See what happens when you get out of your own head?!" Mabel chided.

The rough dirt road ascended quite a bit, twisting into high mountains not far off in the distance. I took it hoping for the best. The road started out half-paved and then turned to deep sand. A mile or so in it started ascending with sharp switchbacks. Broken pavement and dirt most of the way, it ascended sharply and peaked on Cottonwood Pass. It was the road I'd been looking for. From there it was the same, but descending until I hit Carbondale and Independence Pass, highway 82. I had driven it numerous times and had bicycled the beautiful but busy road as well, so decided to take a new route through part of Colorado that I hadn't seen much of. I followed 133 and ended up in Crawford, a tiny and interesting town made up of a single large building that had large, hand-painted signs on it that stated: "Hotel", "Showers", and "Feed Store". Across the street was a coffee shop that sold a few craft beers as well, and across from that was a bar and restaurant. I went in the hardware store.

"Is this where I can get a room?" I called out.

An older woman with long, grey hair was sitting in a small office with two small, fat dogs lounging on the floor next to her.

"Yes. Yes, it is." She answered, getting up and coming to the counter.

"What brings you to Crawford?" she asked.

"Well, I'm heading down to Blue Mesa Reservoir and then home to Texas."

"Can't get there going straight. You'll have to turn around and go back to 92. But I hope you'll stay here for a while. It's nice."

"I will if you have a room."

"I do. I've got a king-sized for $45."

"That's a bargain!"

"We think so. Right across the street there's a coffee shop and over there, behind the cemetery there's a bar that serves food too. Now, the rooms are just around the corner and up the stairs. I've got you in a nice one at the end." She assured me while tapping on her computer.

"Well thank you!"

I parked Mable around back and headed into the room with my top pannier and tank bag. The room was clean but dingy, smelling of mothballs and ammonia but it was immaculately kept, albeit old. The ancient lights were yellowing with age and the mattress had a wide trough in the center from years and years of people sleeping in the middle. I really liked the room. It was devoid of the corporate sterilization that we are all so used to. Typically, clean and shiny, but soulless and cold. I rode across the street to the coffee shop and got a double-americano and a cookie from a good-looking lady, the owner I later found out. Afterwards, I bought a cookie and a few beers to go.

"Oh! I didn't know that you had double IPA's!" I said, looking at one of the cans.

"I didn't either. Are they different than the ones that say IPA?"

"Yes. They have more alcohol for one thing."

"Oh, I didn't know that. I need to charge more for them then."

"How much do you want?"

"Oh. No, not for you. They're the same price. But now I know." She smiled.

Back at the hotel and laundromat I sat out back at one of the tables they had set up. spreading my cooking gear out to make dinner I fell into conversation with three people sitting and drinking beer at a nearby table. We introduced ourselves.

"Did you go to Sturgis?"

"I went through, but it's not for me."

"I don't blame you. I live up there and get away during the rally. I've got a V-Strom too."

"Oh, OK!" I said surprised.

Motorcycle talk ensued for a while.

"How do you guys know each other?" I asked.

"We've known each other since high school and owned a business together for years. This is my wife." He said, introducing the only woman at the table.

"Hi."

"We moved apart about fifteen years ago and have been getting together every year since for vacation."

"That's very cool!"

"It sure smells good." The lady said, smiling.

"Just some veggies and tomato sauce."

"Did you know that Joe Cocker's grave is right in that cemetery over there?" she said, pointing to a forgotten looking graveyard across the road.

"I did not! How cool is that?! Where's his gravestone?"

"Well, we don't know but we're going to go look for it before we leave."

About that time a couple walking a boxer came by and talked to the threesome. They sounded German but I later found out they were from Denmark, a country I'd lived in for a while. I caught up with them later and had a conversation in Danish.

"Yes," the man started, "We love Colorado but our visas have run out and we have to go back. We're on our way now and decided to do one last trip."

"Are you taking the dog?"

"Oh yes!" the lady answered.

"I wish we didn't have to go back."

"I understand." I answered, "I lived in the Denver area and regret leaving it."

"Yes. It is beautiful."

The couple and their friend excused themselves and headed for the nearby bar for dinner. The Danes retreated to their room. As I sat eating and drinking one of my beers the hotel began to fill up a bit. I wrote in my journal when I finished eating.

"In a few days I'll be home; a month-long trip cut short but it just feels right to go back right now. Sometimes time is not what we need and this is one of those times. I'll do my epic trip, but just not now. I just feel like I'm needed elsewhere. It'll be a good few days of riding, but it will be good to get back too."

I glanced up the hill behind the hotel looking for the bored dog that was incessantly barking, and saw numerous trashy looking trailer homes dotting the hillside. Then I heard gunfire in the distance.

"Rednecks and stupidity." I thought, "Well, they may be hunting?"

I thought about the people trying to make Crawford something. They had to deal with the usual suspects that made such progress difficult. I spied the owner's husband walking some dogs and walked over.

"You've got a nice place here!"

"Thanks! We've tried to make it nice. It sure wasn't nice when we got it. I do what I can. Linda's the business head. I'm just the brute strength."

"Well, you guys have really done a good job."

I looked down at his odd menagerie of dogs.

"I miss my dogs, but I'll see them soon." I said, bending down and petting his pooches. One stayed back.

"Yea. These were all strays from up the hill there. Him here, it took a few weeks before I could get him to come. He still won't sleep inside, but he doesn't run away and he always gets offered the chance to come in at night."

"He knows a good thing…" I started.

"I suppose. These others were just strays. I tend to attract strays." He grinned.

I smiled at the implication.

"I guess you're just lucky that way."

"I guess so." he answered, stooping down to pet his fur-babies.

That night I slept great, right in the middle of the mattress. I was up around 4:30 and sat outside after packing Mabel reading a bit. I waited for the coffee shop to open up. It opened up at 5am and had breakfast burritos ready. I guess I was just lucky that way.

There was no denying it: Colorado was great motorcycling country and I decided to check out areas that I'd not been before, the southwest San Juan Mountains. The day started out in the beautiful Curencanti Needles area and then through the Blue Mesa Reservoir. There was very little traffic and blue skies; cold and sunny, a Colorado specialty. Hurtling through the switchbacks I slowed as I saw rabbits scurrying across the road and down into gulches that looked like steep cliffs. A black bear made an appearance. We both stopped for a minute taking a gander at each other. At the end of the twisty, turny, and beautiful Hwy 92 we were spit out on the "the lonesome highway", highway 50, and turned towards Gunnison. We eventually turned on a tiny road, 140 and meandered around soft curves and burmed corners. Colorado was showing off.

About forty miles up the ascending road we hit a strange little town called Lake City. It was a strange mix of four-wheelers, cabins and pickup trucks. It was almost surreal in a way. There were gun and hunting shops beside coffee and hippy shops, restaurants and diners, jacked-up pickups and little four-wheelers with American flags all over the place. I was almost afraid I had entered the twilight zone or a cult of some sort. The road out of Lake City took us over the Slumgullion mountain peak at 11,361 ft dipping, twisting and circumventing ledges and drop-offs with no rails. Mabel and I leaned into the corners with big smiles on our faces. It then dipped into a valley to climb again through the Spring Creek mountains. We were riding high elevation, 10,960 ft. At those altitudes and at this early point in the day things got cold but it didn't matter to us. This was a beautiful road with no traffic. I loved feeling Mabel's weight shift effortlessly as we swung around corners. I heard the foot peg scrape a little around a particularly sharp curve and chuckled a little. We hit South Fork and turned east on 160 towards Alamosa. 160 was a dizzyingly straight road, but fast. It was interesting watching the Colorado landscape slowly change from mountainous forests to prairies and then to desert. Colorado was also typical for having some of the most beautiful landscape and some of the ugliest as well. Alamosa was a dry, dusty town full of fast food and cheap thrills; consumerism at its worst.

Mabel and I rode through the town, almost without looking, and blasted down 285 until we hit a tiny, lonely little road where we turned south-east and headed towards 159 into New Mexico, watching the landscape continually change. The road had been following the Rio Grande River and I spotted a turn-in and slowed to make the turn onto the sandy road. Parking Mabel I took my chair and kitchen and set up by the river, made coffee and watched as two men fished for trout. I fell asleep to the sounds of the shallow water running across the river rocks. Waking and lazily packing my gear, Mabel and I explored the area but found deep, sandy roads and steep, rocky grades. Giving up we turned around and pressed onward towards New Mexico. We passed burned out buildings, desolate poor ranches, starved towns, and hand-painted signs in Spanish. There had been signs of life at some point in the past, but no more. The heat was starting to zap my energy and I started thinking about camping. Having seen nothing for miles but little dirt roads, I turned on one hoping to find a little out of the way spot to sleep for the night. Most of the roads though, ended at ranch gates or fences. A few ended up in odd, out of the way suburbs of beat-up house trailers and burned-out cars. The last vestiges of the Rockies were poking out of the surrounding high desert as I kept looking for camping spots. But everything was either too open or fenced in. Passing the New Mexico border, I started getting a little desperate as it was almost dusk. I was getting too tired to ride, too hot for comfort, and too hungry to make rational decisions. I could have stopped at a diner or just to take a break, but was worried that I wouldn't get going again. My ass hurt by the time I hit Questa. I stopped at an abandoned building in town and considered pitching a tent just behind it. But upon closer inspection, I saw that it was in open view to the nearby houses. Looking on the map for possibilities I spied some campgrounds not far from Questa and took my chances. It was late and I was assuming most would be filled up.

The first spot was nothing more than a pullout with tables. Rocky, uninviting, and close to the road. A few younger people had taken the only usable spot.

"I'm not tired enough to sleep here." I thought to myself.

It was getting dark though and my tiredness was catching up quickly. I started thinking about riding into the night but decided against it when I rode by another campground and pulled in, not expecting much. There were spots to my surprise. I picked one, took the ticket hanging on the post and checked in. Supposedly, according to the sign out front, the camp receptionist would come by and collect the fee. I ate and made camp. After my dinner of instant rice and power bars I retreated to the tent and wrote in my journal before falling fast asleep not bothering to crawl into the sleeping bag. It was around 8:30 and I never saw the camp receptionist.

"Today was a day alone with Mabel. Lots of miles. We seem to be drawn to home. This was not the time for this trip. I am disappointed, rest assured, but I am not displeased. The future is not set in stone, but some things are more probable than others. And a thought:

'Evil is not always in those that kill, cheat or steal. Sometimes it is in the smile of a friend.'"

I didn't know where that last thought had come from.

5.9

The day's ride had been uneventful but the landscape had been interesting. As I meandered through the last twisties that I'd see on the trip, the Rockies themselves started petering out into the earth. The surrounding landscape changed gradually from magnificent mountains to small rock formations in a forested semi-desert. The temperatures had risen as well. The coolness, prevalent at higher altitudes, was gone and the heat was starting to build again. There was a warm, blustery gust starting up as well. I looked to my left at the disappearing Rockies and then to my right where there were the plains, flat and endless, spreading out over the horizon. The end of the mountains seemed to symbolize the end to my own trip. So, I bid farewell to the beautiful, twisty roads and settled in for straight shots through blustery and flat plains. I stopped in Clayton and rode into the little downtown area, looking for a local coffee shop which could often be found in small towns. And, I found it, a tiny coffee shop run by a husband and wife situated in a small train depot of sorts. It was well off the beaten path in the heart of the little town. Their daughter was behind the bar taking orders.

"I'll try an Americano with an extra shot and one of your breakfast burritos."

Upon finishing my coffee and the breakfast burrito a group of cheerleaders bounded in.

"Do you guys have a bathroom?" I asked the lady busily making coffee.

"Ours is broken," she answered, "but you can go across the street to the laundromat. It's clean. They don't mind."

And they were clean. The little immaculate laundry mat was for sale and for a split second I considered my life if I bought it. I was soon on my way to Texas.

The ride into Dalhart was straight and hot and a large grain silo greeted me. Dalhart was a dusty cow town that smelled like fish and dogfood. I rode slowly down business 87 and saw a bright and shiny new Holiday Inn built right beside a huge cattle feedlot, luckily devoid of cattle.

"Very apropos for some reason." I thought.

"You'd sleep there if you were tired enough. And have a steak!" Mabel chided.

"You're probably right." I thought, and rode past.

The further south I went the hotter it got. From Dumas we fought sidewinds that whipped us right into Amarillo. I wanted to find a brewery and drink some beer.

"Let's go out with a bang!" I thought, "Something a little luxurious. I'll treat myself."

I loved to camp but this was a celebration of sorts, at least that's what I'd decided. I stopped just outside of Amarillo, gassed Mabel up, and pulled my phone out. I searched out a brewpub in downtown Amarillo and what was a four-star hotel just across the street. It sounded perfect. When I reached downtown Amarillo, it wasn't what I was expecting. The downtown area was, well…a bit dead. That being said, the little shops and restaurants were really trying. There was a single street with a few empty restaurants and two hotels; the Marriot and an older one which in hindsight I should have stayed at. I chose the Marriot for no other reason than it was closer to the brewpub. Parking Mabel outside the entrance on the street, I walked in and stood behind a customer talking to a short, blonde lady working the front desk. I paid no attention and waited my turn while I froze in the ice-box-like foyer. It was the lobby of an obviously fancy, upscale hotel and I stood there with a dirty motorcycle jacket on and a dusty motorcycle pannier in my hand. I had over two weeks of stubble on my face and hadn't had a shower in a few days.

"Yessir. What can I do for you?!"

The lady greeted me curtly with sugary sweet fakery, served up with a toothy smile.

"I'd like a room at your *fine* establishment." I said, smiling.

"Well, they will be $150 dollars a night." She said primly and returned to her computer, almost expecting me to turn around a walk out. I thought about the exorbitant price.

"That's fine." I said, thinking about the celebratory goal and dismissing the cost.

She looked up, startled for a second.

"Ok…then."

She starting punching her computer keyboard with zeal.

"Email address?" she asked brusquely.

I gave her my email address. It was a bit long, I realized.

"Wha…you're going to have to spell that."

"g-o-w-a-n-p-e-r-s-p-…"

"Wait a minute. One second now."

I waited as she punched her poor keyboard even harder.

"OK. What was that?"

I spelled it again and stopped at p. She looked lost.

"You don't like my email address, do you?"

"No! I don't. I don't understand why it has to be so long!" she replied, obviously irritated and not smiling.

"I like to be difficult." I said, with a smirk.

I spelled it out again and she repeated it back to me quickly, but wrong. I dismissed it as unimportant.

"Are you going to park in the parking garage?" she asked, crossing her ring-bedazzled hands on the little desk and tilting her head a bit.

"I didn't know there was a parking garage. I'm parked on the street right now. Can I get back to you about that?"

"I guess…but you won't. There *is* a cost of $12 dollars. You could just go and park without telling me. There's no way for me to know, now is there!?"

"So, you think I'd do that?" I replied, a little surprised at her attitude.

"Well, yes!" She said with a short and expedient sound in her voice, "Most people would!"

"I would. Wouldn't you?"

I thought a second.

"I don't think you trust people much." I answered, starting to get a little irritated at what I considered an arrogant attitude.

"NO! I don't!" she answered and put her arms to her side. I noticed again that she had rings on four fingers of each of her hands. She had a pat look on her face, staring at me as if I was an alien out of Roswell.

"I don't know what 'most people' would do, but you're in the service business and I would think that you need to trust people a little or at least act like you do. I don't know if you're in the right…"

"I'm in the right business alright. People aren't trustworthy. No one is." She interrupted me, speaking quickly.

"Now I might agree with you, people are not always trustworthy, but I'm not in the service business. I think that you need to at least act like you trust people, even if you don't."

"I don't trust anyone. I *know* people. Believe me!" she said, self-assuredly.

"Well, if I decide to move my bike I *will* come and tell you."

"I'm *sure* you will." She answered snidely, returning her glare towards the computer screen.

She continued, instantly changing her attitude.

"There's the bar over there and they have food, cocktails and sex."

I stared at her waiting for a punchline but none came. She simply continued with the rest of her rehearsed message after pausing a second. I thought I must have misheard it and so said nothing.

While the lady was explaining the logistics and niceties of the hotel to me, a young man had come up and was waiting. I saw him again outside.

"Hey man." He began.

"Yes?" I turned around.

"I wouldn't park your bike out here. It's the hood around here!"

I looked around at an empty but clean street in Amarillo Texas. It was something, but it wasn't "the hood".

"Thanks for that. I'm not. I'm going to the parking garage."

"That'd be best." he said, and got into his pickup truck and drove off.

I rode Mabel around the corner and neatly parked her in the empty parking garage in one of at least twelve motorcycle spots. Afterwards, I walked through the hotel and back to the front desk.

"I'm parked in the parking garage." I told the woman as I passed her desk.

"Just charge my card?"

"I won't charge you." she replied.

"You do what you need to do. I just wanted to tell you."

It was a very nice, but freezing cold room. I took advantage of the luxury. Showered and changed, I walked over to the brewpub. It was empty as well except for six or seven wait staff standing around the kitchen. I sat down at a small table and waited but no one came. I waited some more. No one came. Right before I got up and left a friendly man came over, appearing from nowhere.

"Hey man! You want something to drink?"

I withheld my sarcastic comment. I was in a brewpub after all.

I ordered a flight of beers. He brought them and explained them one by one as I tasted each.

"They're brewed down the street." he offered.

"Oh. But there's brewing equipment here." I replied, a little confused.

"Yea. But the beer's *not* brewed here."

"OK."

"You want something to eat? We got good pizza."

Deciding to stick to the plan, and to be gluttonous, I ordered some fries and a small pizza.

"I will celebrate come hell or highwater." I thought.

The food came and I ordered a second Kolsch, the best of the bunch.

"Hey man… my friend owns the little bar across the street. They've got old video games and stuff. You might want to go check it out."

"I might do that."

I paid my bill and walked up and down the empty, silent street, ending up back at my room where I grabbed my journal.

"The hotel bar is as good as any." I thought.

In the bar, writing, I ordered a gin and tonic. I was on my second when the blonde lady came up again. She was all smiles now.

"You gonna get something to eat?" she asked in a bubbly, friendly voice.

"No."

5.10

I wrote in my journal.

"All endings are anti-climactic and this one was no different. The brewpub was mediocre, more of a basic bar with a few local beers than a brewpub. I'd ridden through the outskirts of Amarillo a few years previous and it had been booming with breweries and restaurants, but downtown there were just a few restaurants and bars hanging on for dear life. The hotel was fancy and Mabel got a parking garage. But this is not what life is. This stuff, these things, are a bubble; air-conditioned and comfortable, expensive and surrounded by people who don't care, don't trust and envy those that do. This sounds dark perhaps. But travelling out in the open, camping, exploring, enjoying coffee on a camp stove and cheese crackers for dinner is oddly…satisfying. It is fulfilling in that deep sense of the word. It makes all these niceties and sugary-sweet people seem vacuous and superfluous. It's always my goal however much I fail. The time spent with Mabel on the road, exploring the backcountry, the dirt roads, the twisty turns and mountains; the time spent pike-shunning, even when things don't work out the way we'd planned, even with the soaking rain, even with a leaky tent is substantial and life-affirming. There is more life in an hour of these times than a lifetime of entertainment in air-conditioned-at-the-cost-of-honesty

rooms. Somehow it all made the Holiday Inn next to the feedlot make perfect sense."

Tomorrow will no doubt be hot and straight. The trip will devolve into the sprawling cement metropolis of Dallas. There will be cars and crowds and consumerism gone awry. And yet I look forward to it because my wife and my dogs are there. I battle the fakery because of them. And I love travelling on a motorcycle. As someone probably once said:

"You have to do what you love."

Home is Where the Heart Is

I'd spent the night in Amarillo in a luxury hotel room full of beer and chips and pizza and somehow, I missed instant oatmeal and camp coffee. I'd meant to leave in the dark of the morning but ended up leaving as the heat rose, around 8am. It was still cool in the sense that Texas can be cool on an August morning. I'd drank several cups of cheap hotel coffee, well not that cheap, and used the freeway to speed my way out of Amarillo when I spotted the Black Bear Diner at a big truck stop. I'd passed it on a previous trip and it had looked interesting then as now. I had to find out if it was as good as it looked. It was. A huge stack of the fluffiest pancakes I'd ever seen and great service to boot. I stuffed myself. But I had home on my mind so I mounted Mabel and headed for 287 South, a pseudo-highway that would eventually dump me into Denton Texas, just outside of Dallas. The heat rose to Texas levels pretty quickly to the point that I stopped at one of the plentiful rest areas and changed into shorts and a light t-shirt under the motorcycle jacket and pants. A sidewind had been building up all morning and by the time I'd made it to Memphis, Memphis Texas that is, it was a full-on side gust. It was hot now and so I hydrated often, stopping at gas-stations and buying bottled water taking a break from being beat by the hot Texas gusts. I found myself buying gasoline two gallons at a time.

In no time I was in Wichita Falls. Since I'd been in Wichita Falls years ago it had grown into a miniature version of Dallas and I found myself on overpasses. By the time I reached Bowie, 285 was just another highway. I was now surrounded by dump trucks, cars and construction everywhere. Dallas was nearing, spreading out over the plains and turning everything it touched to cement and shopping malls, Midas-like. In Decatur the roads couldn't keep up with the traffic and I spent quite a bit of time in traffic jams. When traffic was moving there were loud, jacked-up pickups that roared down the road, and dirty, rumbling dump trucks that seemed like steel dinosaurs risen from some genetic experiment gone wrong. There was "progress" everywhere. By the time I was in Denton, a small college town that I'd lived in eons ago, I might as well have been in the city of Dallas. The feeling of being in Dallas was familiar, but Denton was not. It was no longer that sleepy little cool college town that I remembered. It was filled with too much, too many and had become too big too fast. Traffic on the freeway was typical. Adrenaline-soaked, attitude, and anger. I was back home. My trip had come to its end and I watched as the memories of it already began to fade into the noise and cement of the metropolis. Finally, I pulled into our driveway, worn out by the city, and texted Helle a smiley face. The garage door instantly opened and I was kissing my dogs and my wife, and instantly feeling the city wash away from me.

I had not visited all the states that I had intended but this was how these trips really were. Trying to find sunny weather after being rained on for days, I had followed my gut and they led me to where I went. The trip started out disappointingly, but that was really not a fair statement. My own attitude had had a lot to do with the feel of the trip. My own expectations created my reactions to the inevitable. Shit happens and you have to realize that before taking off. Mabel performed impeccably as usual, but I had not. I'd try to force something at a time when I knew I shouldn't, but was reminded that the universe had a tendency to nudge you if you would only listen. I hadn't listened.

This trip had taught me that every trip on a motorcycle could be an adventure because motorcycles tended to lead us to places that we might not otherwise go. I had ridden hundreds of miles of backcountry dirt roads, battled rain, rode twisties through mountains and witnessed the amazing western sky on early mornings. I had experienced surprises, smiles, anger, tears, frustration, peace, happiness, and excitement which would become fodder for stories told around campfires, around tables, and even in books. A motorcycle drives us to explore, to put away maps and phones and just ride. These things made trips great. If we could learn to leave ourselves room to just live, to catch some air and spread our motorcycle jackets out in the wind, to broaden our perspectives and push our boundaries ever so slightly we would be guaranteed a good trip no matter what. If done right, every trip was what it needed to be. And as I sat in my living room, amazed that I was back, I thought about my great trip. It was, at the end of the day, a great trip because it taught me these things, and I lived to learn another day.

An Addendum

Texas, Louisiana, Mississippi (A Vacation)

A few years ago, I got a call from my uncle. It was a call that I had never expected to get.

"Mark. I'm not riding my Harley anymore and was wondering if you'd be interested in taking it? I've always planned on giving it to you."

I was flabbergasted by this. It was his baby and I knew that. And now he was handing it off to me. It was more surprising given the fact that we had not kept in touch for the past twenty or so years. But I knew this was big. It meant a lot and so I hitched my carpentry trailer to the truck and headed to south Louisiana. Darlene, as I have come to call her, had been sitting in my uncle's garage for a number of years and it pained him to see her rotting away, a garage queen in waiting. I was happy to accept his generous offer and soon had her on the road again. She was a 97' Harley Davidson FXDL and over the next few years she became my daily rider for errands, short trips and just cruises around the city. Loud, obnoxious, and chromed-out, Darlene had attitude. She had moxy. And now it was time for me to get to know this loud and opinionated lady. I had always told my uncle that I would ride her back down to his place to let him say "hi" and the time had come for me to do just that.

I had five days to burn and decided to spend a vacation of sorts with Darlene. There would be no camping and a specific destination: my uncle's house. And it would be a chance for Darlene and I to get to know each other. I had done several repairs on her after getting her road-worthy and now there was just getting her ready for a multiple day ride. First things first, I performed every scheduled maintenance in the manual. But soon I was packed and heading out. No early start for us. Around 2pm we pulled out of the driveway and headed for Hwy 20. Darlene shined on the highway. Big and heavy, she held her own against the trucks and the cars. I leaned back against the backrest and listened to the loud and low grumble of her big motor. She was a sofa on wheels: comfortable and cushy but with the attitude of a big, Harley V-twin.

"I don't know what to expect from you." I thought while trying to get used to the loud monotone of her exhaust.

I did know one thing. Over the past few years, I felt like Darlene and I had hit it off and now I hoped that we were in for a long and relaxing trip where we could get to know each other.

"I hope I don't look like a grumpy, old man!" I thought to myself, smiling.

I spent the night in Shreveport in a non-descript motel, eating a non-descript motel breakfast. Darlene sat out in the parking lot and looked good doing it too. The next morning, I strapped my one piece of luggage on her and we were cruising once again. Just for fun, we dipped into some back roads and explored a little before circling into Monroe. There we took 82 north into Greenfield MS, a quaint little town that had one of the few bridges that crossed the mighty Mississippi river. From there we cruised back country roads down into Vicksburg MS where I stayed at the same dumpy motel that Helle and I had stayed at some years before. When I walked in, back from a quick dinner, the foyer was packed with a bus load of French tourists waiting for rooms in the lobby. I had to do some repairs on Darlene's heat-shields and grabbed a beer and stuffed it into my shirt. Soon I was laying out in the parking lot pulling a broken clamp off the exhaust shield when a man came up.

"Whatchya doin' to er'?" he asked.

"Oh," I got up, "I'm just getting these clamps out. I have to replace them."

"Well, I'm goin' to the Dollar store. Do you need something?"

I was surprised. A perfect stranger. But that's how it was with Darlene. She was an eye-catcher and strangers weren't opposed to stopping, staring and admiring her. People waved from their cars and rolled down their windows when we were at a light just so they could get a good listen to her low and loud thump.

"No thanks! I really appreciate it. I have the clap, I mean clamps." I smiled. He chuckled.

We talked a bit. He was a sailor on a freighter, waiting for his ship to come. He had a Harley that was going to wait for him at home.

I replaced one clamp and decided to wait until I got to my uncle's house to take the heat shield completely off to replace the other. I was in no hurry. This was the beauty of the trip, of Darlene. There was no hurry. Staying in motels was restful and relaxing. It was easy. Darlene seemed to be at home on the road and that made me feel relaxed. I simply followed suit. Comfort is costly though and not exciting in the sense that I liked. However, Darlene seemed pleased and that made me happy as well. It was nice to wake up a little late in a comfy bed and wander out to see Darlene sitting in the parking lot.

"Even standing still, you have an attitude." I thought.

From Vicksburg we followed 61 south. It was a nice and easy road that was scenic enough to make it interesting. The original plan was to follow the Natchez Trace from Tupelo, but after thinking about it I decided I wanted to ride it all the way from Nashville, which meant that it would have to wait. However, on 61 I saw a sign for the Trace and took it. I rode it the last forty or so miles into Natchez. As good on the highway as Darlene was, she really shined on the Natchez Trace. It took me back in time. There were no ugly houses or shopping malls. Just mile after mile of natural beauty. We cruised at 60 until the little road fizzled into a roundabout.

I stopped in McComb, where my family was from but it was no longer the little town that I remembered. So, we made our way towards Covington where my uncle and his family lived. I was greeted warmly and watched with a smile on my face as he took his old bike down the road for a spin; the first time in a long time.

"I'll kill you if he gets another one." My aunt warned me.

The next morning was nice, slow and relaxing. Coffee and talks with my uncle. In the garage I took the heat shield off Darlene and replaced the 2nd clamp while my uncle graciously held the light and kept me supplied with coffee. I was in no hurry but by mid-morning I was packed and saying good bye with promises of coming again soon. I had plans of a lazy day of riding back roads but the universe had different plans. Right out of the little maze of suburbs my uncle lived in I took a wrong turn. Finally, I found 1077 and headed north on 25 to Franklinton. Not paying attention I turned east on 10 instead of west and ended up in Bogalusa. Realizing my mistake, I threw a few profane words into the air and turned around. Heading west I was stuck behind a logging truck looking at long logs pointed straight for me and trying to keep "worst case scenarios" from playing through my head. Back in

Franklinton I missed the turn-off for 10 and ended up on 16 west towards Baton Rouge. A few more choice words into the air, I then relented and followed 16 planning on taking one of the roads back up to 10. When I hit north Baton Rouge I realized that the universe was not done with me yet. Darlene was patient, though. Somehow, I ended up on 10 again and then 1, the road I had originally planned on taking. I stopped at a gas station for dinner and had a free lunch given to me by the attendant, a slice of pizza and boudin balls, neither of which were worthy of the price or being called Louisiana cuisine respectively. That night I paid the price with a queasy stomach.

The nice, lazy day had turned into a day of wrong turns, shitty food and being lost. Finally, 1 led me into Alexandria where I took 49 to Natchitoches and turned off to try to find a place to sleep. The first three hotels were booked. There were two left to check. If they didn't work out, I planned on riding straight into Dallas. At the fifth hotel I got a room and threw myself into the bed with gusto. I called my uncle to let him know that I was in for the night and told him about my day.

"Hey. At least you were on a bike!" he said. I had to agree.

There's always a last day and this was it. It wasn't far to home, about four hours, but I was up early. And after a quick hotel breakfast Darlene and I were cruising up 49, her big motor thumping right along. We took back roads to Tyler Texas and then hit I-20 and dropped into the frenzy of Dallas traffic soon afterwards. This had not been a typical trip in a lot of ways. First, I hadn't really talked to a lot of people. There were several that had admired Darlene in her chrome-splendor and boisterous attitude, but very few conversations. Secondly, Darlene had taught me the idea of a relaxing vacation on a motorcycle. I now knew the difference between the tours on Mabel and a lazy cruise from one hotel to another. Mabel was about exploration. Darlene was about cruising in comfort with attitude.

I had cozily slept in hotels, moseyed down freeways and searched nonchalantly for small roads. I had a destination, a plan, but had plenty of time to make it. The world was not my oyster, but a small portion of it was on the half shell and served with a cold beer. I ate out every night while Darlene waited patiently in parking lots. In fact, it was Darlene that changed the demeanor of the trip and my own attitude towards motorcycle trips. With her reclining position and relaxed ways, she was about exploring but not too much at a time. I found that I was fine with her languid attitude and didn't even mind her small tank which, at times, forced me to keep a lookout for gas stations. Darlene liked small roads but only on sunny days. She was in no hurry but steadfast about her lackadaisical attitude, and her life view influenced my own attitude towards the trip. I found myself thinking more about "riding around" and when I went out to start the day with Darlene it was as if she asked: "Wanna go?". Back from the short stint to Louisiana I found myself thinking that I had had a vacation. It was relaxed, at least as relaxed as a rider like myself could be. Mabel offered something totally different, relaxing in a different but exciting way. But now I had a choice.

"That's the point." I thought to myself, "I have a choice."

I came to the conclusion that any ride is mostly mental. It is what you think it is, and what you think it is, is to a great extent determined before you ever leave home.

A Last Note

I'm not sure what I expect, if anything, from riding a motorcycle. I understand the dangers and often I don't really want to go anywhere in particular. Used to, people would take Sunday drives. Perhaps they still do in small towns somewhere. Not where I live. But on a motorcycle, Sunday drives still seem to exist. I like the motor in motorcycles and the feel, the sound of them, as they rumble or buzz underneath me. I like the mechanics and the necessity of a clutch. I like that a motorcycle can be quick and nimble or relaxing and steadfast. I like the smell of oil and gas and the heat blowing off a hot motor. Ironically, a motorcycle does not seem to be a mode of transportation as such. It is more like a unicycle. It's fun. It can take you places but if that's all you think about then the point of a motorcycle is missed.

"So! What is the point?!" you may ask.

This is a difficult question to answer. What is the point of a Jackson Pollock painting? Of John Coltrane? Of poetry? Answer these questions and maybe somewhere in there will be the answer you're looking for? I like looking at the one and listening to the other, and reading the last. I like riding a motorcycle in the same way. I can enjoy a country road or an excursion to forgotten industrial areas in a big city if I am on a motorcycle. I like how motorcycles look and the sound they make. I like how they smell, their mechanical nature and how that disappears somehow, on a good road. I like knowing that they are there in the garage, just outside of my door. Whatever it is, I like a motorcycle in my life.

I'm not alone but there are times when I like to be. On a motorcycle it's easy if you want to be alone. I've spent miles and miles thinking about these things and still don't have a clear answer to some of my questions. I do know, though, that when we're are finally done with oil and gas I won't ride them anymore. I'm not sure why? And even though I will be glad when we wise up and rid ourselves of fuel oils and the endless troubles that they cause, I will be sad to see my life with motorcycles end. But until then, it's been a good ride and I hope to have more.

Photos

https://www.flickr.com/photos/9747554@N03/collections